Blessed is She

ELDER CARE

Women's Stories of Choice, Challenge and Commitment

Blessed is She

ELDER CARE

Women's Stories of Choice, Challenge and Commitment

Nanette J. Davis, Ph.D.

Blessed is She
Elder Care: Women's Stories of Choice, Challenge and Commitment

Publisher's Cataloging-in-Publication Data

Davis, Nanette J.

　Blessed is she : elder care: women's stories of choice, challenge
　and commitment / Nanette J. Davis. – 1st ed. – Bellingham, WA :
　House of Harmony Press, c2008.

　　　p. ; cm.
　　　ISBN: 978-1-60145-466-9
　　　Includes bibliographical references and index.

　　　1. Women caregivers–United States. 2. Older people–Care–
　United States. 3. Aging parents–Care–United States. 4. Adult
　children of aging parents–United States. 5. Spiritual life. I. Title.
　II. Title: Elder care.

HV1461 .D395 2008　　　　　　　　2008931014
362.6/0973—dc22　　　　　　　　　2008

Printed in the United States of America

ISBN 978-1-60145-466-9
Library of Congress Control Number: 2008931014

Cover Graphic by Meghann Elfering
Design and Typesetting by Kate Weisel, weiselcreative.com

A House of Harmony Press Publicat
Bellingham, WA
www.houseofharmonypress.com

Rare, elusive and tentative
My husband's smile
As illness, paralysis and fear sapped his life.

~ Nanette Davis

If these women do not speak,
the very stones will cry out.

~ Luke 19:36-40

And did you get what
you wanted from this life, even so?
I did.
And what did you want?
To call myself beloved, to feel myself
beloved on the earth.

~ Raymond Carver, *Conversations with Raymond Carver*

The Talmud teaches: One must bless God for the bad in
life as well as for the good. In the act of blessing God,
we begin the deeply personal journey from senseless pain
to meaningful challenge.

~ Rabbi Saul Goldman, *The Fearless Caregiver*

The prerequisite to true freedom is to decide that you do not want
to suffer anymore. You must decide that you want to enjoy your
life and that there is no reason for stress, inner pain, or fear.
Every day we bear a burden that we should not be bearing.
We fear that we are not good enough or that we will fail.
We experience insecurity, anxiety, and self-consciousness.
All of these things burden us tremendously.
[To end this suffering, allow for] the natural unfolding of life.

~ Michael A. Singer, *The Untethered Soul*

*To Jim Davis whose stalwart soul transcended the
years of physical and mental loss.
He will always be remembered with gratitude and love.*

Contents

Preface

When those most dear to us become irreversibly ill, we cannot imagine that our lives will be forever transformed. But while caring for my own dying husband over the course of four years, I recognized that my life was no longer my own. Yet, a longing stirred within me. I *needed* to connect with others who had shared my journey. I soon realized that the common threads of our life-changing experiences would create a fascinating tapestry. *Blessed is She* is the result.

Drawing its title from Psalm 41—"Blessed is she who has regard for the weak; the Lord delivers her in times of trouble"—*Blessed is She* captures the journeys of more than 60 women providing care for frail elderly loved ones. *Blessed is She* also explains how and why the words of these women resonate with countless others facing the daunting task of caring for beloved parents, spouses, grandparents, siblings, aunts, uncles and friends.

Demographically, we live in an aging world—not only in North America, but throughout developed societies—and we desperately need to address social, economic and health issues that confront often overburdened families and communities in their compassionate elder care efforts.

Despite millions of Americans devoted to caring for their older family members and friends, their enormous care efforts remain invisible; their labors are often overlooked or shunned by government, society and even family members. I like to think of this book as a "wake-up" call for our youth-centered society to take action on behalf of those who cherish, watch over and labor for the aged and dying among us.

Life expectancy has been stretched in the elder years. In the 1930s, a retiree could hope to survive for only a few more years. Today, a healthy elder of 65 years can expect to still be thriving at 80. In fact, the biggest increase of all age groups has occurred among those 85 years and older. This population shift translates into a burgeoning number of older people, many of whom will require family members and communities to come to terms with drastically changing needs in a host of services and products: transportation, housing, household management, food preparation and health care, among others. Above all, this expanding population of older people calls for family caregivers, who are both willing and able to turn their lives around for relatively long periods of time.

Modern medical care often means persons with chronic illnesses may linger for months or years. Just as parents have devoted years of selfless attention to growing children, their now-adult children should be alerted to the inevitable turnaround process—parenting their parents. Surveys show that already 12 percent of Americans in the "baby-boomer" years are serving as elder caregivers for parents or grandparents. And we are only at the beginning of this massive wave of longevity.

Unlike my other sociology books written largely for professional and student use, *Blessed is She* does not impose an exclusively sociological voice. Rather, I have interwoven the interviews and scholarly material with my own personal story. After intensive interviews with women serving as elder caregivers and informal talks with hundreds of other women in all walks of life, my story no longer seems so very personal.

Indeed, I feel humbled and uplifted by so many shared stories. Most women I spoke with experienced a similar process: moving from a sense of being imprisoned within the confines of elder caregiving to a deeper level of love, appreciation and even joy. Especially for those of us serving the dying, our sense of purpose and peace was incredibly fulfilling. I discovered that becoming at ease with illness and death was a tremendous gift that could only be earned by participating in the mystery.

Not surprisingly, I experienced an author's dilemma about the tension between the more academic material, the women's stories and my own passages. I was reluctant to expose our family's travail and what I perceived as potentially embarrassing information. But authenticity won out over such misgivings. I came to feel that my own experience had equal, but never more, significance than the narratives contributed by the women whose stories I related. And, yes, for me as well as most others I interviewed, life had become tumultuous—a daily muddle as to how to get through the day.

Other sections of *Blessed is She* could never fit comfortably in a standard academic book. Yet, I felt the need to provide readers with guidance to help them find a way out of the grief and confusion that characterizes so much of elder caregiving. Seizing on a more spiritual model than standard medical or psychotherapeutic solutions, I offer a recipe for happiness that allows us to step into a different stream of thinking and being. In this new perspective, we can experience freedom, love, joy and endless peace regardless of the external state of our lives.

I am deeply indebted to the women in the study who shared their personal stories of choice, challenge and commitment. As a friend told me in an early phase of my study—"get the story out; let people know what's happening." To these women I say: I hope your stories will both mobilize greater public and government support for elder caregivers and provide knowledge and relief for those caught up in the caring process.

I have staunch champions in my daughters Patricia and Susan, who have nurtured and supported me throughout the writing of this book. Not only have their comments, critiques and editing served to keep me focused over the past few years, but also, I am deeply grateful for their tender understanding of the raw feelings that sometimes emerged over the course of listening to other women's heartaches, as well as my own.

My dear friend, Anne Mikkelsen, is the most highly creative research assistant any writer could ask for and is the insightful co-author of Chapter 11. Anne has a knack with language, and her sense of empathy with the women's experiences could not be equaled. Anne continues to serve as caregiver for her husband, Mike, who suffers from Parkinson's disease. If anyone has kept me on target with this book, it is Anne. She has been a constant reminder of how caregiving brings out the most auspicious personality traits we have—and some we would prefer to forget about. Anne's story is suitably highlighted here.

I acknowledge students from my Western Washington University sociology course, "Aging in America," who were willing to confront and understand both the aging process and the crucial role of caregiving. Many admitted to feeling "depressed" and even discouraged about the topic, but most came to recognize that we are living in a transitional period. As more knowledge accrues and more caregivers come forward to share their experiences, we surely shall create a more benign culture of care.

To all of those who have helped me in this journey, including friends and colleagues, I would like to express my heartfelt appreciation. To Kate Weisel, your expertise in the production and design of *Blessed is She* has made publication possible.

To Burl, my ever kind and loving partner, whose grammarian's hand played such an important part of "getting it right," I can only say: bravo, for your insights, persistence and unwavering support throughout the turmoil and joy of completing the book.

Additionally, thanks are overdue to all my children—Katherine, Susan, Elizabeth, Timothy, Michael and Patricia—and especially, Timothy, for their unfailing loyalty, devotion and love for their Dad.

PART I

BACKGROUND

Introduction

While I was caring for my parents, I fought to find meaning in suffering. After my caregiving days were over and colleagues began to experience the throes of parent care, they asked me how I survived. The answer I found was in the journeys described by mystics and shamans as well as in classic mythological and wisdom traditions that reveal suffering as a path to liberation if viewed as a spiritual discipline. These teachings frame **Caregiving** *to provide an accessible, workable guide through this dreaded labyrinth.*
~Beth Witrogen McLeod, *Caregiving*, 1999[1]

The Caregiving Journey

Caregiving has been rightly described as a journey. Beth Witrogen McLeod calls it a "spiritual journey of love, loss and renewal" that transcends the dread of physical decline and death. For most of us, the journey of caregiving for an elder begins with high hopes and a seemingly clear map that plots our course. For a time, it appears we are on track—the patient has been diagnosed and properly medicated. Our goal is to allow the loved one to rest content in this new state of illness, and step in as needed to provide help, companionship and counsel. But the map in our heads is poorly envisioned; it doesn't always take us where we want to go. Instead of a straight road, we find ourselves blocked at different points, forced to reassess our goals, and wondering if we should have started this journey at all. The needs of the patient are draining our hopes, plans and energies. Our optimism has vanished and been replaced with frustration and a bundle of negative feelings about both ourselves and our loved one. Now, we have a sense of being lost—adrift, not knowing where we are going or what the final destination will be. It seems that living under the continuous pressure of giving care offers little more than a permanent detour from our normal life.

As our elder caregivers' stories unfold, we trace their journey from hope to despair to eventual acceptance for their many losses. For most caregivers the task is not easy. Before moving into the final steps of the journey—the place of love, forgiveness and compassion—caregivers must recognize and confront the terrible havoc that elder caregiving brings. This book is the story of their struggle to make sense of the journey, as well as to learn, grow and transcend the difficult, frustrating or painful experiences all caregivers have as they witness their loved one deteriorate and eventually die.

The Heart of Altruism

The caregiving journeys I've studied involve more than personal accounts of hope, loss and acceptance. As the title of this work, *Blessed is She* suggests, family members who undertake this moral commitment come to it out of a sense of *altruism*—a term often used interchangeably with caring, serving, helping, giving and other forms of pro-social and unselfish behavior. Such acts of mercy typically are provided at the risk of family members' own happiness and well being.[2] The literature on altruism suggests that the enduring significance of altruistic acts involves a heightened sense of responsibility, a testimony to the ability to care deeply and a willingness to contribute to another person's enhanced quality of life, while sacrificing one's own preferences and needs.[3]

As early as the nineteenth century, scholars have indicated the profound significance of altruism for keeping society going. Without exception, some form of altruism exists in every society. Emile Durkheim, an early French sociologist, wrote that whenever individuals abnegate their interests in favor of service for the sake of others, they are engaging in altruism. No society could exist unless its members acknowledge and make sacrifices on behalf of each other. Altruism is not merely "a sort of agreeable ornament to social life," said Durkheim, but its fundamental basis.[4]

As a moral quality, *altruism* may also be viewed as a highly developed form of prosociality—the willingness to put the interests and needs of others above our own. As a form of empathy, *altruism* implicitly points to quintessential qualities of humanness, especially self-respect. In turn, acts of care motivated by self-respect are an intricate part of empowerment, healing and the capacity for presence.[5]

As we learn from reading *The Altruistic Personality* by Samuel and Pearl Oliner, even ordinary persons can risk their health and well-being because they are called to undertake acts of human decency and kindness.[6] The caregivers described in this book may not be the heroic rescuers of threatened Jewish citizens of Nazi Germany that the Oliners depict in their penetrating study. However, caregivers do share with these rescuers certain similarities. Many of the caregivers we followed in this research believe they have a revered mission to serve. This necessitated overlooking the risks involved—the loss of careers and financial resources, even jobs, relationships and cherished activities—to carry out their subjectively defined personal commitment. In carving out new relationships and roles and redefining old ones, caregivers—similar to the rescuers of condemned Jews—learn to cultivate contacts and networks to support them through the ordeal, as well as to generate needed resources for the task.

In *The Heart of Altruism*, author Kristen Renwick Monroe defines altruism as "habits of caring."[7] Such habits of the heart challenge the presumed inescapability and universality of the idea that only self-interest characterizes human nature. Altruistic acts essentially raise a basic moral question: Why does one person act out of concern for another, instead of pursuing individual self-interest? Moreover, how does this concern relate to a strong, often overpowering sense of obligation and responsibility? What essentially do we owe our loved ones—and at what cost to our own well-being? What boundaries can be placed around this self-imposed obligatory act of caring? And finally, at what point do presumably altruistic acts of caring degenerate into a pathological condition, where the self has been swallowed up by duty and responsibility? When does the ethic and feeling of caring become lost? In the chapters ahead, I show caregivers' responses when confronting such questions, and how they eventually resolved or failed to gain closure on the contradictions they faced.

In my formal interviews with 61 elder caregivers—and informal conversations with hundreds of caregivers in all walks of life—I was deeply moved by their nearly universal feelings of responsibility. Not that this sentiment was an externally imposed norm dictated by a church, religious body or other institution. Instead, their acts of altruism—giving beyond measure—reflected internalized standards of conduct, which became a normal and everyday part of their value system. One source of this overpowering sense of responsibility appeared to be their empathy for the other—a cognitive and emotional understanding of sensitivity to their loved one's needs and feelings. These women also demonstrated an enormously strong sense of personal integrity that served as the motivator and rationale for giving. The idea that humans are motivated only by rational choice does not stand up among these caregivers. Most admitted they "had little or no choice," but only a compelling sense that no one else could or would assume this responsibility.

Gender and Caregiving

Are these perceptions of personal commitment to care for a disabled elder a socialized response restricted solely to women? Certainly, men find themselves equally challenged to give care to their aging mother or sick wife. But in our culture, primarily women are expected to take on the caregiving duties, and who are more likely to sacrifice careers, hopes and dreams to care for the younger—and in this case—older generation.

A special report by the Family Caregiver Alliance on the status of women caregivers emphasizes that although men also provide assistance, female caregivers may spend as much as fifty percent more time providing care than male caregivers.[8] Caregiving apparently involves explicit gender styles. Women are far more likely to intensify their care, investing more time and being more psychologically involved, especially for spouses. Men who give care to their wives take a different path, tending to delay retirement to bolster declining family finances. Moreover, women's tendency toward intense care contributes to significant economic losses—a point we cannot overemphasize. Along with decreased work hours, failure to receive job promotions or training, being forced to quit their jobs or to retire early, women's caregiving places a significant strain on their retirement incomes. Smaller pensions, as well as reduced Social Security amounts and other retirement payments are the consequences of both reduced hours on the job and fewer years in the workforce. Gender also matters: Women are much less likely to receive a pension than men, and when they do, their pension is about half what men receive.[9]

And, the toll that caregiving takes is not just a financial one. Higher levels of depression, anxiety and other mental health challenges are common among women who care for an older relative or friend. One four-year study found that middle-aged and older women who provided care for an ill or disabled spouse were **six times** more likely to suffer symptoms of depression and anxiety than were women who were not caregivers.[10]

Compounding this dismal mental health picture, physical ailments are a common problem. More than one-third of caregivers provide intense and continuing care to others while suffering from poor health themselves. Elderly women caring for a loved one with dementia may be particularly susceptible to the negative health effects of caregiving, due largely to significantly less help from family members for their own disabilities.[11]

Aside from gender, consider the fact that minority and low-income caregivers face special challenges. For these caregivers, having access to paid sources of care is especially difficult. One study concluded that lower-income caregivers are **half as likely** as higher-income caregivers to have paid home health care or assistance to provide either support or relief from their caregiving duties.[12]

Nanette's Story

Although every caregiver's story is uniquely her own, at the same time, each echoes that of other caregivers. As such, I have chosen to introduce the book with my own narrative. I weave my story throughout various chapters to demonstrate my personal connection to caregiving, and to emphasize how the road I have traveled is like that of so many others.

A heart attack in 1998 on Jim's 78th birthday alerted me to the precarious state of my husband's health. As he was wheeled into surgery by the "swat team" of intervention specialists, he continued a refrain I would hear for weeks: "I don't even feel as though I've had a heart attack; I can't believe I've had a heart attack." And once released from the hospital, he continued "business-as-usual" without taking the precautions necessary to avoid another attack, because, after all, he felt he wasn't at risk.

The doctor's initial prognosis was excellent—stent installed, patient stabilized, family relieved, job done. Jim resumed his normal life, seemingly without missing a beat. On the other hand, I was apprehensive and vigilant, fearing the worst, as he had waited to seek medical care after his initial symptoms, thinking the pain and lethargy would pass. Less than four months later, the day after Thanksgiving, with all the family assembled at the house for the holiday, we received a call from the hospital. Jim had had another, more serious heart attack, after collapsing on the first hole of his favorite local golf course. Hope appeared futile; the crisis had begun.

Over the next few years, as his condition deteriorated, physicians continued to add more drugs to his cornucopia of medicines, and attempted different treatments—all to no avail. Medical crisis followed medical crisis. Trips to the hospital, as well as to various doctors and care centers accelerated. I was in shock, as were our children. What can we expect? Will our beloved husband and father emerge from these trials alive or dead? We did not know then that the answer would be: both alive and dead. Jim was alive, in that his heart beat, he retained the power of speech, he ate (little), slept (even less) and eliminated. But he was dead, as well: dead to the significance of his relationship to self, family, friends and the world. Dead to cherished roles, dead to a life commitment to scholarship and writing, dead to independence and creativity, dead to physical wholeness, dead to the possibilities of a future or even a present that has meaning and purpose. He survived, but without strength, without joy, without courage, and most tragically, without hope.

This personal tragedy started me on a journey that has brought much grief, yet much heart-opening wisdom. I have experienced an intense adventure that has taken me deep into the recesses of myself and my capacities for coping, as well as opened my eyes to the profound contradictions surrounding elders within our culture.

What's Ahead

Our society remains wholly unprepared for the vast number of elderly persons—ten times greater than in 1900, for instance—and their end-of-life needs that further threaten the already precarious American medical institutions. Outside help from family and communities is not up to the task. We are indeed facing a caregiving crisis of major proportions as the baby boomer generation moves into retirement. The elder caregiving deficit—too few people to support the primary caregiver—is a major reason family caregivers feel so overwhelmed.

Talking with caregivers about their burdens, one is reminded of the medieval fable of St. Christopher, who, offering to take a small child across the river on his back, was confronted with a wholly different reality. At first, the child appeared to weigh nothing at all, but as the saint laboriously pushed his way against the current—more fearful each moment they both would drown—the tiny burden became oppressively heavier. The saint could only groan and bewail his fate. Once Christopher successfully navigated the passage, exhausted, he turned to the small one, and asked: "Who are you?"

"I am the Christ Child," he replied. "Whoever takes up my burden will be heavily laden." The story depicts the ultimate price of love and altruism: To give oneself so completely to humanity, whether that sacrifice is collective or individual, implies that survival of self becomes intricately linked to the well-being of the Other.

Chapter 1

The National Picture of Caregiving

People have grown ever more concerned with the aging of the population, both nationally and globally, and worry about the 'burden' of old age that the old present. Natural and social scientists advance careers by presenting old age as a 'problem' to be solved. Furthermore, in a culture that covets youth, 'experts' who help us 'age successfully' can attain the status of gurus. Indeed, one might argue that 'aging well' has become a growing national, if not Western, obsession— particularly given the baby boom generation's increasing attention to growing old.

~ T. M. Calasanti & K. F. Slevin,
Gender, Social Inequalities and Aging[1]

An Apocryphal Tale?

With the new obsession of living to 100 and beyond, here is a heart-warming story circulating among a few contemporary seniors I know.

Gus, a 73-year-old man went to see his doctor for his annual check-up, and after the tests were completed, was told he was in excellent shape for his age: heart, lungs, circulation, blood sugar, muscle tone, sexual potency—all checked out as excellent. The doctor said, "I wish I could look like you when I'm your age. Wouldn't your father be pleased to see what great condition you're in?"

Gus replied, "I'll let him know, doctor, what you said."

The startled doctor said, "What! Is your father still alive?"

Gus answered, "Oh yes, Dad's in peak condition at 93, doesn't take any medicine, and still plays golf everyday."

The doctor, overcome with hearing about such longevity, commented, "Well, wouldn't his father, your grandfather, be happy to hear of his
remarkable health at his age?"

Gus responded, "Oh yes, Doctor, I'll certainly tell my grandfather
what you said."

The doctor, taken aback and barely able to answer, countered back,
"Why, how old is your grandfather?"

Gus said, "Oh, Granddad is going on 114. And can you beat this? He's
getting married next month."

"Married!" the doctor exclaimed. "Why does he want to do that?"

"Well," Gus said, "Grandad didn't really *want* to get married at all…
he *had* to get married!"

State of the Union: An Overview

Before launching into our caregivers' stories, beginning with Chapter 4,
we will need to assess the larger—certainly less benign picture than our
story suggested—of elder health and long-term care needs. This "State
of the Union" overview addresses caregiving problems and challenges at
the national level. In addition, we need to consider how the rapidly growing population of elders contributes to the mounting need for expanded
federal and state support for poor elders. Providing services to infirm
elders and their families should be among the nation's top priorities.

As we discussed in the Introduction, family or informal caregivers are
the backbone of our long-term care system in the United States, providing largely unpaid assistance to loved ones with chronic illnesses or
disabilities. Estimates of the number of family caregivers today range upward to 44 million people who provide unpaid care each year for one or
more ill or disabled family members or friends *of all ages*. Approximately
10 percent of the adult population is engaged in end-of-life care—caring for persons with chronic ailments that require family or institutional
intervention. About 15 million caregivers are middle-age adults helping sick or disabled parents, and these numbers will grow as the baby
boomers and their parents age. Without the assistance of these family
caregivers, many older people with disabilities would be forced to enter
institutions for their care. In addition, policymakers recognize the savings in public dollars when family caregivers help their sick relatives stay

in their own home or that of a loved one, rather than be institutionalized at public expense.[2]

Half or more of family caregivers juggle work, family and caregiving responsibilities, contributing to enormous emotional, physical and financial hardships. A 2007 Report by Evercare and the National Alliance for Caregiving found that nine out of 10 caregivers have seen a decline in their own health while caring for an ailing loved one.[3] At the same time, caregiving and long-term care have failed to command the attention of policymakers and state-funded caregiver support programs. The caregiving burdens often fall directly on the caregiver, who is most likely female, and her family.[4]

"Family caregiving is going to mean the disruption of people's lives," said Emily Friedman, a health-policy analyst, who spoke at the 2007 annual joint meeting of the American Society on Aging and the National Council on Aging.[5] More than 4,000 people who work in aging services heard the implications of the emerging problem. Friedman noted that 20 percent of women caregivers under 65 have no health insurance, 46 percent of caregivers have a chronic condition themselves, and 50 percent of family caregivers live in households with less than $50,000 in annual income.

Friedman and others noted an ugly Catch-22 for women. They tend to be poorer and in greater need of money in later life, so they must continue to work for survival. But caring for a loved one requires that either they juggle two full-time roles, or quit work to serve as family caregiver for one or more relatives. And when women become caregivers, they are 2.5 times more likely to end up living in poverty.[6]

As a society, Americans are confronted with "global graying"—an ever-growing elderly population that has striking consequences in all developed countries. Prior to the Industrial Revolution, only one in ten persons could expect to live to age 65. Today, most will reach that age and considerably beyond. According to the Census Bureau, our nation had approximately 35 million persons aged 65 or older in 2000. By the year 2030, these numbers will shoot up to an estimated 70 million persons over age 65, and by 2050 an estimated 86 million of us will be over 65 years old. Life expectancy is increasing at an unprecedented rate, with those older than 85 now the fastest growing age group in the United States.[7]

Increased longevity is good news. But old age also brings financial woes as chronic illness and intensive care come into the picture. Medical assistance remains very expensive. A report by Lynn Brenner shows that on average in 2008, a home health care attendant costs $19 an hour and an assisted-living facility is $2,968 a month. A private room in a nursing home is $206 each day (more than $6,000 a month), with the average stay in a nursing home at 2.5 years. While long-term care insurance may be an option for some, policies can range from $1500 to $8000 annually, depending on type of services and the age at which the policy was purchased.[8]

Indeed, our technologically advanced society has moved from prolonging life to postponing death, potentially involving years of physical and emotional dependency among older persons, or an extended condition of "total care" as defined by medical personnel.[9]

Writing in *Family Relations*, David Biegel and Richard Schultz emphasize how increased life expectancy and aging of the population have profoundly impacted family caregiving.[10] The changes range from the medical and economic to the social and demographic. Chief among these is how caregiving has been transformed from a private experience into a salient public policy issue. The authors identify several key factors that contribute to increased longevity. First, shifts in the epidemiology of disease from acute to **chronic diseases**, along with a decrease in accidental deaths, has resulted in an increase in the number of persons in the population who will reach old age. Second, **death rates** for heart disease and stroke have decreased, and five-year cancer **survival rates** have increased. Last, **medical technology** now has the capacity to keep very sick people alive for extended periods of time.

The economic, political and social consequences of this aging phenomenon only recently have begun to emerge. One prominent issue is the increasing decline of available caregivers. The nuclear family has contracted, more women work full-time, divorce rates are rising and extended longevity challenges the energy and resources of elderly women, the traditional caregivers, as well as younger family members.[11] For the current generation of elderly, 11 potential caregivers—probably an overly optimistic figure—exist for every chronically ill or disabled person 65 years or older. By the year 2030, only four potential caregivers will be available for every needy elder.[12] Caregiving will preoccupy American families throughout the 21st century, as the baby boomer generation joins the ranks of older Americans age 65 and older. The coming demographic transformation and medical revolution will only intensify demands on family caregivers, and contribute to large-scale family crisis.[13]

U.S. Population Changes and Aging

The U.S. Administration on Aging has prepared "A Profile of Older Americans: 2007," which includes the latest information about the aging population from the U.S. Bureau of the Census, the National Center on Health Statistics and the Bureau of Labor Statistics. To appreciate the special issues and needs confronting older Americans, a summary of major trends follows.[14]

Highlights
General Facts
- The older population (65 and above) numbered 37.3 million in 2006, an increase of 3.4 million or 10 percent since 1996. This figure will grow to 54.6 million persons by 2020 (see Table 1.1).

Table 1.1   **Number of persons 65+, 1900–2030** (numbers in millions)

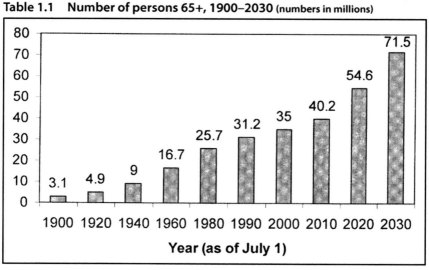

Reprinted from Administration on Aging. "A Profile of Older Americans: 2007."

- The 85 and older population is projected to increase from 4.2 million in 2000 to 6.1 million in 2010 (a 40 percent increase) and then to 7.3 million in 2020 (a 44 percent increase for that decade).
- The number of Americans aged 45 to 64 who will reach 65 over the next two decades has increased by 39 percent during this decade.
- About one in every eight, or 12.4 percent, of the population today is 65 years or older.
- Members of minority groups are projected to increase from 5.7 million in 2000 (16.4 percent of the elderly population) to 8.1 million in 2010 (20.1 percent of elderly) and then to 12.9 million in 2020 (23.6 percent of elderly).
- Persons reaching age 65 have an average life expectancy of an additional 18.7 years (20.0 years for females and 17.1 years for males).
- Older women outnumber older men at 21.6 million older women to 15.7 million men (65 and above).

Marital Status

- Older men were much more likely to be married than older women—72 percent of men versus 42 percent of women. Approximately 43 percent of all older women in 2006 were widows. More than four times as many widows exist (8.6 million) as widowers (2.0 million) (see Table 1.2).

Table 1.2   Marital Status of Persons 65+, 2006.

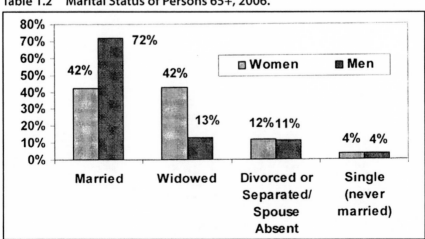

Income

- About 30 percent (10.7 million) of non-institutionalized older persons live alone, but women are much more likely than men to be living alone (7.8 million women vs. 2.9 million men).
- The median income of older persons in 2007 was $23,500 for men and $13,603 for women. Median income for 34.8 million persons over 65 reporting income was $17,045 (see Table 1.3).
- About 3.4 million older persons (9.4 percent) lived below the poverty line in 2006. Another 2.2 million or 6.2 percent of the elderly were classified as "near poor," or those hovering near the poverty line. An estimated 4.5 percent of elderly persons live in abject poverty (under $5,000 in annual income).
- As of 2006, older women have a higher poverty rate (11.5 percent) than older men (6.3 percent). Older persons living alone were much more likely to be poor (16.9 percent) than were older persons living with families (5.6 percent). The highest poverty rates were experienced by older Hispanic women who lived alone.
- For more than one-third of Americans age 65 and above, Social Security benefits constitute the majority of their income (90 percent).

Table 1.3   Persons 65+ Reporting Income, 2006

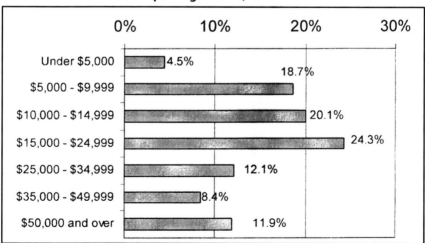

$17,045 median for 34.8 million persons 65+ reporting income. Reprinted from Administration on Aging. "A Profile of Older Americans: 2007."

Caring for Grandchildren

- About 670,000 grandparents aged 65 or older in 2006 had the primary responsibility for grandchildren who lived with them.

Today, more than twelve times as many Americans 65 and older exist than in 1900 (from 3.1 million to 37.3 million). Population changes in the United States and throughout the world have transformed society. In 2006, the elderly comprised about 13 percent of the U.S. population. That number is expected to grow to be 20 percent of the population by 2030. With the added pressure of the baby boomer population—ages 46 to 64 retiring by 2011—we can expect to see the ranks of the older population swell to more than 71.5 million persons in 2030, far exceeding the number of children (40 million)[15] (see Table 1.1).

In 2006, 19 percent of persons over 65 were minorities; 8.3 percent were African-Americans. Persons of Hispanic origin, who may be of any race, represented 6.4 percent of the older population. About 3.1 percent were Asian or Pacific Islander and less than 1 percent were Native American.

Minority populations are projected to increase from 5.7 million in 2000 (16.4 percent of the elderly population) to 8.1 million in 2010 (20.1 percent of the elderly) and then to 12.9 in 2020 (23.6 percent of the elderly). Between 2004 and 2030, the white population over 65 is projected to increase by 74 percent, compared with 183 percent for older minorities, including Hispanics (254 percent), African-Americans (147 percent), Native Americans (143 percent) and Asian and Pacific Islanders (208 percent).

Regardless of race, ethnicity or immigrant status, older women now outnumber older men in the United States just as they do in most developed societies. According to the Census from the year 2000, there are 141 women for every 100 men. By age 85 and older, there are 237 women to every 100 men. This disproportionate sex ratio resulting from greater female life expectancy has some important implications for caregiving: among them, long widowhood, women living alone and late-life poverty. By age 85 and older, nearly 80 percent of women have lost their husbands. The largest proportion of women whose husbands survived into their late 70s will have been caregivers, using up family funds to meet the needs of their sick elderly spouses. When these women eventually need care, they will have to rely on adult children, and failing that, government assistance.[16]

Fewer older Americans are high school graduates, compared with those 25 to 50 years of age. Whereas the 25-year-old and older group of whites had more than 80 percent of persons with high school diplomas, only 65 percent of blacks and 46 percent of Hispanics graduated from high school. For the 75 and older group, less than 20 percent of Hispanics graduated from high school, with somewhat more than 20 percent for blacks.[17]

Because higher levels of education are associated with longer and healthier life expectancy, racial and ethnic minorities experience more job insecurity, lower pay, bleak opportunities for advancement, a greater number of illnesses at younger ages than whites and far greater financial anxiety in old age. And, when those who lack retirement benefits and savings can no longer care for themselves, it places a heavy financial burden on their families, local charities, state funding sources and federal Medicaid and Medicare programs.

Living arrangements play a critical role in older persons' lives. Congested urban areas with high noise pollution, high crime rates and dense traffic are least desirable for older people, but may be all that is available for elders living in poverty. In 1999, 57 percent of blacks lived in central cities, many complaining of moderate to severe problems with their housing (15 percent). Income is the best predictor of comfortable housing in one's older years. Owner occupancy remains reassuringly high for whites (82 percent own their own homes), while blacks and Hispanics are more likely to live in rental accommodations (about 33 percent). For most Americans of modest or few means, the chance of bettering oneself economically simply does not exist.[18]

Older workers are increasingly targeted for cost-cutting measures, with early retirement buyouts and layoffs becoming commonplace. The U.S. Bureau of Labor shows that African Americans, Latinos and women aged 51 to 61 are more likely than white men to be displaced.[19] By age 65, 59 percent of women are no longer in the labor force and only one third of workers (men and women) have been re-hired after being let go from their job. Involuntary job loss takes its toll on physical and mental well-being, especially since few lower-income workers have health insurance or other benefits. The Administration on Aging charges that such job displacement smacks of age, race and gender discrimination. In a special hearing on older workers in the U.S. Senate, observers contend that older workers continue to be at risk because of inherent ageism—"a systematic stereotyping and discrimination against people simply because they are old."[20] Ageism promotes discriminatory practices in housing, employment and services, as well as contributes significantly to elder abuse.[21]

The Administration on Aging has the job of monitoring the health status of older Americans. The organization's 2007 Report indicated that in 2005, more than 13.2 million persons aged 65 and older were discharged from short stay hospitals.[22] This is a rate of 3,596 for every 10,000 persons aged 65 and over—which is more than three times that of persons aged 45 to 64. The average hospital stay for persons aged 65 and older was 5.5 days. Older persons averaged more annual office visits with doctors in 2005—6.5 visits for those aged 65 to 74 and 7.7 visits for persons older than 75. The 46 to 64 age group averaged only 3.9 office visits during that same year. In 2006, more than 96 percent of all older persons reported that they did have a usual place to go for medical care.

This information reveals the level of vulnerability for many elderly persons, who remain in need of outside help from families and communities because of entrenched poverty, living alone, disabling or chronic illness, housing problems, inadequate income, especially for medical and drug bills, as well as physical, mental and social deficiencies. The persons who step forward to give aid and sustenance to America's elders are, more often than not, family members. Their support—socially invisible and often unacknowledged by policymakers—constitutes the difference between two opposing outcomes. An elder could end up living in poverty, isolated from kin and friends and dying alone. Or, best case scenario, the older person could have a rich network of sustaining, caring relationships and die deeply comforted.

A Profile of Caregivers

Who are the family caregivers who look after their aged relatives and friends? According to the National Family Caregivers Association, the number of family or informal caregivers for the elderly in North America has grown more than 300 percent in a nine-year period (1990 to 1999), involving 25 percent of the U.S. population. Nearly 80 percent of family caregivers are women, and about 90 percent of persons providing formal care in facilities are women. Among adults 51 and older, 12 percent are providing assistance with basic, everyday activities to their parents. This translates into 7 million adult children serving as primary caregivers to their parents.[23]

Other pertinent facts demonstrate the depth of commitment and challenge faced by family caregivers, based on a sample of more than 1,000 persons.[24]

- The typical family caregiver is a 60-year-old married woman with annual household income between $20,000 and $25,000, who has been caring for her husband at home for five years.
- More than half of family caregivers work outside the home. An estimated 14.4 million full-and-part time workers are balancing caregiving and job responsibilities.
- Nearly 60 percent of caregivers showed symptoms of clinical depression.
- A profile of caregiving emotions includes frustration (67 percent), sadness, anxiety and, more promising, compassion. On the positive side, 70 percent found an inner "strength" they did not know was there.
- Between 20 and 40 percent of caregivers have children under 18 to care for, in addition to their disabled relative.
- Caregivers of persons living in institutions or residential care facilities provide an average of 36 hours per month or 8.5 hours per week of care, while caregivers of community or home-based patients provide an average of 286 hours per month or 66.5 hours per week of care. Despite caregiver reservations about placing their loved one in care, institutional services are lifesavers for those caring for the very frail elderly.
- One in three family caregivers indicated they receive no help at all from family or friends.
- Long-distance caregiving is a fact of life in our highly mobile society. About 7 million Americans provide or manage care for someone

age 55 or older who lives at least an hour away. When caregivers are unable to see how their sick elder is doing, distance can compound feelings of guilt and anxiety. The caregiver may also feel overwhelmed by the challenges of arranging services from afar.[25]

Research concludes that being a high-level caregiver increases the odds of not getting enough rest, not having enough time to exercise, not being able to recuperate from illness and forgetting to take prescription medications, compared with women who are not caregivers.

Yet, families and informal caregivers play a central role in both the decision-making and delivery of long-term care to the estimated 13 to 15 million Americans with adult-onset cognitive impairment (e.g., Alzheimer's disease, stroke, Parkinson's disease, traumatic brain injury and other old-age related illnesses). The economic costs of these brain disorders are conservatively estimated at more than $130 billion annually (1997 dollars). The economic *value of care* provided by families is even more staggering. At an estimated value of $196 billion nationally, informal caregiving eclipses home health care ($32 billion) and nursing home care ($83 billion). This trend is likely to continue in the decades ahead with family members taking on even greater caregiving demands.[26]

A study conducted in 2000 by the National Family Caregivers Alliance focused on 51 caregivers and their 51 care receivers who were cognitively impaired.[27] The research objective was to elicit both "voices"—the caregivers' world view and the daily care wishes of the care receivers. Caregivers reported the importance of paid service to prevent them from being overwhelmed with duties.

Family caregivers tend to minimize financial strain, asserting they have enough money to cover the costs of care. Despite their ostensibly positive financial viewpoint, nearly 40 percent of the caregivers admitted they had "just enough" or "not enough" money to make ends meet at the end of the month. Most struggled to keep their loved one at home, rather than move them to a nursing home, even though they were often dealing with debilitating or very severe problems caused by progressive dementia and other illnesses. Their loved ones had declining mental health, incontinence, an inability to eat independently or recognize

family members. Some demonstrated such irrational and aggressive behavior that they posed a danger to themselves and others.[28]

The research concluded that families experiencing the multiple and
long-term stressors that accompany caregiving are not tuned into the
care receiver's daily care wishes, values and preferences. Instead, caregivers worry about how they are going to get through each day. This has
serious implications for disempowering the care receivers, as well as increasing the strain on family caregivers. In the absence of more support
services for these caregivers, getting through the day may be the most
that can be achieved.[29]

Given all the stresses, it should not be surprising that some studies
have found caregivers have moderate to very high rates of both mental
and physical illness. Dr. Andrew Weil (2003), the guru of "aging well,"
points to an important article in The *Journal of the American Medical
Association*, which reported that elderly people who were experiencing
emotional strain from taking care of a spouse had a 63 percent higher
risk of dying within four years compared with non-caregivers.[30] Among
the more than 30 million people currently caring for an elderly, disabled
or chronically ill family member or friend, the likelihood of premature
death is a real possibility.

The caregiver, then, plays the central role in the family drama. Their
ability to tolerate—even embrace—the multiplicity of physical, emotional and social tasks that daily care of a disabled person requires is the
key to a mutually harmonious and satisfactory outcome. What has been
termed the "caregiver burden" strongly interferes with this objective.
Susan Hughes and her co-authors write that the caregiver burden has
both objective and subjective components.[31] Age, race, income, level of
care, residency and type of relationship are at the objective level.

- Younger caregivers experience greater burden than older caregivers.
- White caregivers exhibit greater depression than black caregivers,
who express lower levels of stress, burden and depression.
- Caregivers with lower incomes and lower levels of education experience a greater sense of burden than caregivers with higher incomes
and education.

- Wives and daughters demonstrate a greater burden than husbands and sons.
- Persons who live with the care receiver have a greater burden than those who do not.
- Caregivers who assist care receivers with activities of daily living (e.g., feeding, bathing, dressing) and/or who care for persons with behavioral problems, especially dementia, exhibit greater burden than caregivers who assist with other care needs (e.g., financial management).
- Elderly wives caring for their older, terminally ill husbands displayed an objectively very high score for caregiver burden.
- Husbands who have transitioned into the caregiving role will be more likely than non-caregiving husbands to report depression and declines in marital happiness—a fact strongly linked to divorce.[32]

Hughes' research also demonstrates the subjective component of care: Overburdened caregivers are more likely to experience problems with mental health, physical well-being, financial resources and social participation. Severely reduced vitality, clinical depression, a diminished immune response and withdrawal from social activities commonly afflict high-level caregivers, such as those who care for spouses, conditions which actually undermine their ability to provide care. Subjective burden plays a significant part in the overall functioning of a caregiver, as well. Emotional problems interfere with normal daily life. Chronic feelings of nervousness, depression, sadness and anxiety accelerate the sense of one being out of control, and raise the stress level for both caregiver and care receiver.[33] In short, the caregiver role results in enormous emotional, physical and financial hardships, even when it is willingly undertaken and considered a source of great personal satisfaction.

Long-Term Care

The 21st century will be marked by a dramatic increase in long-term care needs for the elderly. *Long-term care* refers to a broad range of personal, social and medical services required by populations with chronic illnesses and disabilities. An estimated 12.8 million adult Americans of all ages need assistance from another to carry out everyday activities.

Approximately 1.5 million individuals have more substantial needs and are in nursing homes. The number of older persons needing long-term care is expected to double over the next 25 years. In fact, estimates are projected to be 14 million by 2020 and 24 million by 2060.[34]

Long-term care becomes necessary when a chronic condition, trauma or illness limits an individual's ability to carry out activities of daily living (ADLs) or household chores, known as instrumental activities of daily living (IADLs).[35] Long-term care involves the most intimate aspects of people's lives—what and when they eat, personal hygiene, getting dressed, using the bathroom and moving themselves from place to place (see Tables 1.4 and 1.5). Other less demanding long-term care needs may involve household tasks, such as preparing meals or using the telephone. By age 65 and older, many elders will be requiring extensive care for even their most basic needs, including walking, bathing and toileting. Only about 30 percent will be able to handle heavy work. Moreover, approximately 55 percent will require help getting around

---

Table 1.4 Percentage of Persons with Limitations in Activities of Daily Lving by Age Group, 2005.

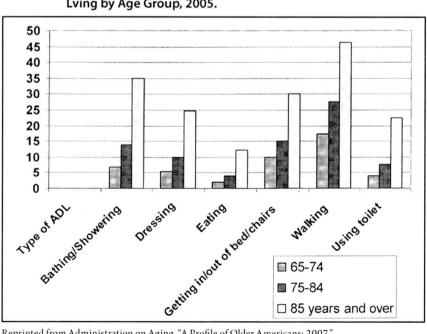

Reprinted from Administration on Aging. "A Profile of Older Americans: 2007."

Table 1.5   Average Percent Needing Help with Instrumental Activities of Daily Living (IADL), 1982–1984.

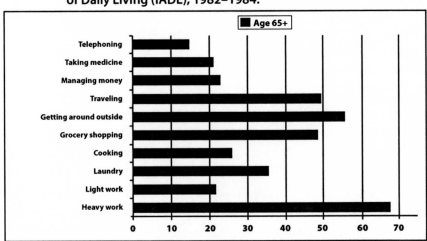

Source: K.G. Manton, E. Stallard, L.S. Corder. "The Dynamics of Dimensions of Age-Related Disability 1982 to 1994 in the U.S. Elderly Population." *Journal of Gerontology: Biological Sciences,* vol. 53A, no. 1, B59–B70, 1998.

outside. For elders 85 years and older, the proportion of people needing help will rise significantly.[36]

Frail older adults who are unable to manage daily care needs clearly are one of the most vulnerable groups in the nation. A 2006 study of the frail elderly by the Urban Institute indicated that the elderly disabled population is sizeable—about 8.7 million people—disproportionately female, widowed and in their 80s and 90s with little education. The frail elderly also tend to live at home with inadequate care and have limited financial resources, with nearly three-quarters of them depending exclusively on unpaid caregivers.[37] But needing care and receiving care are often not compatible. Despite their intensive medical and psychiatric needs, only 53.1 percent of frail older people living alone received regular care.[38]

Persons with chronic illness and disabilities need a broad array of information, education, services, research and advocacy over a prolonged period of time—and *so do their family caregivers.* In a 15-state survey of caregiver support programs, the authors concluded that states should have an increasingly greater responsibility for financing and delivering long-term care services.[39]

Policymakers show the beginning of a new interest in providing help for family caregivers. States can act in one of two ways to ensure that the needs of families are recognized and supported. They can promote distinct state-based programs for family caregivers that are linked to other services, such as hospitals or nursing homes. Or, they can integrate caregiver support into existing home and community-based programs.

Currently, the caregiving/medical support systems across the country are woefully inadequate (as we will discuss in Chapter 6).[40] Funding is seriously limited. Low wages for professional caregivers prevents successful recruiting and retention, while public awareness of caregiving services remains abysmally low. Moreover, low visibility of services particularly impacts needy families, virtually excluding them from available programs. As for middle-class families, income restrictions effectively prevent their participation. It is within this context that caregivers give day-to-day support and care to an elderly relative.

The Next Step

The chapters that follow are based on interviews with 61 Northwest Washington caregivers who are now (or formerly have been) providing long-term care to an elderly relative or friend. Their stories demonstrate how this group of primarily middle-class women cope with the burden of care. What values sustain them? What kind of physical, emotional and financial circumstances are they facing? What kind of outside assistance do they have—both from family or friends and from elder care agencies? What type of illness and care needs typify their loved ones' situations? What level of care are they actually providing, and what constitutes especially difficult or burdensome care? What are typical perceptions of their role and their sense of responsibility? What choices have they made about their own self-care, as well as the day-to-day care management of their disabled relative? What is the nature of their commitment to their loved one? What wisdom can these caregivers pass on to others, as they confront the physical and mental decline—and for some—the death of a deeply cherished person?

Chapter 2

Caregivers and Care Receivers: A Statistical Profile

The longing to tell one's story and the process of telling is symbolically a gesture of longing to recover the past in such a way that one experiences both a sense of reunion and a sense of release.
        ~ bell hooks, *remembered rapture: the writer at work*[1]

Introducing the Caregivers

To better understand the caregivers' stories, let us take a look at the women who participated in the research study. We interviewed 61 caregivers, almost all from Washington State, from October 2003 to June 2005.[2] More than 90 percent of the interviews were conducted in the caregivers' homes. Our caregivers' group spent an average of three or more hours responding to 133 questions. Almost all wanted to converse beyond the parameters of our questions. In one case, a distraught caregiver was unable to finish the survey in a three-hour period, requiring another visit. Her apprehension over her husband's imminent return home from the hospital, and what she said were his "incessant demands," kept her very edgy throughout the interview session. However, for almost all of the subjects (and myself, as well), the interview proved to be a cathartic experience. In addition to formal interviews, I have spoken with hundreds of caregivers over the course of my study—friends, neighbors, colleagues, acquaintances—who shared their stories with me.

Caregiver Interview

The caregiver interview explores eight major aspects of their lives: (1) *personal history*, including age, ethnicity, occupation, and other personal data; (2) *home community*, which entails the length of time they have lived in a particular house or neighborhood and level of involvement in their community; (3) *quality of life*, regarding their health status and concerns; (4) *finances*, which inquires about their housing, medical costs and other expenses during the period of caregiving; (5) *health condition of the care receiver*, involving location of care, as well as care receivers' specific illnesses and other physical and mental symptoms, and the type of support the caregiver has had from both the care receiver and family members; (6) *caregiving activities*, detailing caregivers' actual duties and tasks, and the intentions, attitudes and emotional responses to caregiving; (7) *problems and issues with caregiving*, examining their available resources and financial obligations over the course of caregiving, psychological problems of the care receivers and changes in the caregivers' identity over the course of their providing care. This section also inquires about their general response to self-sacrifice, self-respect and meeting others' needs before their own. Also included in a portion of the interview is a description of their relationships with their loved one over time, as well as their sense of responsibility and stress reactions. (8) A final section explores *religious values and spiritual sense of self* among caregivers. These issues are further explored in the chapters that follow.

Let me cite two examples of how the research questions elicited specific information. First, in order to appreciate the level of commitment these women were making to the caregiving task and their ability to cope, caregivers were asked how many hours per week they provided care, what specific types of care, how extensive the physical and emotional demands and what strategies they developed to deal with the often seemingly impossible workload.

Second, to clarify the nature of the relationship between caregiver and care receiver, these women were invited to talk about what kind of relationship they had *before* the caregiving began, and what changes had occurred in that relationship *during or after* the period they had provided care. For example, a loving spousal relationship tended to remain intact, greatly easing the caregiving process. But some women had suffered

under the rule of an oppressive parent. Now, as adults, they were taking
on the care of a mother or father who had been emotionally or physically
abusive to them as children, and remained hostile over the years. This
situation compounded the difficulty of their caregiving.

Caregivers were also asked to assess their intentions, feelings and
personal responses associated with giving care. The results are often
surprising. Despite the sometimes onerous nature of the physical and
emotional demands placed on them by their sick or disabled relative,
almost all indicated they felt a "strong commitment to my loved one's
care."

Caregiver Profile

To more succinctly address the social backgrounds of the interviewees,
here is a brief overview of relevant information that depicts selective features of the caregivers' lives (see Table 2.1).

Table 2.1   Selected Caregivers' Data

	N	Minimum	Maximum	Mean
Caregivers' Age	57	28	90	66.84
Loved one's age	57	59	106	83.00
Number of children	58	0	8	2.31
Total number of organizations/clubs (CG)	56	0	8	2.64
Visits to alternative health providers	57	0	144	4.51
Number of medications	50	0	21	6.14
Length of time providing care (months)	56	2	180	65.14
Annual income	52	0	$200,000.00	$47,310.92

Caregiver sample. The sample was drawn from Washington State,
mainly from residents of Bellingham and greater Whatcom County. The
sample includes 61 women currently serving or having served as caregiver for a family member or friend (mother/father, 47 percent; spouse, 38
percent; sibling, 2 percent; grandparents, 3 percent; friend, 10 percent).
I gathered these interviews through a process called "snowball sampling,"
or referral sampling. For instance, I personally know Mary, a local caregiver, who is also in touch with three other caregivers. Mary provides
their names, and often makes phone calls to these friends and neighbors
on my behalf. I then follow up with calls and set up appointments if the

potential subjects are willing. It is not a scientific sample, since it is not based on random numbers pulled from the known population of caregivers. Rather, the convenience sample I employed serves as a suitable method for gathering subjects who share in one or more salient characteristics—in this case, being female and being a family caregiver for an elderly relative or friend.

Education. Eighty-five percent of the study's caregivers attended college, most had college degrees and almost all had technical, administrative or professional training. Four women had Ph.D.s, and had been involved in college teaching as their lifetime career. Obviously, this more highly educated group of subjects mark the sample as biased. A strategic consideration, though, is that such subjects are highly articulate, familiar with social and political issues, open to sharing and quickly grasped the significance of the questions.

Caregivers' age. Ages ranged from 23 to 90 years of age, with one-third of caregivers being 75 or older. The average caregiver's age was 65.4. The mean age of working caregivers, who were most likely caring for parents, was 57, whereas the mean age for retired caregivers, tending to care for spouses, was 74.

Marital status. Fifty-one percent were married, 18 percent were widowed at the time of the interview and another 18 percent were divorced or separated. Seven women had never been married (12 percent) and one caregiver was in a long-term relationship.

Children/Grandchildren. Slightly more than 79 percent had children; among those with children, 76 percent had grandchildren. Seventy-four percent visited with their children or grandchildren at least once a month or more often, indicating very close or strong family ties.

Work/Retirement. Thirty percent of caregivers were working full-time, and 69 percent of caregivers were retired or semi-retired. Fifty-six percent of those retired did so before age 60, some to serve as full-time caregivers. One caregiver in her early seventies taught full-time at the local university, while another woman in her late seventies worked as a personal assistant for an even older woman in her eighties.

Ethnicity. Ninety-five percent were white and 5 percent were Hispanic, a distribution that closely matches the Hispanic population of the area. Whatcom County has a population distribution of 5.2 percent

Hispanic, although many other ethnic groups are also represented, albeit in smaller proportions. Despite my efforts to contact our local Native American population for interviews, I was unsuccessful in securing names of women interested in participating in the study.

Living arrangements. Fifty-nine percent of caregivers had lived in their home for 11 years or more. Another 32 percent had been in the same home for 21 years or more. Even with this very stable population, nearly 30 percent had been forced to move in order to provide care (e.g. living in their relative's home, buying a different residence to accommodate the elder, etc.). Occasionally, living arrangements can be very demanding, as in the case of a caregiver who spends weekdays caring for her sick parents and weekends in her own home with her family while teaching high school full-time.

Income. Our sample consisted of primarily middle-class professionals, with 52 percent having incomes of $35,000 or more yearly. Another 27 percent of the women reported their yearly incomes to be $24,000 or less, with the overall income ranging from no income for a 23-year-old college student who cared for her father as a teenager, to a high of $200,000 for a woman who owned three businesses.

The significance of income is directly related to the relative ease or increasing difficulty of care. With abundant resources, caregivers are able to hire competent nursing assistants, take time out for themselves and maintain relationships with family members and friends. Sources of income vary widely, as Table 2.2 shows, with 44 percent employed, 48 percent receiving a pension check, 56 percent receiving Social Security, 36 percent with investment income and only three percent dependent on public assistance. For 10 percent, their primary sources of income were savings or family assistance. Nineteen percent indicated that they have had financial problems since they began caregiving, often because of job reduction or loss.

Cost of care. Medical expenses for a normal month among care receivers ranged from $500 or less to more than $6,000 monthly. For four families, the higher sum entailed nursing home expenses and/or around-the-clock home care for their dying elder. Families carried the largest burden of financial costs (82 percent), with Medicare contributing only ten percent and Medicaid about three percent of total medical costs. All but a few of the families were covered through health insurance, which typically did not include skilled nursing care.

Time served as caregiver. The length of time caregivers have been providing care was an average of 65 months (about five-and-a-half years), with a range of two months to 180 months (15 years). More than half of the caregivers previously provided care to at least one other family member. This information supports the idea that families have informally targeted certain women in the family (e.g., eldest daughter, wife, granddaughter, daughter-in-law) to serve as the "designated caregiver," when an elderly family member becomes stricken.

The amount of time devoted to caregiving has a direct impact on social participation. Many women report they had withdrawn from cherished activities, such as attendance at church or community organizations. This well-educated sample tended to remain relatively active in organizations, as Table 2.1 affirms (on average, the women identified 2.56 organizations they were moderately or somewhat involved in during much of their caregiving).

Likewise, self-care becomes compromised when the physical and emotional demands of the sick elder occupy the day. To this end, we inquired how often they sought alternative medical providers, such as chiropractors, massage therapists, acupuncturists, spiritual counselors or other forms of physical or emotional help outside the medical field. While a few women engaged very regularly in alternative practices, the majority of caregivers tend to regard such practices as largely ineffective. Still, for many caregivers, even irregular massage or chiropractic work eased some of the strain of the day (the average number of visits was 4.58 yearly per caregiver, although a significant proportion had *never* tried any alternative procedure).

Hours worked weekly. The average number of hours per week involved in giving care was 57.7, with a minimum of 5 hours and a maximum of 85 hours. More than half of these caregivers provided care for 81 hours or more per week during their most recent caregiving experience. And, for about one-third of the sample, it was a 24/7 job, with no relief in sight. Overall, these caregivers demonstrated a profound commitment to care. This means that their entire life was oriented around meeting the physical and emotional needs of their loved one.

Functions of care. Different functions of care include standard housework, assisting with activities of daily living (ADLs) and special needs, including monitoring life support equipment, distributing medication, wound cleaning and other specialized care (see Table 2.3). Overall, these caregivers provided an average of about 10 different functions. For one caregiver, the only significant function involved feeding her stroke-affected husband in a nursing home, whereas some caregivers provided as many as 15 different tasks to sustain their elderly loved one.

Measures of stress. Significantly, those caregivers caring for parents experienced more stress than those caring for spouses. Intergenerational conflicts appear to be the cause. We found that the greater the family support, the lower the stress reactions. Conversely, the highest level of negative reactions was associated with a total lack of family support (e.g., sharing time, money, concerns, etc.). The stress issue will be covered in subsequent chapters, and serves as a primary element in the burden of care reported by caregivers.

Levels of caregiver compassion. Our statistical data also reveal that as care receivers become increasingly frail and ill, caregivers are more likely to become sick. In fact, the incidence of caregiver illness tends to increase both in numbers and seriousness. Among this group, the average number of illnesses was 4.4, nearly double the illnesses of their care receivers (a topic we explore further in later chapters). At the same time, the more severely ill the caregiver reports herself to be, the higher her compassion level. At the end of life, pain and suffering can hardly be avoided. The one gift caregivers can provide their loved ones in distress is empathetic understanding.

Care Receivers

Most research on caregivers for the elderly ignores the all-important significance of those persons receiving the care. In this elder caregiving study, we have mainly a very elderly population receiving care, with the youngest at 59 years old (but with diseases typically afflicting the elderly) and the oldest person at 106 years old. Fifty one percent of this group were 83 years or older. Fully twenty percent of those receiving care were 90 to 102 or above. The majority of care receivers suffered from severe

Table 2.2 Caregiver Sources of Income

Source	Percentage
Social Security	56
Pension	48
Job	44
Investments	36
Other (family, savings)	10
Public Assistance	3

Financial problems since caregiving: 19%; all numbers have been rounded.

medical conditions, including advanced cancer, Alzheimer's disease, stroke, Parkinson's disease, terminal heart disease, depression and other ailments of old age (e.g., arthritis, osteoporosis, lung problems, kidney failure). The cumulative number of diseases plays a role in the relative ease or difficulty of caregiving, as well. For this group, the average number of diseases for care receivers was 2.38 (mean), with a range from one disease to 11 different maladies for two elders (see Table 2.4).

Table 2.3 Activities of Daily Living (ADL) and Special Needs of Care Receiver

Activity	Percentage
Shopping	95
Housework	85
Cooking	87
Transportation	90
Feeding	28
Interacting w/loved one	85
Personal care	45
Transferring (chair to bed; bed to toilet)	47
Walking	58
Dressing	60
Financial Arrangements	70
Giving daily medications	72
Facilitating/lifting equipment	27

All percents are rounded.

Table 2.4   Number of Medical/Psychological Conditions of Care Receiver

Condition	Percentage
Anxiety	73
Sadness/Depression	68
Memory Problems	66
Sleep Problems	60
Eating Disorders	60
Irritability	50
Acute Pain	47
Despondency	42
Danger to Oneself/Others (self-injury/suicide/violence)	38
Heart Disease	25
Cancer	25
Alzheimer's Disease	18
Dementia (non-AD)	18
Stroke	13
Blindness	13
Parkinson's Disease	13
Diabetes	8

Cumulative number of diseases: 2.38 (mean)

Among these elderly care receivers, 53 percent took five or more medicines each day, and 19 percent took 10 or more prescription medicines daily. The average care receiver's necessary daily medications were 6.38, with one elder taking no medicine and another elder taking 21 *different* medications. The actual amount of individual doses, though, may have far exceeded the number of drugs, as many drugs had to be given every few hours over the course of both day and night. For most of these sick elders, drug administration needed to be provided by others—usually the caregiver—unless hired help is available or the elder is institutionalized.

Multiple medications clearly complicate the caregiving process. Medications tested on younger people may be contraindicated for older persons. Providing appropriate dosages for very frail elders may turn out to be simply a trial and error approach. Moreover, drug interactions (where certain drugs cannot be combined, because of severe or lethal

**Table 2.5   Locations of Care for Care Receivers
Over the Course of Caregiving**

Location	Percentage
Care receiver's home	75
Skilled nursing facility	25
Assisted living	21
Caregiver's home	16
Residential facility	10
Other (YWCA, motel)	8
Other relative's home	5
Friends	2

reactions) are a constant threat to the sick elder's precarious medical condition. Multiple medications have the potential to create a toxic stew. How many care receivers in this sample were afflicted with this condition remains unknown. We suspect the number was high for those taking 10 or more medications.

We can sum up the caregiver situation as one that entails profound physical, mental and emotional contributions of time, energy and compassion. Most of the care was provided in the caregivers' own homes, although over time, about 46 percent of the elder care-receiving group spent some time in an assisted living or skilled nursing facility, when their level of care needs exceeded their caregiver's capacity (see Table 2.5). In one instance, a caregiver in her seventies took over the care of her older indigent sister by moving both of them into the local YWCA, where care delivery could be shared among volunteers.

Substantial mobility characterizes end-of-life care. A sick elder may begin receiving care at the family home, then shift to a residential care center for greater ease of mobility and self-care, and later into an assisted living facility, where medications may be dispersed, and food and transportation provided. The fateful move into a family group home (usually limited to six or fewer elders) or to a skilled nursing home occurs when the care receiver is nearly or totally incapacitated, or at least, incapable of normal self-maintenance because of physical limitations or dementia. At the point of dying, most elders live out their days in a hospital.

Such shifts in locations of care further contribute to destabilization among sick elders. "Sundowners," a condition of confusion and disorientation that occurs around dusk, is typical among the aged living in assisted living, family group homes, skilled nursing facilities and other institutional facilities. I spoke with many residents of such facilities during the years my husband lived in these settings, and very few cognitively present elders recognized this "place" as home. Among those with severe memory problems, literally crying out for "home" and "family" was an ongoing lament.

Caregiving as a Family Crisis[3]

Why is caregiving a family crisis, and not merely an individual caregiver's burden? This question opens up the issue of profound shifts in family alignments that must occur to accommodate this new, very consuming role, and raises the following issues:

What must be done to actually carry out the caregiving role? What impact will it have on the caregiver and her family in terms of time, finances, psychological state and other areas?

Who must be involved? Are all family members expected to contribute, and what happens to family relationships when one or more of them declines to participate? Or will they participate only reluctantly, and with a negative attitude, which undermines the caregiving enterprise?

What are the financial costs involved? What are the government and health insurance companies doing to support the family facing unexpected medical expenses?

Where will caregiving occur? Will the elderly person or couple be obliged to sell their home and move into their adult children's household, or more likely, into institutional care? If care is provided in the care receiver's home, will this require the caregiver to move out of her own home? What about care for her own family? How willing are family members to sacrifice their wife and mother for the older generation?

What are the hidden social and psychological costs? How will this impact the caregiver's marriage, career, relationship with her children, friendships and community groups, as well as her lifestyle? What kind of services will be needed for the caregiver and her family to adequately deal with these burdens?

How can family members support the designated caregiver, in the absence of assistance? Will support come at too high a price to be maintained over the long run?

What is the government doing to help the overloaded family, as well as the caregiver and care receiver? These and other questions emerged from my two-year study of women caregivers. And, their responses to my questions form the bedrock for understanding both the problematic nature of caregiving and the steps needed to change existing social policy.

Research Considerations

Invariably, one of the first set of questions any social scientist asks when undertaking a research study is: How representative is the sample? For example, do these caregivers have similar qualities and experiences as other caregivers in the United States? (A tall order!) Also, to what extent can I generalize these findings from this study to the larger population, and in this case, to other caregivers and their care receivers across the country? Again, if differences exist between samples or between findings in other studies, which ones are significant? And, which are incidental ones? Two other issues exist, as well. Namely, how do we address the reliability and validity of the research? If I repeat this research using the same set of questions and using the same or a similar sample, would I get the same results? As for the validity of the study, do my questions actually measure what I intend them to measure, or are they off the mark?

Let me take up each of these questions in turn. First, this research offers an *exploratory* and *qualitative* analysis, rather than testing hypothesis on a known population. As exploratory research, it includes a variety of ways I prepared myself to address the caregiver issue. This includes: (1) reading a wide assortment of pertinent literature in the field; (2) teaching "Aging in America" to upper division college students over a six-year period; (3) extensive participation in various organizations that provide services to the elderly or their families or conduct research on caregiving (local and national Alzheimer's societies, elder care provider organizations, sociological associations); (4) informal and often heartfelt conversations with countless caregivers; and (5) my own hands-on experience as a caregiver over a four-year period.

Most recently, I talked with a number of family caregivers as "fellow travelers" en route or while visiting South America, and even on local shopping expeditions. When I've told them some of my findings, I invariably find them vigorously nodding and saying—"yes, this is how it is," "what can I do about it?" and "where can I go for help?"—all of which support my belief that this research is on target.

The reason I feel so affirmative about the truth of this report is simple: The challenges of caring for a loved one for months and years remain the same, whether we are talking about our next door neighbor in Washington State, or the former first lady, Nancy Reagan, who lives in California.

I daresay if I asked the same or similarly situated women the same questions, I may or may not receive the same response. Caregiving, as this book hopefully demonstrates, is a process, not a product. As process, change is inevitable and dynamic. A woman may reassess her response to a question from a negative evaluation *before* her loved one died, to a positive appraisal of the experience *after* that person's death (not an infrequent situation).

Did my research results yield the information I was seeking? Certainly, that answer would be "yes." I sought to uncover not only the material conditions of caregiving, but also the psychological, medical, social and spiritual conditions these women experienced. Their stories repeatedly confirmed and reinforced the reality I believed to exist, and wished to expose: The caregiving burden is real, intense and at times, nearly unbearable. And, it remains one of the most demanding, yet transcending experiences of one's life.

The caregivers' narratives often appear repetitive. More often than not, the caregiver returned to a topic or an issue about which she felt particularly strongly and wanted to emphasize. In other instances, I included sections from earlier narratives in later chapters because they exemplified the point so well.

From a critical sociological perspective, research focusing on the authenticity of the human experience remains inherently valuable for its own sake. As a culture, we have historically treated our elderly with scorn, rejection, neglect or worse. As studies show time and again, nursing and home care in this country is lamentable. Elders are regularly overcharged for medical services and denied even the most basic information and assistance, often when they need it most. At the extreme, frail elders are at risk for physical, emotional or sexual abuse.

Caregiving invariably opens up a larger discourse about the way our society treats the elderly, and those who serve them: the underdeveloped, costly and discriminatory nature of our health care system; our out-of-balance economic and taxation system; our government's active avoidance of sound social policy on aging; ongoing mismanagement and bungling of public funds for elder care; and the public and professional foot dragging on end-of-life care reforms to relieve most elderly from languishing and dying in impersonal hospital or nursing home settings.

Although, this research may not address all of the issues I have discussed in this chapter, the caregivers' concerns I have documented provide a foundation for exploring the private, often anguished, responses to a deeply flawed elder care system in America.

The next section—an Interlude between chapters—contains "Caregiver Snapshots," a brief biography of each caregiver interviewed for the study. Whereas ages of the caregivers vary, as well as their economic, social, marital and psychological circumstances, each of them merits our recognition as a lifeline for a chronically ill, aged loved one in her life.

Caregiver Snapshots

The following brief biographies introduce you to the women whose stories of their caregiving experiences are featured in the chapters ahead. The "snapshots" provide information about the caregiver, her care receiver, some of the circumstances surrounding the giving of care, and in some instances, caregivers' words of wisdom that helped them through difficult times. All names except for Anne and myself have been fictionalized to preserve the anonymity of the participants.

Anne (written by her husband, Mike): Anne was a 100 percent atypical, fully-engaged mother of four; she is now a 100 percent fully-engaged caretaker. The main difference in the roles is her ability to treat me as an adult, capable of making decisions for myself, even though I am incapacitated by Parkinson's disease. She encourages me to continue doing what I am still able to do and she does not fret over what I cannot do. All the while, she continues to care for herself physically, intellectually and spiritually.

Antonia: A life-long caregiver, Antonia's first memories are of looking after her single mother. Enduring a life-threatening accident at age 12, Antonia believes she lived because she had a higher purpose—"I have always felt I survived for a reason." Today, she serves as a professional administrator in a care facility, as well as takes care of her elderly stepfather. She remains upbeat while confronting her own health challenges. Her advice: "Give and get a lot of hugs so you can recharge—and look at the lighter side. Even in the darkest moments, hold a spot for laughter."

Betty: An elementary teacher, Betty treasured the shared caregiving of her 88-year-old mother in assisted living with her sister. Betty's life continued as normal, with no dreams abandoned, no losses, no regrets, no guilt, and a stronger relationship with her mother. She continues to experience a feeling of being important and doing her best, cooperating with her sister to assist their mother at the end of life. "I know that I did my very best to assist my mother in her final challenging years of life."

Billie Mae: An independent, retired business woman, Billie Mae became frustrated with the management of her inept 24-7 "care force" for her husband with Parkinson's, blindness and heart disease. Billie Mae abandoned nothing and always moved forward with gratitude. She was her husband's eyes, his driver and companion. He "finally gave up at 95." She adds, "I have only been a widow for one week and though my feelings are deep my greatest loss is the death of my husband."

Carla: A professional caregiver and friend to a 60-year-old positive, appreciative, terminal breast cancer patient, Carla tried to live in the moment, but was overwhelmed by the denial of the patient's daughters. She remained grounded by her religious beliefs as the cancer kept coming back. Eventually, she helped her friend prepare to die, and stayed through to the end. "I owed her the best job I could do. One day I'll probably need someone to look after me."

Carmen: A professor, Carmen served as a facilitator for six years for her 75-year-old friend with Alzheimer's. Since home care was not an option, she used "the gentle care approach." She was frustrated by the disease, the deterioration of her once independent, capable colleague and the lack of professional input. In the latter years, she felt trapped and a sense of danger that finally merged into relief and loss of a friend and a mind. "Try not to think of yourself, think of the other person's needs and comforts. Don't lose your identity, but recognize this person's life isn't going to last much longer and you have time to do other things."

Carrie: As soon as she could walk, Carrie was a caregiver: first for her mother with multiple sclerosis, then her father, then a sister, then a neighbor, then children, postponing so many dreams. She has never known anything else, but remains philosophical. "Everything is temporary. Everything changes, it all passes—materials, emotions, life… it's all temporary."

Catherine: A competent, creative manager and working professor, Catherine remained socially active and managed to easily and happily fold the care of her 85-year-old flexible, uncomplaining mother into her professional and personal life for ten years. She provided social and spiritual stimulation, denying nothing pleasant either to herself or her mother. "I just kept up a normal life, interweaving my life with my job, weaving many threads together to form a pattern of life; hers was one of beauty. I suggest learning all you can from the person you're caring for."

Charlotte: A nurse who has multiple sclerosis, Charlotte has been married for 40 years. With good skills and a supportive family, she serves as a mutual caregiver with her 71-year old husband, who has Alzheimer's. Charlotte's role changed from physical to emotional. "When I had no legs, he held me up. I didn't owe him, I just wanted to take care of him. Reciprocity. I was sad to lose him but grateful for the time we had. I recommend worrying efficiently."

Cindy: A nurse, mother and reluctant daughter caregiver for her alcoholic father, Cindy felt annoyed and inconvenienced, with no support and no relief in sight. She dreaded the fights, as well. After three years, she placed her father in assisted living with much remorse and guilt and little contact. "He got exactly what he asked for."

Claire: An extrovert, walker and homemaker, Claire is also a resourceful and accepting caregiver who speaks of the "wheel of life." Claire suffered a stroke, kidney failure and high blood pressure during the care of her husband. She accepted their way of life, and truly felt loved and supported by her husband. She said she believes in a higher being. "Live so there are no regrets. We always assumed that we would go on forever. Now, I sort of live day-to-day."

Clarice: A never-married student with a 19-year-old, Clarice reiterates that "no one was good enough for Dad." Before Clarice "got custody" of her 79-year-old father in 2003, their relationship was distant. She moved him 2000 miles to her home. Caregiving ultimately took over her education, her finances, her home, her health and her emotional stability. "I just had to do it: get dressed, put on red lipstick and go do it. I believe there is a bigger plan, bigger than I and I can play that plan."

Claudia: As one member of a beautifully choreographed four-sibling team caring for their mother, Claudia and her siblings allowed their roles to be determined and adjusted by their mother from her room in a nursing home. She felt fortunate that her mother was able to call the shots and raised her to know that "...this is the best thing I can do with my time." She adds, "Let your life be your message."

Denise: In her middle years, Denise enjoyed sailing and sharing quiet times with her husband and her two boys. But in later life she was struck a bitter blow when a son committed suicide, and her husband developed inoperable lung cancer. The tragedies she faced led to serious illness, and eventually the inability to speak for months. Despite the setbacks Denise has encountered, she has done much inner work and feels healed and renewed. "It was such a difficult time; I felt so alone, but I felt good about helping him through the dying process. I kept my promise—to help him through the end."

Eva: A product of the circle of abuse, Eva was angry, guilty and overwhelmed. She also suffered from multiple personalities. She admits to having "a lot of hang-ups." While caring for her mother, she wished she would die, yet still wanted to make her mother happy. Ultimately, she felt healed as result of caregiving. "Let it go, let it go, let it all go, and it does."

Evelyn: Having retired early to care for husband with Alzheimer's, Evelyn accepted her role. "I never gave it a thought, it was no sacrifice, never longed for anything else. He was grateful; other people were very kind. We couldn't live in a condo—nothing for him to do. It was peaceful knowing I was doing the right thing: fulfilling God's will."

Faith: A community health educator who retired early, Faith became the designated caregiver for her difficult, negative, 87-year-old mother, an alcoholic with Parkinson's, heart failure, dementia and blindness. When Faith was nine, on crutches from polio, she began her caregiving career with multiple family members. After a lifetime of commitment, Faith felt "a sense of finality of care, an internal feeling that it was as good as it could be." She acted on her strong sense of connectedness with all others and her complete sense of democracy—no one more privileged than the other, the rhythm of human life and a sense of personal responsibility as an intelligent woman.

Fran: A 61-year-old with two knee replacements, Fran has been trying to prove herself to her husband and his family. She has been married for ten years to a demanding husband with Crohn's disease and short bowel syndrome, and who is numb from the waist down. Fran inherited the care of her mother-in-law, as well. Her husband's two unresponsive grown sons said, "You married him—you get Grandma, too." She has experienced both mental and physical devastation and almost complete isolation. "No care for this caregiver. Restoration? I go to Costco and get help loading the car."

Gloria: Remaining positive and upbeat despite her own health challenges, Gloria provided care for her husband, who suffered from heart disease, as well as her 85-year-old quadriplegic mother in a nursing home. She expected to care for her husband, adjusted to their new lifestyle of illness and traded their separate independent styles in favor of companionship, interdependence and sharing of interests. "What gets me through? Be appreciative if what you have now—you really have to live in the moment—next year I may be looking back and saying, 'I never had it so good.' Stay grateful and positive. It doesn't help you to look back. Find something positive to be and do."

Hazel: A Catholic housewife who once worked as a welder during World War II, Hazel is a self-sufficient woman who lives an uncomplicated, small-village life in Mexico. She has an ideal, holistic support team. She is a willing, yet no-nonsense caregiver of her husband, who had a debilitating stroke. "If he fell out of bed, Carlos came over, put him back. If we needed food, Louis arranged for it. When I needed a lifting device rigged up, the kid across the street built something. If I got fed up, I took it outside, walked it around, waited fifteen minutes, it was over. I didn't have to make any changes, kept playing cards and feeding the birds, just used common sense, that's the way to deal with things."

Helen: A homemaker and skeptical Christian with a good income, Helen consciously took on the role of caretaker for twelve years. Her husband of 60 years, an academic who was always pleasant—"a saint"—had neuropathy. "Love conquers all. Do and say the most loving thing at this moment for this particular person no matter what."

Ina: A retired teacher, Ina cared for her husband of 48 years, who had mesothelioma, a lung cancer caused by exposure to asbestos. She had a good son for support, and was able to maintain a normal lifestyle, never feeling confined or having to live alone. Her husband made most decisions and the future was simply not a topic. "Life changes completely during caregiving—just stop in your tracks. Do the best you can."

Jane: A self-acknowledged angry, out-of-control, highly stressed, bi-polar and driven daughter, Jane was often in denial about the consequences of her caregiving commitment to her father. Jane left her own young family to care for her abusive father with Alzheimer's, making choices "he can't argue with." She adds, "I'm going to keep trying until *he* gets it right."

Janice: Janice never sacrificed her spiritual development, but learned how to give up household chores and hobbies for more time with her mother at the nursing home, which was a half-hour drive away. Janice says she slowed down, took deep breaths and brisk walks. She laments a loss of free time, but acknowledges getting a great opportunity to hear wonderful family stories. "A positive, privileged, lucky experience."

Jean: A duty-bound daughter, Jean sees no end to the caregiving. She struggled through the death of her best friend and confidant in a constant state of stress, anxiety and grief while caring for her mother. She felt her own stages of life slip rapidly and regretfully away while her mother lived well past anyone's expectations. "The elderly are living so long."

Jill: Trying to remain spiritual throughout, Jill never felt loved by the negative, super-critical mother she cared for through the final passage of life. Jill triumphed because she knew well the skills of *The Eightfold Path to Personal Peace*. She practiced compassion moment-by-moment; she sought to see and appreciate the child-face of her mother before she was wounded. Jill believes, "You can't do any better than the best you can."

Joanne: An editor and Quaker, Joanne is enormously generous of spirit. She assumed the care of her 94-year-old mother, with whom she was estranged since she was five-years old. She embraced her final opportunity to know her mother, abandoning nothing, regretting nothing. "The world provides fascinating opportunities to ease the suffering. I did the best I could. I kept the covenant."

Joyce: Joyce tried to be a good person, even though she was deeply depressed. Her 94-year-old mother was a deaf, gullible, hard-hearted controller who was never loved as a child and showed little affection or appreciation to her daughter during the 14 years Joyce cared for her. "But, I'm so glad my mother's taken care of. I would feel terrible if no one had taken care of her."

Kali: Originally a residential care aide, Kali became a premature caregiver. She felt lonely, worried and bored, yet also validated by caregiving. She later moved in with her grandparents, providing care 24 hours a day; she couldn't go home anymore. Kali's grandfather was contrary, obstructive and controlling, while her grandmother with Parkinson's was sweet, happy and appreciative. "I got to know her better, keep her warm. She was like a mother to me. I don't believe this is a just world. He even cheated at cards."

Kathy: A fitness trainer, Kathy moved to care for both parents, ages 102 and 92. She copes by meditating, praying and walking. Sometimes, she feels overwhelmed, tied down or wants to run. "How long can people live?" Kathy changed her thoughts, worked on intentionality, advocated and cared for herself. "I can do this—take care of my parents, and I'll come out stronger, healthier and more in tune."

Kendra: Between the ages of 15 and 21, Kendra cared for her father when her mother left to care for her own father. Too young to make a conscious choice or be a caretaker, she was left exhausted, sad, hopeless and helpless. Kendra remained a caregiver until her father's death. Her mother continues to be resentful, blaming and controlling, while Kendra feels too mature for her age and hopes to move on. "Don't sacrifice everything—save something for yourself."

Laura: Laura retired early from clerical work and didn't see herself as caretaker. With multiple illnesses herself, she took on the complicated role of care in two separate locations for her 90-year-old mother with Alzheimer's and her 85-year-old father with stroke and depression. She spent countless hours driving over, driving back and delivering dinners daily. She learned much, though. "See the humor. You can laugh or cry—we chose to laugh."

Lenora: A professional caregiver who earned $250 a day, Lenora cared for her friend, who was adamant about staying in her own home. Lenora felt little disturbance in her life, did an adequate job not wanting to "leave her in the lurch," and had a theory that things aren't as bad as they seem.

Marianne: A professional caregiver for two-and-a-half years with only weekends to herself, Marianne eventually got tired of the job. "[You] can't take on their energy. I realized it was time to get out." She could no longer make the adjustments necessary. "Take responsibility just for your own things—not others."

Marsha: Marsha took medical leave for two-and-a-half years to care for her appreciative father, who had Alzheimer's and cancer. She says she has no regrets, doing it all because he had always loved her. She loved having him around, appreciated the opportunity to hear his end of life storytelling and learned a new kind of patience and kindness. "I didn't do very well taking care of myself."

Martha: A 78-year-old retired researcher with high coping skills, Martha meditates and reviews choices daily. She strives for an open heart, but lacks privacy and free time. She is usually fairly patient and is sustained by strong friendships, good neighbors and an active support group. After everything, she has learned "the bureaucratic dance." Her husband of 52 years with Alzheimer's has a Ph.D., but is not a real people person. He is sometimes positive, sometimes negative, living in a very confusing world. "We're on this earth for a short time; we've been given all sorts of gifts and it is up to us to use them. The natural world is incredibly wondrous. We need to be respectful of things in this world and not do violence to them."

Mary Beth: A retired high school teacher with high blood pressure and a history of mini-strokes, Mary Beth prepared herself for her husband's care. She retained a good lawyer, got Power of Attorney and access to a good pension, and sought out a support group. She then chose her fights. She saw it coming—the Alzheimer's and Parkinson's—and experienced it all, from his thoughts of suicide, despondency, memory problems to the controlling, argumentative elder filled with self-doubt and worthlessness who exhibited paranoia. His final stage at age 85 was one of "absolute appreciation," and repetitive apologies for any transgressions. "You are allowed to feel sorry for yourself for three minutes, then it's over—you cannot succumb to self-pity. You have to have friends, you have to have friends, you have to have friends" (said with emphasis).

Mary Ellen: Mary Ellen went rapidly through the stages from happy wife, fun companion, black-jack dealer to that of angry, resentful, burned-out, depressed caregiver of two, living on food stamps. Her husband had Alzheimer's and dementia, while her adopted nine-year-old son is totally disabled. "I believe in honesty. I pray and meditate. No one is perfect. I am surviving."

Maxine: A semi-retired secretary, Maxine "carried her 87-year-old sister on her back," to live and care for her at the YWCA. She says she did the best she could with no one else to help. Sometimes she was cross, sometimes frustrated and impatient; but she trusted in a Higher Power and gained understanding and compassion for someone suffering from indescribable, untreatable pain. "This experience was necessary for my own growth and understanding. Without it, I would have less compassion for others ill or dying. I believe you create your own thoughts and it's important not to let yourself be pulled down into negative thinking."

Melanie: Viewing caregiving for two sets of grandparents and her father as an opportunity and an honor, Melanie experienced very few frustrations, inconveniences or losses. She successfully teamed with her mother and sister for round-the-clock care until the very end-of-life. "Everything in life has a reason and purpose. We may not know it, but it is there. Don't let the little things bog you down—enjoy them all!"

Nanette: A dedicated scholar and student of caregiving, Nanette felt inadequate and overwhelmed. She feared the ineffectiveness of medications, financial pressures and her children's reactions. She witnessed her brilliant husband's rapid deterioration, keeping him at home until he resisted living, and observed evasive and cynical professionals. She also saw her dreams of travel and spending their old age together dissolve with each obstacle. She will never forget her late husband's depression and the oppressive smells of the dying in the nursing homes. In the end, she learned the full range of care and life's expanding spiritual lessons. She urges all caregivers: "Get the story out!"

Natalie: A loving, responsible and compassionate daughter and niece, Natalie gave for 10 years, even beyond her ability to care for herself. As a new bride, she took care of her father first, then her mother, then her uncle, seeing each commitment through with intentional grace, dignity and some private tears and resentment for the little that was left over for her patient, supportive husband. "Seek support, accept help. Don't isolate yourself from friends."

Nora: A nurse and eldest daughter, Nora became the caretaker of her 89-year-old mother with Alzheimer's and her 89-year-old father with depression and heart problems. The worst part? Not being able to fix everything, as well as the constant crying and shutting down. "Am I a horrible person for not bringing them to my home?"

Patricia: A conscientious Mexican Catholic, Patricia is the wife of a very sick, deeply stubborn and profoundly controlling American husband twenty years her senior. She prayed on her knees every day so she would be able to talk on the phone with her distant family, to ask God to make her husband more cooperative and take his medications, to get help from her husband's children and to transform miserable people. "It is our commitment in our culture to care for all humans."

Rachel: A 63-year-old teacher, Rachel grew up caring for her suicidal, alcoholic mother. As an adult, she considered herself a burned-out caregiver. Rachel was detached, passively unable to cope, and decided to hand over the care of her husband with colon cancer to her willing and very capable adult children. "I recommend getting all the help you can, do no harm, and do everything you can to avoid grief."

Renae: A grieving rescuer and caretaker of three—son with Down's Syndrome, mother with Alzheimer's and sick live-in boyfriend—Renae has also recently dealt with the death of her former husband. Renae was conflicted, uncomfortable and stressed about the appearance of caring for and living with her boyfriend, who declined rapidly with pancreatic cancer only one-and-a-half years after moving in with her. "I lost myself in all the illness, gained weight, lost interest in everything, gave up."

Rita: Performing an act of love for her stepfather, Rita left her husband and children to fulfill her promise to let him die with respect and dignity in his home, all the while, allowing him to call the shots. "Keep your cool and all falls into place."

Roberta: A Christian who retired early from teaching, Roberta continued to be a friend and musician as she cared for her husband with dementia for three years. It was "like taking care of a toddler." She tried to think ahead and prepare, as well as advocated on behalf of Alzheimer's and dementia patients. "Don't try to do this alone. Get your spiritual life in order."

Rosanne: With a good husband, no children and a spacious home, Rosanne gave up her job to care for her mother. She felt very fortunate to have plenty of room for her mother to sit in the sun. She and her husband tried their best to make her mother "feel like a duchess and look like a million bucks." But then her mother suffered a frightening and devastating attack of vertigo and Rosanne had to place her in a home.

Rose: Sometimes despondent, sometimes just worn out, Rose learned how not to "blow her temper" while caring for her cantankerous, opinionated, independent, smart 96-year-old mother. "Like mother, like daughter."

Sally: A single mom of seven, with three children in college, Sally is an only child who rode the caregiving roller-coaster for fifteen years. Her mother suffered from Alzheimer's, while her father had heart failure. Sally was sucked dry by three homes to finance, countless arguments, the horrible decline of her parents and wrenching life support decisions. At one point, her mother almost died, and then bounced back. The confusion and depression was overwhelming as Sally faced homes to sell and papers to shred. "It's a painful experience, like having a baby, but labor's easier when you know what to expect; make it through naturally, you can't prevent it. Women I knew who weren't prepared for labor, screamed. I wasn't prepared for caregiving. I screamed, but that's the cycle of life."

Sandra: Sandra's unappreciative and negative husband was only 59 when he died of heart disease and cancer. Their relationship remained rocky throughout his illness. "Intentions were there, but I didn't know what it would be like… financial stuff, guilt, his anger, no power, dreadful medical system, turbulence. Our emotions just did us in. Breakdown or breakthrough? 'God grant me the serenity to accept the things I cannot change, courage to change the things I can, and the wisdom to know the difference.'"

Sarah: A feisty, self-educated octogenarian and former actress/singer, Sarah began ten years of care for her blind, estranged husband, Jack, who lived in a separate but connected apartment. Sarah was anxious and tired, proud that she didn't put him in the veteran's hospital. At the same time, she did not feel any gratitude for the situation, either. "Gratitude? In a pig's eye." Meditation, movies, girlfriends, dinners out and making Jack laugh altogether made Sarah's years of caregiving easier.

Sharon: Married for fifty years, Sharon "never really worked" because her husband didn't want her to. She became a willing but exhausted caregiver for her husband, who had lymphoma. "He would have done it for me, if I'd been the sick one." Sharon and her husband belonged to the Hemlock Society, but physician-assisted suicide was not available.

Eventually, her husband died of pneumonia. Sharon makes crafts for sale and belongs to a co-op. "I get lonely sometimes, but I know I've been fortunate all my life—blessed. I feel he shouldn't have died, but we all have to do it."

Sylvia: An exhausted 86-year-old retired secretary with strong family support, Sylvia was happy for a "good day," that is, one without unmanageable pain from her broken wrists. She cared for her 93-year-old husband at home with congestive heart failure, memory problems and despondency. "Sometimes when he gets out of line, I used a little shock treatment: just do what has to be done, but pleasantly, and put us both to bed." Sylvia suggests something she deems healthy neglect. "Let people do as much as they can without trying to help them."

Teri: A premature caregiver of her grandparents, Teri felt impotent and angry at those who normally would assume the role of caregiver, but declined. Teri lost an important stage of early adulthood, but through faith and belief in a Higher Power, did the best she could with the limited tools, power and respect she was granted. "I believe it's good karma— that somewhere, somehow, it's good to do good deeds."

Theresa: A retired librarian, recovering alcoholic and intentional caregiver, Theresa felt no burden and learned from her mother's example how to give. Caring for her 94-year-old mother was a privilege. Theresa relaxed by dancing with seniors in the nursing home where her mother played in the rhythm band. Together they shared support, convictions, values, expenses and a love of each other. "Give till it hurts. Love with all of your might and it will come back to you. Amen!"

Toni: After six years of caring for her 81-year-old mother, Toni feels resigned, frustrated, trapped and angry. Now facing menopause, she resents her loss of freedom and privacy, and feels there is no good part of care except fulfilling responsibility. She is simply not prepared to be the "mom." She said, "I expected to help but not do every single thing. Run around, run around, solve one problem, another pops up."

Virginia: A retired professor who was divorced with a strong social life, Virginia accepted the challenge of caregiving. She was always close to her mother, who had Parkinson's. What began as home care ultimately led to a nursing home. "Coming to the end, I could see it more clearly.

I think I did my part—a job well done. I recommend: Don't look too far ahead, one day at a time. Your attitude affects the patient. Try to rise to the occasion."

Wendy: Now 80 years old, Wendy was a 65-year-old writer/illustrator and recent Christian convert. Wendy became a caregiver to a complaining, unappreciative 93-year-old mother, who had been "whittled away by age." Wendy resisted resentment of her mother's disapproval, and was grateful for the opportunity to do something for her, to expand her love—a "strong element of my conversion."

And finally, a tribute to our sole male caregiver.

Ramone: A gentle, male caregiver, husband, father, rancher, boiler-maker and native of Chile, Ramon, 80, cared for his wife, who had atypical face pain. He'd have it no other way. "I am proud. It's payback for 50 years of caring." Her illness involved nine years of excruciating, horrifying, untreatable pain, as well as unpredictable behavior. His loyalty, commitment and sacrifice were unfailing, as were his prayers. He remembers the thousands of breakfast, lunch and tea trays set with fine linens, pewter and flowers he toted up a spiral staircase to Lola's sickbed. "This is my life till death do us part." Lola died September 8, 2006 at home in Bahia D'Kino, Mexico on the Sea of Cortez.

PART II

THE WOMEN'S NARRATIVES

Chapter 3

Caregiver Burden

It is not unusual for family members to feel alone in their struggle with a chronic illness. People may drift away... it may seem impossible to get out of the house, and life narrows down to a tight circle of lonely misery.
~ *The Thirty-Six Hour Day*,
Nancy L. Mace and Peter V. Rabins[1]

Defining Caregiving

From an objective viewpoint, caregiving is neither a negative nor a positive experience. Sociologists Toni Calasanti and Kathleen Slevin observe: "Caregiving involves rendering physical and emotional care, as well as instrumental or mechanical services."[2] They point to two dimensions: "caring for" involves the physical activities of seeing to another's needs, whereas "caring about" entails the emotional or affective dimension, including the ethic of feeling responsible. This means that *caring* is a relationship that involves at least one caregiver and one care receiver. Although caregivers ostensibly have greater power, the "success" of the endeavor may depend upon the care receiver's reactions. Soothing a disturbed elder, encouraging a reluctant mother in a nursing home to eat her meal and helping a feeble family member to the toilet appear to be minuscule tasks, but once achieved, these accomplishments provide mutual gratification.

Caregivers and care receivers are locked into a delicately balanced dance. Under an optimal balanced order, caregivers intuitively know when to press forward with an activity, and when to back down. Care receivers, wishing to please their benefactor within their comfort level, willingly accept the caring assistance, or gently modify it to fit their needs.

We have all known cases in which this intricately patterned juggling act works. The relationship between giver and receiver deepens over time; each understands and accepts the limitations of their situation. Both are spiritually informed, have a sense of humor and validate one another in myriad ways—for example, with displays of love, support and gratitude. Even within difficult caring relationships, moments may arise that make all the effort of both giving and receiving worthwhile. The balance is restored, if only momentarily. Even when the balance has been restored, a caregiver knows she will have to repeat the same exercise over and over again.

For the most part, however, the neutrality of our sociological definition masks the everyday conditions caregivers experience. Caregiving is not a monolithic experience—either all bad or all good. Rather, it varies with the situation, personal expectations of the parties involved and the capacity and willingness of givers and receivers to behave reciprocally in a gracious, loving manner. Such an ideal model is fairly rare. As our caregivers demonstrate, the act of giving care is fraught with deep losses, insecurities and concerns. Caregivers face ambivalence about their own capacity for benevolence. They also confront physical and emotional exhaustion as they wrestle with family baggage. And, caregivers must strive to overcome the cultural ethic of individualism, which wreaks such havoc because the act of giving care is genuinely a self-less endeavor.

Levels of care vary greatly in terms of time, special demands on the caregiver, her personal resources and the quantity and quality of care required. Regardless of how much care was given, all caregivers reported they experienced a variety of physical, mental, emotional and other challenges that caused excessive stress. Problems include conflicts with family members over the type of care, medical indifference or neglect, the excessive financial costs of care, as well as the loss of friends and family for daily support. If the caregiver pushes too hard, the loved one may resist—refuse out right to cooperate—or regress and take on childish behavior and otherwise act irrationally. Sometimes, the difficulty of care has to do with the nature of the loved one's response to his or her illness. They may demonstrate obstinacy, rejection, hostility or become overly demanding, among other reactions.

According to medical persons I spoke with, many emotional conditions associated with terminal illness prove resistant to intervention. A caregiver must simply bear up under the strain. When a loved one becomes a danger to himself or others—a condition afflicting nearly 40 percent of these care receivers—legal, medical and social challenges come up for caregivers. Such circumstances contribute to hopelessness among both caregivers and care receivers. For caregivers, not being able to help their loved one was a major source of psychological and emotional distress.

In many circumstances, then, care becomes burdensome, an unwanted, even despised obligation. Part of the burden resides in its inevitability—the lack of choice involved—because of moral and emotional ties to family members. Certainly, another part of the burden of caregiving is its apparent all-consuming nature. Robin West, a feminist writer, suggests that caregiving, by its nature, essentially impoverishes or diminishes the opportunities of those who engage in it, whether freely chosen or not. Unlike other "chosen" paths of life, caregivers cannot simply leave their charge, because *by definition*, they are emotionally and ethically committed to the work of caring for their dependents. Family caregivers, unlike employees, enjoy no autonomy, cannot walk off the job, unionize or strike for better working conditions, nor can they anticipate a termination date. "Consequently, caregivers receive all the vulnerability but none of the solace and certainly none of the security from the "at will" aspect of their employment.[3]

To appreciate the burdensome aspect of caregiving, we must acknowledge both qualitative and quantitative aspects of what has been termed the "36-hour day"[4] or the "burden of care."[5] The following sections examine the caregivers' narratives, which describe the problematic nature of caregiving. Also included are the stories of those who face the challenges of days, months and years of giving care.

Losses and Imbalances

The sense of loss seems pervasive, at least during earlier stages of caregiving. Not only does the caregiver recognize her own life as undergoing radical change, but also, she perceives the monumental losses assaulting her loved one. We mention a few hardships that profoundly affect both caregivers and care receivers: loss of independence, self-control, financial security, predictability, future dreams, physical and mental health, normal role relationships with one another and other family members, leisure time, preferred lifestyles and a sense of personal balance. At the same time, an overwhelming sense of responsibility hovers over the giving of care. Role relationships are especially fragile. Illness evokes frustration and anger and the care receiver often lashes out.

Anne, a 61-year-old caregiver looking after her 70-year-old spouse, Mike, who had been recently diagnosed with Parkinson's disease, became the object of her husband's wrath, when he blamed her for everything that was going wrong.

> 'It's your fault. If you didn't have that job, I wouldn't be sick. If you would be nicer to my children, I wouldn't be sick. If you'd just behave differently, I wouldn't feel sick. If you weren't so hard on me, I could stand up straighter, speak in public without being nervous and write a legible sentence.'

Kali's experience was wholly different. At 28 years of age, she became the "designated caregiver" looking after both her grandparents at the same time, one diagnosed with a stroke condition and the other with Parkinson's disease. Her burden was not only the loss of her young, carefree life, but also her inability to communicate with this older generation, and the feeling that she simply could not meet their needs.

> It was such a dark time for us. I tried to work with them to make life decisions, but problem-solving was very difficult. Trying to explain why things are the way they are [about their age and life situation] was truly impossible. I wish I could have done more to help them during that time.

Jean's experience echoes that of Kali's in that other family members failed to come to her aid, and her sense of futility about the situation undermined her sense of competence. Jean, a 50-year-old married woman, suffered deeply over the course of her caregiving career, including the death of a supportive friend, her mother's nearly total dependence upon her—even living in her home for three years—and her belief that she has sacrificed one dream after another without adequate compensation for the years of providing care.

Jean said:

> *While I was taking care of Mother, I was in a car accident, I suffered*
> *the loss of a loved one, I was exhausted, and the year Mother moved*
> *here from Spokane, I had pneumonia. She moved in with us for a while.*
> *I was afraid I would have a heart attack.* [But] *I felt duty-bound. No*
> *one else in the family helped. My mother's been ill for eight years. She's*
> *90 years old.*
>
> *Mother had dementia, osteoporosis and Parkinson's disease. I was*
> *really taken aback by the Parkinson's. She was incontinent, confused,*
> *sometimes unable to communicate, sad and depressed, suffering from*
> *eating and memory problems, feeling worthless and easily distracted.*

Jean felt the full weight of moral and emotional commitment.

> [Although] *she's very polite, she expected I would provide care. I spent*
> *11 to 20 hours a week providing shopping, housework, transporting*
> [her] *to medical appointments, bathing* [her], *cooking, calling medical*
> *providers, personal care, dressing* [her], [making] *financial arrange-*
> *ments, encouraging her to participate in activities. I try to encourage*
> *her independence.*
>
> *I've tried to prioritize between my mother and my daughter. I've had*
> *to abandon my dream of going back to school. I see myself getting older*
> *and older as she gets older and older.*
>
> *My greatest loss is the opportunity to engage in this stage of my life.*
> *I've been doing this since I was 44. I didn't realize how great the flex-*
> *ibility was before I began caregiving. I miss the time alone and with my*
> *children. I felt relief when she left to go back to her house* [assisted liv-
> ing]. *I was tired and resigned. I have a parent who has lived long and*
> *I couldn't imagine she could live this long. Now, I no longer feel this is a*
> *stage of my life—it is my life. I don't see an end to it.*
>
> *My main support comes from my husband and another friend, my*
> *walking partner. I miss my friend. She died in a car accident. Mother*
> *would have liked me to be her friend. I tried, but I didn't feel that. She*
> *didn't have many friends. I felt better about myself* [after] *I asked my*
> *mother to try assisted living.* [Now] *I visit her every day and when I*
> *get home I know my time is my own. It's difficult and frustrating just to*
> *have to go—repeatedly.*

My advice to caregivers: Start immediately reminding yourself [to] hold onto the dreams of what you want to do with your life, so you don't lose that—especially with the elderly living longer and longer. We need to take care of ourselves.

Many daughters, reluctant to give care, feel imposed upon by family and/or the sick elder. They may resist, but with a perception of having no choice, ultimately become the "designated caregiver," as one inter-viewee explains it. At the same time, daughters feel burdened with a deep sense of obligation and responsibility.

Cindy, who commuted between the West Coast and the Midwest for years to supervise her mother's care, observed:

I was responsible for taking care of my mother because I'm the old-est daughter. I'm the medical professional—that qualifies me. It was an obligation, but one person should not have to shoulder such a responsibility.

Inability to Define Moral Boundaries

Caregivers tend to react against, rather than respond to the feelings and losses of their loved one. Without a strong sense of "I can do this, but not this," they take on any and all responsibilities, regardless of their age or capacity. Carrie, now 39 and a student at the local university, has been caring for her blind father and his companion over the last few years. However, her earliest "training" was nurturing her mother as a small girl, then as an adult. She has also been caring for her stepchildren, and over the last few years, meeting the needs of her sister, who recently died of cancer. In a significant sense, Carrie qualifies as a "progressive caregiver"—an expert, but without pay or public recognition.

In a written disclosure she sent to me about her multiple caregiving roles from childhood to the present, she said:

When I was born in 1965, my mother had already been diagnosed with M.S. (multiple sclerosis). Pregnancy and delivery escalated her symp-tomatology. By the time I could walk, I was caregiving for my mother. We did have some neighbors, who would 'stop by' and check on us, but basically, I would retrieve or reach for things for my mother (lunch, etc.) and assist her in getting to the bathroom 'on time.' She was wheelchair-

bound at this time, and was progressively worsening, so by the time I started attending school full-time (first grade), no one was home any-more to care for her (with the needs that she had), so she moved into a nursing home. From then on, I would ride my bike to the nursing home every day after school to see her... then I would get home by 5:00 p.m. to cook dinner for my father, who was returning from work... During the time Mom was in the nursing home, I would read to her, fix her sheets and blankets, give her water, help her eat, and there would be many times I would communicate her needs to the staff at the nursing home. She would get upset, needing something, and I would 'go get them' and communicate her wishes, and follow-up with them [staff] to make sure they were carried out.

Because of her continuous caregiving responsibilities since childhood, Carrie said that "part of me feels as if I've never known anything else [except caregiving]."

For others, like Faith, now in her sixties, whose early life was colored by her mother's alcoholism, it is as though caregiving defines one's entire existence. Faith said: "Caregiving is a life imprint" that began early and continued throughout her life.

I was the designated caregiver. Some of us are programmed for this. You don't make a choice. I was responsible for all of the five older genera-tions and one of my uncles had Alzheimer's. For three years while I was in high school, I was the enabler [for mother's alcoholism], then for two people in my extended family, cousins and others. When I was nine, I contracted polio, and was in a wheelchair, even on crutches, but that didn't seem to matter. I was sent to my grandmother to look after her. On crutches! Later, I took care of the father of my cousin.

Now, as an adult she faced caring for her mother, who never acknowl-edged her.

When she was 87, I took direct care of her for 18 months. She had con-gestive heart failure, dementia, Parkinson's disease and paranoia. She called the sheriff once to protect herself against taking a shower. I was so relieved to get a diagnosis of Parkinson's: relieved that symptoms were not related to alcoholism. Mother was always able to talk—verbally aggressive.

Faith was notified that her mother had been hit by a nursing home aide. The incident caused her to lose an eye. So Faith brought her back to live with her in a four-room cottage. Faith said: "She was supposed to die over the weekend, but she lived for 18 months." The relationship had never been a healthy one, but her sense of responsibility was paramount over any other considerations. Faith pointed out:

> *I really felt devalued when she said, 'You've never been any good,' or 'I should have never had you.' She was alcoholic. I'd heard all that before. And, yet I felt a strong commitment to my mother's care… a lifetime commitment. I felt responsible for every bite she took.*
>
> *I had been a professional woman, intellectually growing and providing for my security. After a few months of caregiving, I was tired and confused about the future—no closure happening. I was responsible for so much. My terrible concern is that I left her in a nursing home where she was hit [by an attendant]. So I owed her this [care].*

Joanne is a middle-aged woman confronted with the long-term care of a mother who was never there for her. Yet, like most caregivers we interviewed, she had an all-consuming sense of responsibility. The story begins with abandonment at age five by a mother who dropped her off at an older sister's, and showed her little or no support throughout her life.

> *I never really lived with my mother. That was part of my mental problem with her.*

Many years later, she encountered her mother again—a feeble 80-year-old woman, suffering from mini-strokes, heart problems and osteoporosis. Helping her effectively required that Joanne seek a more secure housing situation. She placed her mother in an assisted living facility two states away, a solution that appeared to work for two to three years. At one point, Joanne realized her mother was not receiving adequate care.

> *They brought her a commode—a dirty, used commode. I took her out of there within 24 hours.*

When her mother required skilled nursing care, she transported her to a nearby facility, where Joanne could supervise her care.

[Once she was ill] *she couldn't come live with us. My husband was not very supportive. I had to make all the decisions alone. I feel some anger and resentment about that.*

For seven years, I spent 31 to 40 hours a week transporting my mother to appointments, calling or interacting with medical providers, dressing and walking her, dealing with financial arrangements, constantly filling out forms, taking care of her little room in the nursing home. The food was atrocious, so I took her out for dinner.

The most physically or emotionally demanding were things that involved paperwork. Conversations with my mother and the medical details with the dentist and the skin doctor took so much time. I took her over to our 'secret garden' and walked around the apartments. I got her a child's sleeping bag to keep her warm. I took her for drives—so she could talk. That didn't work. She couldn't hear a thing. She didn't enjoy errands and things.

I mostly didn't express my feelings in front of my mother. She was so fragile. I never had a conversation with her. She avoided conversations. I dropped out of all social and professional clubs; dropped most of my friends, too. Eventually, I talked to a counselor.

I do feel sorry for my mother, because of her life. My emotions always go to my children. I owe my mother something. There was the conflict of caring for a mother I didn't know—yet I knew her better than she knew me. There were things she gave me. Still, I had so much trouble picking out Mother's Day cards.

My greatest gain was time spent with my mother. It was an unusual situation: the first time we lived in the same state. She loved hymns, so I sang her favorite songs. During the holidays, I brought her a little gift every day.

I felt overwhelmed one time when I took my mother to the Fountain [drug store]. *She had an episode, probably a stroke, and then she looked dead. She loved parades and horses. I always took her to the fair on the bus with other nursing home residents. At the end, she missed the parade.*

Before caregiving, my relationship with my mother was distant. I took care of her like I was her mother. I learned to keep her routine in the seven years I cared for her. I was able to sit with her all day while she died. And when she died, I had [a] strong feeling that I kept my covenant. 'I took care of you.' It was very satisfying. It was very hard, but I saw it to the end.

Caring For Someone Who Will Never Get Better

Since long-term elder care is most typically resolved with the death of the care receiver, caregivers must, early on, incorporate the death and dying of their loved one into their every day thinking and planning. This means that for caregivers, "letting go" early in the caregiving stage serves as the most effective strategy for coping with the declining health of their loved one. Since we live in a death-denying culture, which strenuously rejects death not as an option, but only as a failure, most caregivers woefully fall short at maintaining the necessary distance. They often allow whatever is happening to the loved one to unfold, without processing the experience, and then blame themselves for both their own bad feelings and any negative outcomes.

After Fran received her husband's medical diagnosis of Crohn's disease, she flew into a rage. A sense of futility absorbed her attention as partial paralysis set in, rendering him immobile, incontinent and impotent. Months later, she was still trying to deal with his death.

I was pretty angry. I still deal with it [his dying]. *He was numb from the waist down. I was losing my husband, and changing from wife to caregiver. I know he will not get better. I was so disappointed in myself in terms of giving good care, because of my own medical problems.*

Carla, a 50-year-old mother of two, who cared for a friend during her terminal illness with cancer, felt overwhelmed on two counts: her own emotional crisis over her friend's dying, and that of her friend's daughters, who refused to acknowledge the reality of their mother's death.

I felt overwhelmed when her cancer came back. When people die on you, you lose part of yourself. You give so much of yourself. It's hard to see them get relapses. I worried about her. Was she really going to be

OK? Was she ready to die? Had she made her peace with everyone? I felt overwhelmed with [my friend's] *daughters. I tried not to say harshly, 'your mom's dying. She doesn't want to eat, I can't force her to eat.' I tried to give them information, but her daughters denied their mother's illness.*

The Balance Between Freedom and Attachment

Caregivers frequently have deep ambivalence about achieving a balance between freedom and attachment. In giving herself too freely to another, a caregiver tends to lose herself, contributing to feelings of exploitation or even abandonment by the loved one. This is particularly true when the sick elder has dementia or has lost the capacity for rational thinking.

Rosanne, a consulting editor, brought her ailing mother to live with her and her husband in their large house. Initially, she had no idea of how taxing this caregiving project would be. She sums up the time she devoted to her mother.

The caregiving role is so draining, [that] *you don't have the energy to read the usual books. But the lighter literature doesn't give you what you need! You read mystery stories, preferably ones with lots of humor. It's like having a baby (and you need to listen). Mom would have good and bad days, but she never was herself. I could see the* [deteriorating] *process going on.*

Rosanne's mother had vertigo, dementia, congestive heart failure and was subject to mini-stokes. As a result, she needed constant supervision. At first, caring for her mother was a joyous, loving experience, but over time her mother's sense of entitlement and self-centeredness wore Rosanne's material and emotional reserves down. Another solution needed to be found.

We lived in this neighborhood for 10 years. Taking care of Mother was easier because I lived in a very large house. My husband was very supportive. We had no children, and my father paid most of Mother's expenses. When we realized Mother was not receiving adequate care in her assisted living facility, we brought her to our home, where she stayed for 10 months.

I had always had in mind that there was room in the house if we needed to. I thought we could manage with in-home care.

The best part was seeing Mother have a good time, seeing her appearance come back—like a duchess again. We hugged her and smiled at her. We indulged her and made sure she looked like a million bucks!

I provided shopping, housework, transporting [her] to appointments, bathing assistance, cooking, cutting up her food, calling and interacting with medical providers, versatile care, transferring, walking her, financial arrangements, giving medications. We did a great job! [However] there's a big price to pay: trying to show her a good time 51 to 60 hours a week, even though I had 30 hours of help per week. We used a baby monitor. I was happy to do it and so was my husband.

A good chunk of our monthly expenses was for Adult Day Health (ADH). Once I took her to ADH, [and] I figured things out, it got a lot easier.

During the time we were caregiving, I lost work, so I lost money. I couldn't concentrate. I lost freedom—that's the thing. Even if someone was there, I was on a short leash—a caregiver continuum. My relationship with my mother had always been good, but that relationship changed as the dementia progressed. With dementia came entitlement feelings.

A difficult decision for me was to send my mother back to Eastern Washington. She had a devastating Transient Ischemic Attack (TIA). I thought she was going to die or be a vegetable. I told my dad she needed to go home. There was an opening at the home. On Wednesday, he picked her up, and she looked like death. I visit her in Eastern Washington. They let her eat anything and now she's overweight.

If I could wave a magic wand, I would wish for a big house and deep pockets for all caregivers. That's what I would do. Take care of yourself. Just sit down. Go outside. Unless you have that time, even a book won't recharge you.

For Kendra, a young teenager when she took over the care of her father, freedom of choice evaporated when she felt "forced" to replace her caregiving mother, who "deserted" the family to look after her own father. Kendra's optimism carried her through the earliest sacrificial period. However, it did not enable Kendra to heal her mother's continuous grieving over the loss of both her father and her husband, or put an end to the animosity her mother had for her.

Before I started caregiving, I was young, with the world at my feet. After a few months, I'm hoping for this to end. I'm in high school, a busy student athlete. And after a year, I'm wanting to change my life.

I didn't choose it, but was more or less forced into the situation when Mom left to care for her father. I took care of Dad 31 to 40 hours a week for six years, [including] high school. He took 25 medications for heart disease, kidney failure and lung problems. The most physically and emotionally demanding was transporting him to appointments and calling or interacting face-to-face with medical providers. I didn't mind at all—he was there and needed me. I did feel hopeless and wished there was something more that I could do.

I had a dream of playing softball in college and I was accepted to my first choice school, but I turned it down to stay closer to my father. I lived with him and he had given me all he could, so I gave him all I could when he needed me. The best part was that I could change things for him. I was helping someone and he showed his appreciation. I loved making him happy. He was my mother and my father. We had a stronger relationship and an unspeakable trust as a result of my caregiving.

The burdens I carry involve an impossible relationship with my mother. She is very resentful, blames me for making my dad love me more than her, thinks I get between her and her men. On the whole though, taking care of my father was an accomplishment. I felt more mature than my peers and more knowledgeable. I value integrity and I try to do the 'right' thing. [I am] too forgiving sometimes… I don't like to drag out arguments or hold grudges.

I did a good deed, I guess. I felt blessed for sacrificing some things I cared about.

For seven years, Roberta cared for her 85-year-old husband. She has worked through her loss of freedom by having a strong faith in God and deep forgiveness, but clearly recognizes the severe constraints of her life.

You have to let go of the things you had in the past. If there are things [that need resolving] *in your marital history, you'd better get into the business of forgiveness, or it will eat you alive.*

My husband suffered from dementia, Alzheimer's-like symptoms, hallucinations, Parkinson's-like symptoms and incontinence. He experienced confusion, [an] inability to communicate—using the wrong word. He was also in denial about his health problems, had memory problems and [was] prone to moments of despondency.

This meant that Roberta needed to take over all the responsibility of the household, prop him up emotionally, as well as structure her husband's time to give him a sense of feeling *useful*. She likened it to looking after a small child.

I do everything: 80 or more hours a week. This is my life. There's really little Raymond can do. He can vacuum (Oreck) and do the dishes. I try to find any little job to help him feel useful—folding napkins, sweeping. He can't dust or determine what needs dusting. The most physically demanding is cleaning the bathrooms—the times he's incontinent.

He takes my arm when we walk in the wind. I tell him, 'We'll get through this. It will be okay.'

I do feel overwhelmed sometimes. I need to work on patience. It's answering the same questions over and over. Our relationship has changed. I have to do everything—make all of the decisions—no shared decisions or activities. There's a lack of initiative on his part.

My greatest loss is my freedom to do things in the evening. I can't just say, 'I'm going to a concert or a lecture. I'll see you in a couple of hours.' During the daytime, Raymond goes to Adult Day Health (ADH), otherwise I take him everywhere I go. I have no independence.

Raymond was home for four days. ADH was closed. Those conditions presented a difficult pattern. There's a lot of pressure to keep him occupied and structure the day to keep him busy. I have to deal with my own understanding that he really doesn't know how to do something anymore. I tell myself, he does not know how to do that. He can't remember. My own work is learning those behaviors so I can respond to him in the most Godly way.

I've lost touch with my family and friends. It's like taking care of a toddler. I'm grieving that. It's okay. I have [a] strong desire to serve my husband. I made a clear and conscious choice to be Raymond's primary caregiver. Yes, I could have divorced him, but that would not be compatible with my calling in Christ. Part of serving God is to serve Raymond. I want my life to be a reflection of God.

The most unfair experience I had over the course of caregiving is [that] the whole medical care system is out of whack. I think the rich don't have to care, but for the lower-middle class the costs are exorbitant. There's a lack of attention by the political community of the magnitude of dementia and the care that's going to be involved.

Gender and Caregiving

Women carry out the brunt of caregiving, a task seriously devalued in American society, and one accorded little respect. This fact has to do with historical legacies, traditional gender arrangements, expectations of "feminine" behavior, cultural conventions and arbitrary definitions of reality, rather than with the mandate of biology or human nature.[6] In addition, gender stress exacerbates the caregiver burden. Whereas men are more likely to focus on task orientation, women emphasize emotional relationships, with the latter far more problematic. The dark side of caregiving for women involves the limitless obligations and positive emotions they are expected to express.[7] Affinity, sympathy, compassion and affection are presumed to be natural properties of the female gender, rather than cultivated social-spiritual practices.

As a result, women are likely to suppress their true feelings, eventually to be overcome by the volatility and persistence of their negative emotions.[8] They are also likely to succumb to chronic health problems, depression and unrelenting feelings of futility and worthlessness, topics we later explore. Additionally, early mortality haunts elder caregivers. As noted earlier, 63 percent of caregivers die within a four-year period of taking on the caregiving role.[9]

Wives may be especially prone for gender-related expectations and conflicts.

Mary Beth, married for 47 years, took loving care of her much older husband for 10 years. Despite having a stroke, and for a period unable to read or write, she prepared herself for the worst. Until the final stages of

Alzheimer's, her husband proved to be an intrusive, obstinate, if not impossible, patient. Mary Beth recognized that it was the disease causing the problems, but that did not ease the day-to-day difficulty of managing their lives.

I didn't have much time for relaxation. He became absolutely attached to me. I didn't have a minute to myself, totally, totally. He would talk and talk and talk. Every evening at six or seven, he wanted to go to bed. He wanted me to go to bed. He would pester me for two hours until nine when I went to bed. I did everything for him except transferring. The most difficult physically was bathing and coping with his not knowing what was going on. Early on, he went to a lawyer to get a divorce. He thought I made him sick. I took over the finances. He was a money freak, and I had Power of Attorney. It was important to get his signature while he could sign. Four weeks later, he couldn't. It was awful, awful, awful... When he had bright moments [of lucidity], his desperation took over.

Daughters are next in line for stepping up to the caregiving task. In the midst of a busy college career training to be an X-ray technician, Clarice, a single mom, received a phone call from Florida, thousands of miles away. A relative informed her that her father had deteriorated significantly. Now, having quit school, forced to sell her home and two cars to make ends meet, she serves as a full-time custodian for her 79-year-old father, afflicted with heart disease. Clarice feels *trapped* with an over 80-hour week of looking after her dad.

Because she was unable to care for her dying mother, Clarice feels especially obligated to take care of her father. "Besides, I'm the only one who is going to do it; there's no one else in the family who can." I asked her what activities of daily living or special needs she carried out for her father, and which of these was the most difficult.

[I do all] *the shopping, housework, transporting him to appointments, cooking, calling and interacting with medical providers, financial arrangements, giving him medications and walking with him.*

[The most difficult was] *transporting him to medical appointments and calling/interacting with* [medical] *providers. He insists nothing is wrong with him, but hides behind my apron. He's too scared to go to his medical appointments alone.*

Parenting her parent, Clarice expresses her concern for her father, even while admitting, "I have no choices left; caregiving has taken over my life." Still, when she feels cranky and overworked, Clarice manages to be kind and thoughtful. "I tell him I love him every night when I tuck him in and give him medications."

Overall, how does she feel about her caregiving experience? Clarice said of her loving burden:

> *You know, I quit school to care for my father. During the time I've tak-en care of him I've suffered from multiple chronic problems—low back problems, high blood pressure, always, always exhausted. I buy TV din-ners and plan meals ahead when I know I'm going to crash.*
>
> *I have always been an advocate [for the elderly]. I like disrup-tions—find them refreshing. I'm so in the hole financially—don't have anything—lost my house, sold two cars. If he gets much sicker, I'm screwed, but so far nothing's been shut off.*
>
> *No one wants to visit me with my father here. He can be positive, ap-preciative—also sometimes negative and unappreciative—that's when I say you're more than welcome to do it yourself and he does.*
>
> *If I hadn't brought him here, he would be dead. Sometimes I think people look at Dad's weight and think I'm starving him. I'm restoring order in my life with Valium. I did advocate for myself once: a Christmas tree really helped. I put it by the window.*

Kathy, who was in her 60s, sold her house and moved into the home of her parents. At the time, her mother was 92 and father was 102. Her idea was ostensibly to simply monitor their medicine, as well as gener-ally keep track of their lives. Setting up housekeeping for herself in the lower level of their comfortable home did not resolve the problem of the 24/7 schedule. Kathy has become a child again in her newly formed relationships with her ailing, elderly parents. "I was just the one—the designated caregiver."

> *Who else would do it? I never told my parents about my problems. I keep them at low key, but sometimes I feel overwhelmed when I come*

home and Mother yells at me because I didn't call. I feel like I want to run away. What am I doing? I need to get a life—this is dreadful. I guess I've given up freedom; [I] never go anywhere without telling them. As long as my parents are alive, I don't believe I have choices.

Distinctions Between Child Care and Elder Care

The uninformed public and caregivers who have been mothers often assume that child care and elder care run on parallel tracks. But this is not the case. Elder care offers a distinctive care syndrome that varies greatly from well baby or child care. For elders, illness episodes vary and chronic disease, likely to be very serious, implies no remission or ending. Children's illnesses are typically of short duration. Elder care recipients have experienced high levels of autonomy, initiating choices and decisions, as compared to children's dependency. Community services for elders differ from those for children, requiring a range of help for the specific, ever-changing needs of the sick elder. Schools serve as central repositories of services and referrals for most children; elders lack a similar institutional framework. Additionally, the caregiver has a far more multi-faceted relationship with her spouse, parents or other sick loved ones than a mother caring for her young child. At the same time, caregivers often equate their efforts with child care, because most women have deep familiarity with that stage of life. It is as though the aged mother or husband is childlike—dependent, helpless and non-rational.

Certainly, the level of sacrifice that one makes to one's own child is not comparable to the care and concern in other relationships. Unfortunately, treating the sick elder as one's child simply muddies the emotional waters, and drives the elder into deeper dependency and mental confusion. Finally, there is a downward spiral in elder care—"things only get worse." This phenomenon is unmatched in the typical illnesses of children, as caregivers sadly come to realize.

Seventy-nine-year-old Helen has been caregiving her husband of 62 years for an extended period of time. Despite the fact that he had seriously deteriorated, she remembers him when he had all his faculties. Now, she ministers to his multi-dimensional needs. I asked Helen what activities she carried out for her husband during the 10 years she provided care.

Shopping, housework, transporting him to appointments, bathing assistance, cooking, feeding, calling and interacting face-to-face with medical providers, personal-care, transferring (from bed or chair to toilet), dressing, financial arrangements, giving medications—he couldn't do anything. He didn't understand me the last six months. He was in a wheelchair for seven years—he wouldn't push himself. He lost his volition—he was very accepting—accepted life in a wheelchair, me taking care of him, the kids visiting him. He lost that edge in the 1980s. He said he didn't want to drive anywhere in 1985. We were still square dancing—he got so that there were three beats he was off—he had a lack of connection with everything.

Helen did *not* identify her husband as a child, an awareness that allowed her to take a more balanced view of the situation, although some women felt they were dealing with small children. Instead, her husband served as a role model for her decision-making about his care.

When Roy died, I had been caring for him for so long I wanted to put it behind me. But people kept coming around with a long face, and it was hard to stop thinking about it. But I've adjusted—I've prepared for this for seven years. As he deteriorated I got more and more technology— handicapped van, hydraulic chair, sling. Roy was very successful, he was a money man, went after his goals with energy and zest. My goal in life in taking care of him was just to keep him out of a nursing home.

The more information the caregiver has about her loved one's disease, the more aware she becomes of the futility of her efforts to make him better. Mary Ellen's angry reaction to her husband's decline with Alzheimer's disease was not untypical of caregivers we spoke with. She said:

I was angry. I fought with my husband and yelled. It was so frustrating answering the same questions over and over; he opened and closed the refrigerator constantly. I cried a lot—depression, frustration and anger. I don't feel I've gained anything. The knowledge of that disease—it's depressing.

When is Caregiving *Not* a Burden?

We easily recognize caregiving as a terrible, and often unanticipated, load that full-time caregivers assume. But when is caregiving not a burden? Among these caregivers, I discovered certain conditions that appear to mitigate the burdensome aspects of providing care: (1) sharing the caregiving load with other family members; (2) having only a short-distance commute to the care receiver living in a residential facility; (3) looking after a neighbor or any person for whom the caregiver does not feel deep attachment, subjectively minimizing the time and effort involved; and (4) feeling a sense of commitment that is so deep, the word "burden" simply does not enter the caregiver's mind.

Betty is a retired elementary teacher, married with one stepchild, who shared care for her 88-year-old mother with her sister over a five-year period. Because this older sister lived near her mother, Betty handled most of the organizational tasks. She also filled in a few weekends a month for around-the-clock care. She said she was pleased to be "able to assist, comfort and love my mother during her aging years and death." While Betty was furious with her two brothers, who would not get involved, she focused on the positive aspects of her loving care.

> *The needs of my mother determined my involvement. Some weekends, I spent 11 to 20 hours; other weekends, less time. My husband supported and encouraged me to be involved. I enjoyed doing it and felt it was my role as a caring daughter to help my mother. Yes, sometimes I felt overwhelmed because of her failing health, but I always empathized with my mother and tried to suggest options that would help her. I've always tried to be sympathetic, helpful and caring. So, I've had no loss at all because of my caregiving. The best part of caregiving my mother? I loved spending time with her, talking about literature, movies, theater. She had a great sense of humor.*

Betty's strategy for dealing with her sadness over her mother's poor health was to live as full and joyous life as she could.

> *I've tried to spend time with special friends and continued doing what I love—read, walk, cook, volunteer, entertain friends and attend cultural*

events with my husband. I try to get through the rough times by enjoy-
ing myself. I guess you could say I laugh, laugh, laugh and spend time
with friends!

Joyce, a retired teacher and family-oriented person, exemplifies a caregiver who shares her caregiving load. She lives in close proximity to her
96-year-old mother, who is in assisted living, and is able to get assistance
from her three sisters when they visit. Joyce's life remains normal, and
visiting her mother is an event she looks forward to. She also recognizes
that she has much less personal time, a situation she accepts.

Mother and Father moved to [their facility] *December of 1999. Dad*
died February 28, 2000. Mom was very arthritic, and that, combined
with her grief and loneliness, led naturally into [her] spending time
with me. Mostly, I am privileged to have quality time with Mom, and to
hear stories from her childhood. I tell her I love her often. In sum, I feel
positive, privileged, lucky.

In instances where caregiving is perceived as a part-time commitment, or caregivers subjectively minimize their involvement, feelings
of being overwhelmed are rarely expressed. Lenora takes care of her
90-year-old husband. She also has temporary power of attorney for her
neighbor with Alzheimer's, Lilly, for whom she serves as financial manager. Lenora's help enables Lilly to live in her own home, her avowed
wish. Lenora enjoys feeling "useful," adding, "When I'm needed, I go
over and see what has to be done."

While Lenora admits to feeling obligated at times—running errands,
buying groceries and accompanying Lilly to the doctor—she also has
a fall-back position, in that she can call Michael, Lilly's nephew, should
the situation become too difficult. Part of the ease that Lenora expresses
("it's okay doing this") can be attributed to the many years she dedicated
herself to community service, working in a volunteer capacity with the
American Cancer Society, local hospital and university. Lenora further
described her caregiving involvement:

Lilly had her stroke, and her nephew came over here to ask for my help.
Then, Lilly approached me too. She was definitely urgent about staying
in her own home. She's had spells when we all thought that she should

be in care. But she's adamant about that [staying home]. *I wanted to help just to see that she was adequately taken care of: that people wouldn't take advantage of her. I think I'm helping her to the degree I can. I try to practice patience, and after all, things aren't as bad as they seem.*

Finally, caregiving is not perceived as burdensome when the caregiver has dedicated herself—heart and soul—to a dearly beloved person, and simply cannot imagine doing anything other than giving care. For the past 50 years, Sharon has been happily married to Carl, a university professor. She has enjoyed a rich life as the co-owner of a gift store, occasionally interviewing job-seekers and making crafts. But her heart was always at home with her husband and their daughter. Sharon believes she has been "truly blessed … and fortunate all my life," feeling especially grateful that she and Carl were able to "celebrate our 50th anniversary with our daughter and son-in-law [with] over 100 people."

Shortly after the event, Carl was admitted to the University of Washington hospital for surgery, where he was put on a feeding tube for the last nine months of his life. Sharon confided to Carl's brother her greatest fear: "that something would happen to me. What if I couldn't take care of him?" His brother responded: "You can't fall apart. Everything is up to you." And, Sharon rose to the occasion, fully determined to do her best. She described herself as a "competent and caring" caregiver.

I guess I coped all right. I managed to take care of him. He wanted to die at home, and I was able to do that for him. I was right proud of myself for being able to do it—the daily care, the wound cleaning, the feeding tube. I guess the worst thing was the wound care—it was terrible to look at. It was very sad, but necessary [and] *I didn't object to doing it.*

Death was not something either Sharon or Carl feared. They both belonged to the Hemlock Society, and would have chosen the organization's assistance with dying, but the feeding tube prevented that option. A matter-of-factness characterized Sharon's discussion of death and dying, as well as her willingness to let him go.

When we found out he was terminal, he would have ended it then if we had [legal] *physician-assisted suicide. Carl got pneumonia at the end.*

Hospice asked if he should have antibiotics. [But] *I saw no point in prolonging his life.*

Reflections

What emerges from the stories of these women is unpredictability and the constraints of giving care to elderly loved ones as physical and mental health decline. Life has seemingly shifted from a normal working and family self with a set of reasonable routines and relationships to a heightened reality, whereby selflessness and vigilance must take over to meet the ever-changing and complex needs of the loved one. At the same time, the caregiver burden is not absolute. Rather, it is mitigated, and given significance by love, commitment and a sense of duty.

Chapter 4

Identity:
Who Am I, Anyway?

Self and identity are central to understanding the human condition… and making sense of the thoughts, feelings and behaviors of individuals. [They] *are also important to explaining the formation, maintenance and dissolution of interpersonal bonds—both personal relationships and role relationships.*

~ Richard D. Ashmore and Lee Jussim,
Self and Identity[1]

Self and Identity

What happens to our identity and sense of self over the course of caregiving and after the death of the loved one? Do these events dramatically alter the sense of self? Do caregivers exhibit social and emotional stability through their challenges, or do they succumb to mental confusion and emotional distress or breakdown at one point or another? In a word, is our identity fixed, despite outward circumstances? Or the reverse—is it subject to change with alterations in our roles and relationships? For example, a caregiver who says, "I was a competent mother and nurse, but now I'm nothing since my kids left and my husband died," demonstrates not merely a loss of roles, but more important, a loss of selfhood.

Let's review two important terms here: self and identity. Scholars remind us that *self* and *identity* are crucial to making sense of the human condition. In fact, self and identity mainly determine our thoughts, feelings and behaviors, but not in a simple, straightforward way.[2]

Self refers to the character or essential qualities of a person, including awareness of one's own person as distinct from all others. To have a sense of self is to be conscious of one's own welfare, interest or advantage as separate from even our most intimate others. Kurt Danziger, a social psychologist, points to the complexity of the self as both knower and known. He says, "The self knows, evaluates and controls itself as it knows, evaluates and controls other people, and, as other people know, evaluate and control it."[3] While we speak of the self as a unified, singular entity (myself), the self should also be recognized as a multiplicity, a kind of paradox. Think how we take for granted our multiple selves: parent, wife, worker, son or daughter, friend, artist, writer, caregiver and so forth—until we are challenged with the loss of a significant self. What happens when the wife aspect of self confronts the accelerating role of nurse-caregiver as a husband lapses into dementia? When challenged too deeply, the unity of the self may dissolve completely.

Identity refers to our sense of individuality, and entails an emotional attachment to a specific self or role. Identity, like self, is inherently multiple and social-based. Identity commitment refers to the number of social ties or the affective importance of the social ties upon which each identity is predicated.[4] The notion here is that the higher the awareness of a particular identity, the more time and effort one will invest in its enactment. This implies that a caregiver who experiences a lack of supportive social ties for this role does not merely work harder at the job, but actually experiences a weakening of commitment, a withdrawal of self-investment.

Both terms, *self* and *identity*, capture the significance of consciousness—a cognitive, emotional and social orientation to ourselves and others. Thus, a mother continues to have a maternal identity, even though her children have grown and moved out of the home. She may play out this aspect of self through her caregiving of a parent or spouse in emotionally stable or unstable ways.

Earlier, we showed how vulnerable the self can be, even to the point of loss, as in *self-abnegation*—a self-denial that borders on lack of consideration for ourselves or our own interests, and placing the welfare of others before our own, even to the point of illness and beyond. At the extreme, *self-annihilation* involves the *loss of* awareness of self: an obliterated self, which is found among some extremely mentally ill or cognitively damaged people. *Self-abasement*, a humbling or lowering of oneself may be opposed to *self-actualization*, the full development of one's abilities and ambitions. These common understandings about selfhood all imply that the self is *not* a fixed entity, but rather, is subject to change, as in upward cycles (self-actualization) or downward cycles (self-abasement). When we have a sense of personal enhancement from an experience, it cycles us upward; when we are fatigued and plagued by self-disgust, we cycle downward, even into depression and despair.

Erik Erikson, a distinguished psychoanalyst, captured the element of change in his concept of "identity crisis," a condition of being uncertain of one's feelings about oneself, especially with regard to character, goals and origins.[5] When our lives have become deeply disrupted, with conditions changing fast and seemingly out of our control, we often experience an "identity crisis." When we have lost our jobs, experience divorce or death in the family, the "who am I" issue looms large, as people with profound losses attempt to understand who they are/will be under deeply changed circumstances. As we turn to caregivers' sense of "Who Am I?" over the course of caregiving—and for some, the death of the loved one—we find enormous variability in their sense of themselves and their altered identities.

Normalizing Caregiving Over Time

Normalizing the caregiving role entails treating the additional duties, issues and problems as ordinary, part of a day's work, a problem-solving task, and nothing too special, once a strategy has been devised or help could be summoned. Despite years of selfless devotion, some women pulled off the courageous feat of adapting to changing conditions in ways that can only be described as unflappable. You hear this in the following stories. Ina talks about her life before, during and after caregiving, following her husband's death.

> *Before caregiving, I always challenged myself to do something new and different. I was a retired teacher, traveling with my husband and actively involved with my children and grandchildren. I had an attentive family—two daughters, both nurses. We had good medical coverage, lived in the same house forty-one years. I'm a reader. I never felt confined.*
>
> *It was a year before doctors could pinpoint the reason for* [his] *chest*

pain. After my husband's diagnosis of mesothelioma and subsequent surgery, he became anxious and started feeling too sorry for himself. My son took him off and they had a good discussion about how important it was to face this and not pull everyone else down. My son is a bright, calm man; I rarely see him react.

I took intense physical care of my husband for a year and then it was 80 or more hours a week. He was physically exhausted and I was emotionally exhausted. I had to sleep, so I slept on the davenport. I tried to maintain a normal lifestyle—birthday parties, grandchildren, videos, Fourth of July and ice cream cones when he went to the doctor.

We skirted the issue of death. We never talked about the end until the very end. I fed him his food only once—the day he died, once and only once. We were just setting up for Hospice and he died two days later.

It's been nine years since he died and I know caregiving was hard, really hard. Our future was not a topic. You just stop in your tracks about all the things you were going to do. I ate over the kitchen sink the first year after he died—couldn't sit down at the table. The best thing I did was keep up with a normal life.

Today, I try to challenge myself with new interests and new friends— take a class, do something different. I want to stick around for my grandchildren and my children—son, daughters, sons-in-law and daughter-in-law.

A stable self is actually a state of mind, as Evelyn, our next caregiver shows. Regardless of how objectively difficult living with a husband who had Alzheimer's disease was, Evelyn made it work for both of them, even if "normal" was anything but.

I gradually realized Scott's diagnosis of Alzheimer's disease—it wasn't dramatic at all. We continued living a normal life for ten years. I'd sit beside him while he paid the bills to see that it was done right. He's happiest in the kitchen. He's still conscious about being polite, and he is so grateful for everything. His character came through.

I don't feel I've had a change in my identity. I am content with my situation and I don't struggle with problems. I'm not aware of stress, but my daughter sees it in me. I know I'm doing what's right. I don't ponder it at all. I go on with my normal day's activities, and never feel tied down. Caregiving hasn't compromised my values; it's reinforced them.

What would my life be like if I had never taken on the caregiving role? It would be nice if he were active and mentally alert. I would enjoy it. But I owe him my best. He'd given me so much. I knew he would do the same for me.

The wisdom I can offer is the peace you receive from taking care of your loved one. It's reinforced every time Scott says 'thank you' or 'the food is delicious.' Sure, I missed being with other couples. He couldn't interact normally with other people. But no loss around sociability. So many women have husbands with Alzheimer's. I see other women at Alzheimer's support groups, and they tell me that they sleep in separate beds. But I couldn't sleep without Scott.

Sylvia, a former college professor, now retired, has a long history of caregiving. Like Ina and Evelyn, she rationalized caregiving in terms of living a "normal life."

I've always been a high-energy, optimistic, focused and liberal person. I got along well with my family. When Mother moved from Wisconsin to live with me, I was fifty years old. She was 85 and in good health. She stayed for ten years; never complained. I kept my schedule—teaching management. Mother and I went to professional meetings together. My sister called Mother and wrote frequently. One of my friends spoke Norwegian with Mother.

I had to change some of the ways I did things. I was willing to make changes, but mostly I just interwove caregiving into my life with my job—the weaving of threads—your life goes together to form a pattern. Her pattern is one of beauty.

Mother decided to move to a nursing home and lived another one-and-half years. I was there every Saturday and Sunday. I slept in the same room with her and helped with personal care. One day while I was feeding her, I said, 'I wonder how long I can keep this up?' She died a week later.

The process was gradual. I kept up a normal life in spite of caregiving. My life was not disrupted. My life management and high energy, my creativity and optimism gave me coping skills then and now. The only difference in my life now is that I am a retired person.

My grandmother and older aunt were role models—very strict, but they gave me a great deal of stability. Caregiving is a gift if you look at it in a positive way. It enables you to do something for another human being—especially one you love.

Not all elder caregivers who exhibit stability express noble emotions about their contribution. Sarah, our oldest subject at 90 and a former actress and singer, had been married for 65 years. She realistically faced her responsibilities in the face of her husband's decline without remorse or guilt. When asked how she felt about herself before caregiving began, during the caregiving experience, and after her husband's death, she replied:

Before it began, I felt free to do what I wanted. It wasn't a good marriage... still, we had a good relationship just the same. After a few months, I never thought of that word [caregiving] *for what I was doing—it's just something one has to do. After one year or so, I just got used to it... doing for Jack.*

Continuity of self certainly depends upon honesty: being honest with oneself, especially, but also being selectively honest with the loved one. Sarah, who suffers from heart disease, confronted her husband about her limited capacity to manage caregiving. Combining humor with psychological know-how learned from her psychologist daughter, Sarah often "faked" her good feelings, but on crucial issues, let her husband know that caregiving was not a forever thing.

Now, Jack, I will do this as long as I know I can do it. When the day comes that I'm too old and too sick to do it, you will have to go to the veteran's hospital. I'm not forcing you. I'm just telling you that I could be struck down... I could have a heart attack any old time.... Be aware and alert that something could happen to me. It happens everyday in anybody's home.

Sarah retained a sense of being in the moment, a useful tool for maintaining the self during difficult periods. She recognized being a caregiver or helping others may have few or no rewards and many headaches. Her greatest fear remained her own loss of capacity before her husband's death: "I was terribly nervous that something was going to happen to me." A philosophical attitude helped her through the process of learning that caregiving does not involve paybacks.

And it doesn't mean that because you did the right thing, you're going to get paid back. It means that life has a way of altering every situation. But fortunately, it didn't happen. He died just before it could happen to me…. I was lucky because I still had some time left. Today, I'm free… totally free. I'm so looking forward to visiting Tuscany. I'm young at heart, you see.

Stability of self over time does not necessarily flow from inner resources. In some instances, caregivers play out helping roles learned in childhood and reinforced by family members in the here and now. Claudia provides us with a glimpse of how a group of siblings could rally around their afflicted mother over a six-year period without major loss of self or shifts in identity. Instead, in recognizing their strengths and limitations, they learned mutual tolerance and acceptance. Essentially, mom was still running the show despite her repeated strokes. Claudia clarified how the "team" worked.

I shared the caretaking role with my siblings. We each had a part to play with the roles partly determined by Mom. For example, one sister handled the financial part, one sister was responsible for the medical, one brother visits regularly and offers emotional support to everybody and another brother [disabled and living with mother] *reads the paper to her. I read to her, too, and fixed her hair and giggled with her.*

After her first stroke she was in a wheelchair. Then we jockeyed around in our positions to figure out where to fit into the changed patterns of her life. My siblings and I found each others' weaknesses, both glaring and sometimes hard to deal with. But I know we each did what we could. After all, Mom raised children willing to do what needed to be done. If we hadn't taken care of her as we did, I would have regretted it.

Some caregivers normalize their caregiving commitment by assimilating the activity into their everyday life, and "feel good" about the responsibility. Antonia, who has been on a life-long caregiving journey, considers herself a heart-centered person. Currently working as an administrator in a skilled Alzheimer's unit, as well as caring for her step-father, Antonia depicts the "ideal" caregiver: positive attitude, sense of humor, strong values and a desire to serve. When I asked her how she first became involved with caregiving, she replied:

> *Since I was two, my mom said I would place a pillow under her head and a blanket over her when she came home from work—she was a single mom. I was a nursing home caregiver at 16 and Red Cross volunteer in high school at the Geriatric Psychology Unit at Northern State Hospital.*
>
> *My car accident at 12 made me feel I survived for a reason. How do I cope with caregiving? Well, I understand and value the need for family, the need for respect and dignity during this passage in life.*

The Transitional Self

Caregiving is often perceived as a transitional role, a temporary loss of oneself to be restored as one learns different ways of being alive *now* and *after* the caregiving task has been completed. Certain diseases place very heavy demands on caregivers. Old selves must be shed to accommodate new demands. Such is the case with Alzheimer's disease for many caregivers. Learning to live with progressive dementia is a vast challenge. How can one maintain a sense of oneself as a competent, independent decision-maker and partner under conditions of constant shifts in the loved one's mental capacity? One strategy is to simply "go with the flow" and balance out the confusion and disturbing behavior of the loved one with memories of former stabilizing experiences, such as raising children. Another is to accept the shift from the wife role to that of companion or nurse. Yet another is simply to endure the sometimes unendurable until the care receiver passes on. These stories embody different transitional experiences.

Perhaps the most tragic situation for many caregivers, as with Martha, involves the cognitive loss of a high-achieving husband. Martha talks about how she adjusted to her husband's gradual decline, accepting rue-fully the new circumstances.

> *I don't know if it was my intention to be my husband's caregiver. You*

say, 'for better or worse.' We've been married 50 years. We always did things together, but we also had separate lives. We shared all the responsibilities. Now the hard part is getting some private time. I need to get him out of the house, but I can't imagine getting him ready for the morning Adult Day Care. He has a Ph.D. in physiology research—and he has Alzheimer's.

For me, the shift of roles came gradually. I had just retired and was enjoying being a "crone," having free time and the sense that I had done the things I really enjoyed in my life.

After a year of caretaking, I realized my freedom would be limited. Remember when you had toddlers and they interrupted every five seconds? That's the way it is—the interruptions. I haven't figured out a good way to ignore them. I've abandoned the idea of control and that helps. I had to let go of standards—so he sleeps in a sweater, that's okay. As he's less and less able to do things, I have to do more and more. There's no one else to be responsible. I had to stop him from driving the car. I supervise when he dresses and simplify the feeding—food on his plate not served on the table. He sometimes thinks I'm taking over everything. I'd like to see my grandchildren more often, but Alzheimer's and a toddler don't mix.

After his death, Martha had an opportunity to review her life, and to grasp the wholeness she had lost while caregiving.

Today, I'm back to the crone. I had no escape while he was alive. I'm incredibly grateful I could arrange respite care. I think I should move to a place that doesn't take so much of my time [large home]. It's wonderful to have kids and grandkids. It's also wonderful to have friends who seek you out for discussion. I read a lot. That keeps me young.

In the next story, Gloria traces the shifts in her marriage, beginning with the period before her husband's illness to the present day, where interdependence and a companionable relationship have replaced her former roles as an independent, professional woman, in a moderately conflict-oriented marriage.

I retired to have more time with him. I'd always thought independence was important. My life was disrupted by caregiving. It made me less independent and less able to do what I want to do without thinking of the consequences. Our futures lie out differently now. Before he became ill, we were more independent from one another. We had some shared interests, but we disagreed fairly frequently over things—a little pushy interaction and shouting, but only one major fight in our 37 years of marriage.

I remember the first time I heard, 'You are his caregiver.' I am his voice. After a couple of years of caretaking, I grappled with my changing role. I am more of a companion to my husband. We are closer as a result of caregiving. There's a sense of less independent activity. He doesn't attempt to curtail my activities, but he needs more attention. He is taking 15 to 17 medications for heart disease and a stroke, and I need to supervise this.

I wish it weren't happening. Sometimes I feel low, but I need to stay okay—sometimes it's hard to stay optimistic. It's not that I am uncomfortable, but I'm aware that the role itself will change. I'm learning to be grateful for what we have, rather than what we've lost.

We're closer now that we're interdependent. He's happier now than he's ever been. He enjoys spending more time together. It's a plus— we've adjusted to the new lifestyle. The greatest gain has been more communication and sharing of interests. I think it's made me a much more patient person. I'm a better person than I used to be. It's taught me to be more accepting about things I cannot change.

I know this situation will progress. I don't know how I'll take care of him when I'm not physically able.

Gloria's narrative demonstrates how one can change one's identity (from independent to interdependent) and social roles (conflict marriage to companionable one) without sacrificing the self. Instead, Gloria gained a greater measure of personal integrity as her primary relationship developed renewed strength and vigor. At the same time, she remains haunted by an unknown future of her own possible inability to continue care indefinitely.

When a friend steps in to give care to a longtime companion, the obligation feels not much different than when a sister or brother requires care. And when the friend's family fails to respond to the call of their family member's decline from Alzheimer disease—much less show up and take over care management—the sense of responsibility can be overwhelming. When confronted with the unwelcome intrusion of her dearest friend's illness, Carmen, a highly successful professional, realized she needed to act. Under the pressure of uncertainty about her decision-making role, Carmen's sense of who she was shifted over time:

> Before caregiving began, I am a friend of Mary, a single woman. I am an educator. After a few months of caregiving, well, the disease was so gradual, I didn't really notice stuff happening. Once I realized what was wrong, I felt so much dismay and sadness that something can happen to someone with a brain like that—her family died early. After one year or more of caregiving, I became an apprehensive person. I was feeling more trapped. I had a continuous sense of danger. I didn't know how to cope. I thought: I shouldn't have to give up my friends to look after Mary. Today [after her death] I am relieved. I feel sadness because part of my life was no longer there. But now I've retired, and I have my life back.

Once Carmen learned "to set priorities, and just deal with it," she could work as an advocate for her friend. Later, she was able to locate an excellent care setting for Mary. This decision reduced Carmen's 30 or more hours of caregiving a week to a reasonable number of visits and interventions with the nursing staff. After six years of looking after her friend, Carmen offered a wise approach to preserving oneself through the caregiving process:

> Just take the situation as it comes. There are more options for you than you think. But the more you think of yourself, the worse it gets. Think of the other person's needs and comforts. Don't lose your identity, but recognize this person's life isn't going to last much longer, and you have time to do other things.

Young women are particularly tested when they leap generations to care for grandparents. In her early thirties, Teri took on the six-year task of supervising home care and very frequent hospital visits for her grandmother, and after her death, her ailing grandfather. Deeply attached to both, she endured 31 to 40 hours a week of caregiving along with a full-time job, to carry out the myriad of tasks required to keep them going:

shopping, housework, dressing, financial arrangements, interacting with medical providers and resolving day-to-day decisions about their lives. She felt she owed them "love and time." How did these care functions impact her over the years? Teri replied:

> *Before caregiving began, I could describe myself as fun-loving, newly into a relationship and self-centered. I am a lot of fun. After a few months of caregiving I am getting more concerned; I am a worried person. I am a strong activist. I am responsible for them.*
>
> *After one year or more of caregiving, I am stressed. I am deeply concerned. I am short on time—never enough time for me or anybody. My biggest loss was lack of personal time.*

Teri faced not only the care of two deeply ailing elders, but also the failure of other family members to get involved. Yet, she moved beyond the call of duty to provide daily care for her elderly relatives, persisting through the most egregious situations.

> *They both needed assurance that they were okay. I would advocate for them. Sometimes everything was too much, especially when Grandpa got combative. Then I just broke down. I was angry for so long, especially about his medical care. They were negligent with his* [grandfather] *care* [at the nursing home]. *They didn't give him enough morphine for his pain. He was screaming into death.*

Now that her grandparents have both died, how does Teri define herself?

> *Today, I am strong. I am appreciative. I try to help others. I try to make a difference. I realize how short your life is. I'm grateful I had the good sense to look after them. I stepped forward at the right time—not a lot of people feel the calling* [to be a caregiver]. *If I hadn't done this, I wouldn't be as altruistic. I believe it's important to leave the world in a better place for having the opportunity to be here.*

In Teri's case, the transition from a fun-loving self *before* caregiving, to a responsible politician who advocates for the elderly and other needy people *after* caregiving, involved a steep learning curve. Today, gracious and confident, Teri has emerged as a major community leader, overcoming enormous odds, including cancer.

The Turbulent Self

Under the duress of caregiving women frequently confront the hidden or shadow part of themselves. Emotions and sentiments, normally buried, burst forth under the pressure of daily demands, as well as the loss of a loved one's health, companionship and life. Sandra clarifies how "different" her life became once she took on the caregiving role. I asked Sandra to describe herself in "I am" statements for four time periods: before caregiving, after a few months of caregiving, after one year of caregiving and today. Here is her response.

> *Before caregiving began, I used to be a different person. I am a married woman. I am a daughter. I am a good friend. I am a lover. I'm an active woman. I am a business owner. I'm the only one left in my family since my brother died, so I had that responsibility, too. I first became a caregiver for my brother, who died of AIDS.*
>
> *After a few months of caregiving, I'm a devoted wife, I'm a loving woman. I'm a business owner.*
>
> *After one year or more of caregiving, I am an emotional wreck. I'm unorganized. I am not a good friend. I'm moody. I felt helpless, frustrated and full of conflict. It's hard to watch someone you love suffer and die and not do anything about it. I was overwhelmed. I'd go on autopilot— do it and think about it later. Only when it stops do you think about it. I broke down a lot.*

When I asked Sandra if she could pinpoint the source of her turmoil, she indicated it was her reaction to circumstances, including frustrations surrounding medical care.

> *At the beginning, I was so committed. But the sicker he got, the angrier he got, and I couldn't deal with his feelings. He was angry at being sick. I wasn't angry at him, but at circumstances. I took things out on him; he took things out on me—heat of the moment. And the medical system up here* [Canada]—*it's dreadful. That's why he's dead. He died while having kidney dialysis. My husband was in a drug-induced coma.*

When I asked the doctor what was happening too him, the doctor told me, 'Everything's fine.' I'm so mad that I didn't speak up enough to the doctors about their lack of care, and that I got short and spoke up to my sick husband instead.

Sandra also complained that her husband's lack of appreciation of her efforts further compounded her sense of incompetence and futility.

He went from an expectation that I would provide care to a totally negative attitude. He was so unappreciative. It got to be overwhelming.

Additionally, Sandra felt guilty about leaving him to go to work. She commented:

I felt terrible about not being with him all the time, but I had to work. No work—no pay.

Clearly, Sandra had over-identified with her personal shortcomings and succumbed to anger and helplessness about the quality of medical care. Her former self-image—competent, energetic and in-charge—had deteriorated over the course of caregiving and had given way to one imbedded in anger, guilt and remorse. Only after her husband died could she reconstruct an integrated self. This time, the "who am I?" question yielded a highly positive response. Sandra said:

Today, I'm a loving wife [remarried]. *I'm a business owner. I am a spiritual person. I'm a good friend. I am an independent woman. I'm seeking balance and prioritizing my life. I've learned to 'let go and let God.'*

My own struggle over the course of my husband's illness clarifies how I first resisted the notion of "normality" or living an "ordinary" life. Instead, a sense of the tragic prevailed; the perpetual question surrounding the loved one and all caregiving activities was, "Why did this have to happen?" And the answer: "Because I wasn't prepared; I didn't know what I was doing."

I was overwhelmed, but caregiving was a necessity. In retrospect, I wish I had spent more time on practical thinking, maybe caring for an adult person, or maybe volunteering at a nursing home.

I could not easily resolve my husband's precipitous decline, and my own need to restructure my life around this new turn of events. A major issue involved my husband's repeated medical crises, requiring frequent hospitalizations and nursing home follow-up care (at one point, four hospitalizations in a six-week period). In my interview, I describe myself in "I am" statements over the course of my caregiving:

Before caregiving began, I am a married woman with children. I have a strong identity as a professional woman, actively teaching, researching and writing. I am optimistic, a take-charge person, a fun-loving person, a feminist, a politically aware person with strong family values. My values were ordered very highly, and I worked hard to implement them in my daily life.

After a few months of caregiving, I am a frightened, disorganized, panicky, out-of-control, reluctant caregiver, which was fast becoming my central role. I couldn't keep up with my research and writing; I felt at loose ends. I continued teaching full-time because of financial pressures. My biggest hurdle was putting my husband in care. I couldn't believe I could put a dearly beloved in a nursing home, and walk out the door.

Once I surmounted that early period, which went on for a couple of years, I realized I had to learn the full range of care—whatever was out there. It's as simple as choosing a walker or giving loving/caring services; the gamut of care. I had a strong sense of personal obligation and commitment, which sustained me. At the same time, I always felt off balance; I felt totally responsible. I couldn't let him down.

After two years or more of caregiving, I am an experienced caregiver, developing the compassionate side of my nature, learning one of life's lessons—a spiritual truth—to overcome any difficulty, and to be more patient. But I remained frustrated with the medical system and incompetency of many of its practitioners. At the same time, I had a sense of myself as a courageous person, strong family centeredness, a friend. So, I guess you could say I even transcended the medical system and just did the best I could for him.

The Declining Self

Among some caregivers who embraced the caregiving role as a single, focused experience, the post-caregiving experience was less positive. These women report a sense of loneliness (sometimes, years after the death of their loved one), deep depression or emptiness. For a few, once the ordeal was over, they experienced a collapse—a "kind of falling through space," in the words of one caregiver, with no landing in sight. Disengaging from care-centered activities, the grieving caregiver may believe that life has been lived already.

At the extreme, they die with the loved one's passing. Their state of being may be masked by normality—they clean the house, answer their phone and e-mail, attend social events and participate in family gatherings—but reluctantly and as little as possible. They speak as one who has withdrawn from life. As a result, energies wane, life's possibilities dwindle, the decline seems inevitable, the future appears bleak.

For Sally, the caregiving journey seemed to be interminable, with no end in sight. An only child, she assumed full responsibility of both parents after they were diagnosed with terminal diseases. Having recently buried her mother, she now looks back over the last four years, which she describes as "totally" disrupted by the caregiving task of two ailing, and often obstinate, parents. Sally describes her shifting self over the course of her caregiving.

> *Before caregiving began, I would say I am an outgoing person; I am adventurous, involved with community, friends; I am a wife, a mother.*
>
> *After a few months of caregiving: I became stressed, disorganized. Like when I went to their home for Thanksgiving to sell their house. I was devastated at the shambles. Mother was totally argumentative. She wouldn't cooperate. I had to travel with two sick people who needed hospitalization. Dad had respiratory failure. Once we got here [Sally's home], I had to decide whether to put him on life support. We did it for three weeks. Meanwhile, Mother needed care, so I put her in a nursing home for two months. I thought she was going to die, but she bounced back.*
>
> *After one year or more of caregiving: I was thoroughly depressed. I didn't find a lot of joy. I was going downhill, as they get sicker and sicker.*

It's so debilitating. I just couldn't cope with it. But I felt it was my moral obligation. I was an only child… my mother lived vicariously through me. My whole life was confused by it all.

Unlike some, Sally is currently trying to re-establish herself after the rigors of caregiving.

Today, it's been a few months and I'm just now beginning to snap out of it. I've had to deal with it: selling the house, supervising their medical care, organizing their finances, sorting out their personal effects, taking care of everything. The entire thing [caregiving] took so long. I'm still in process. It feels real funny… sometimes I feel I'm going to the nursing home again to visit Mom everyday.

Finally, I'm glad I don't have to do it again. I'm sorry that it's over, but I'm sure glad it's done. It's kind of hard when your loved ones pass away. It's kind of hard to visualize what your life is going to be. It takes a long time to even figure out you have a life. I'm just learning to go back to some of the things I used to do. It always feels like something's just hanging right out there.

Rose never recovered from her husband's death. After he died from a sudden illness, she immediately—albeit with deep resentment—took on the care of her mother. Having experienced a "crash course in dying"—her husband survived three months after diagnosis—Rose remains uncomfortably attached to her 93-year-old mother, who refuses to talk about Rose's beloved husband or her own imminent death.

My husband had brain cancer—three months and he died. I was devastated after Bradley died. I felt lost and I didn't know who I was. Even after years, it's still the same. It never goes away. I'm caring for my mother now, no choice. There's not a day when I don't think about Bradley. I want to walk again and play the piano again.

Caring for my mother makes me feel like throwing things sometimes and she doesn't want to talk about Bradley. I get nervous and shaky—it plays on my emotions. I tell myself not to be mouthy, to be kind. I get frustrated. She's my mother, so I can't get unhinged with her. She's controlling and makes me feel like a little kid. She has always pulled my strings and I'm aware of it, so I can't express sympathy. I've just learned not to blow my own temper.

I sometimes feel like a failure at what I'm doing; I can't deal with it, but I know I have to. It's difficult to maintain your sense of self when you're caregiving. It's tough to be told by my mother that I treat her like I don't want her; that I have 'mud in my eye,' that I don't care about her. It's a real tough one. I can't talk death with her.

If I hadn't taken on the role of caring for Mother, I would have gotten my individuality back. It wouldn't always be 'we.'

Like Rose, Mary Ellen has lost her purpose in life. Caregiving for her husband with Alzheimer's disease over a decade has drained her both physically and emotionally, and she has no perception that anything could be different than it is. Neither the prospect of hope or a different life sustains her.

Among other things, I watch the fish tank for relaxation. I'm depressed, frustrated and angry. Ron has had Alzheimer's disease for nine years. I watched him go downhill, answering the same questions over and over again. I went from being happy, loving, employed, married and a good companion to quitting my job and living on food stamps. My main concern was medical testing.

Now, I'm lonely and uncomfortable most of the time. Basically, I don't have a life since caregiving. I'd never marry again. I just want a corner to be alone and play an online game for escape.

Cindy, a well-educated occupational therapist and nurse, has a family background that significantly contributes to her role as solo caregiver for both parents. Childless, Cindy's parental commitment undermined the relationship with her husband. Eventually, they parted on negative terms, and Cindy lost her stake in their jointly owned family farm. Cindy struggles to make sense of her five years of caregiving for her alcoholic father, whom she remorsefully put in care. Now, she dreads the future. She will need to convince her sister to take over the duties of her aging mother's care or it will again fall to her. Cindy's story illustrates the special problems of caring for an elderly alcoholic.

All my brothers and two sisters are alcoholic. I cared for my father. My morning wake-up was my father vomiting. Do I have the right to make choices for myself? Yes, yes, I have the right, but will I have the strength to do it? My dad was alcoholic for 25 years. He is very small-minded; he has a tiny little world; he is so immature. It began a long time before because of his long-standing alcoholism—on the wagon, off the wagon. When does the fight begin? Always the dread, always the dread.

He went into alcohol recovery in 1973 and five more times after that. I was the eldest child; my obligation was to care for him. He was an incapable caregiver for my mother, who had lupus and strokes. I cared for both him and my mother who developed ulceric stomach. Both of them had 'dumping syndrome' [a spastic bowel condition].

I have the niggling guilt about not seeing him enough. I'm not looking forward to Mom—she's 75. All my brothers are alcoholic. It's my sober sister's turn. This has really tested my values. Am I an ongoing server—tending to every need? A stronger Christian would be more involved than just maintenance and it ain't much. Caregiving has taxed my spare time, taxed my relationship with my husband, no time to heal—healing did not happen.

Cindy regards the personal changes she has experienced over those years.

When I first began caregiving, I was a married woman, employed. I am the eldest daughter and responsible. I am a friend and highly active, exploring the world around me. After a few months of caregiving, I am confused and frustrated struggling with multiple decisions every single day. My dad used alcohol on top of his dementia, then he insisted on driving (which was his hobby). His behavior was so bizarre; he just left his disabled wife behind.

After a year or more, I'm failing to have a significant level of control and comfort in the decisions that I need to make on a day-by-day basis. So I said to myself: 'I know you can't dance, and it's too late to plow....' It just needs to be done [placing her father in care]. *After three years, he's in assisted living. I think I lost a great deal of compassion. It was a task-oriented project. I didn't have any emotions after that.*

Today, I am a woman whose husband is 'out of the way.' I have some remorse and lack of contact with my father—big guilt. I am guilty.

Kali moved into the basement of her grandparents' home for two years so she could care for them. Her 81-year-old grandmother had Parkinson's disease. Her grandfather, a taciturn and competitive character, had a notoriously bad attitude. She describes two vignettes of their intergenerational relationship.

It was Grandfather who I had problems with. My grandmother was my support. When Grandfather thought I was cheating at cards, Grandma said: 'Just let him win.'

When I was there I kept sweaters on Grandma to keep her warm. But when I wasn't there, Grandma was always cold. It was so hard to see her so uncomfortable. Grandfather didn't want her to have a lot of clothes on. He insisted it would be too hard to dress and undress her. Everything with him was an argument. It was too hard to make both grandparents happy.

What was Kali's life before caregiving began? And how did she become, at 28 years old, the designated caregiver for the older generation?

Before caregiving, I was single, living at home with my parents; I was worried about my direction in life. I was a residential care aide. What am I going to do with my life? I try to please everyone—make everyone love me. The care of other people always came first. I felt like no one noticed me or knew I existed.

Because of Grandma's illness, I took the RCA [residential care aide] courses, when what I really wanted to do was to take human resource classes working with the handicapped. The RCA work seemed the right thing to do. But now I'm still paying for my student loans for those courses.

A few months after caregiving, I am lonely and bored. At the same time, now people are praising me, happy for me, proud of me for being there for Grandma. My patience is being tested time and time again. I guess I managed. But, after a year, I was trying to get away, trying to get my own space. I made excuses not to be at home with my grandparents.

At the end, I am lost, lost fulfillment. I don't know if this is the right direction.

Kali clearly has second thoughts about whether she should continue caring for her grandparents, but feels trapped, as well as lacking job options. She had been fired from her RCA job shortly after she assumed full-time care of her grandparents.

> *Maybe this is not what I should be doing. Maybe I don't have enough patience to deal with certain situations. I need a break. I feel like a bad person saying this, but I was there 24 hours a day. It wasn't like I had an 8-hour job and went home.*
>
> *I knew it was either a stranger or me to care for Grandma. I knew I could give her proper care and once I started, she didn't want anyone else. I didn't know her before, but during the process of caretaking, we bonded. She became more like a mother to me, but Grandpa made my job very difficult. It was hard to make both grandparents equally happy.*
>
> *Dealing with death and seeing her sick, seeing her on her down days is the greatest emotional burden. I've been tested too many times. Even though I'm a loving, caring person, I need a break.*

Kali invested all she had emotionally and financially to care for her grandmother. The nearly impossible task of her grandmother's care was further complicated by her grandfather's distracting interference with her grandmother's care. Kali's spirit is broken, and her premature involvement with the death and dying of someone she loves deeply keeps her in a suspended state. Jumping the generations for caregiving could backfire on the family. Who will care for Kali's parents when their time comes, as their daughter remains weary and disillusioned from her earlier caregiving experience?

Considering Selfhood Among Caregivers

We have traced the caregivers' self-concept from the period prior to taking on the role to their final assessment at the time of the interview. The most distinct finding from these interviews involves the relationship between normalizing the caregiving role and the self-concept. The more the caregiver can perceive illness and the dying of her loved one as ordinary events, part of the order of things, the more likely a caregiver can thrive without abrupt identity shifts or losses. Among those whose loved ones have died, the women report they experienced a renewal; most were able to resolve negative feelings or experiences and forgive onerous burdens. For about 10 percent of these caregivers, though, there has been no sense of resolution or fulfillment. Instead, another kind of self exists, which is suspended in a state of remorse, emptiness or guilt. Such feelings can accompany caregivers under a variety of situations—those whose loved one had died, those who had placed the elder in care, or those who were currently providing care. But, invariably, it occurs for caregivers who lacked supportive ties through the caregiving experience.

Considering the intensity of care, perhaps it is not surprising that more caregivers have not succumbed to a sense of futility. Rather, a remarkable resilience prevails among most of these caregivers. Life may be difficult, but it is not impossible. Transitions and turmoil can be endured. Sometimes, it is only a matter of time until the situation changes: the loved one dies; the difficult patient can be placed in care; the loved one's slide into illness has entered a plateau period; a relationship is renewed.

Certainly, one of the more challenging commitments involves care of grandparents, especially when the elders' own sons and daughters withdraw from participation. A different set of moral imperatives exist for women in their twenties or thirties than for those in their middle or later years. Caught up with an older generation's biological unwinding and demise is never an easy task. When this process holds a woman back from pursuing family and career goals, it can have devastating results. One of our young marrieds was obliged to postpone childbearing until care responsibilities ended, only to confront her inability to carry a child because of ovarian cancer.

Expectations—what we hold as our prospects in life, our achievements, what we look forward to—play a crucial part in what appears "normal" and "ordinary." When most of our goals have been achieved and are now behind us, it may be far easier to slip into a sacrificial mode compared with those women who identify themselves as remaining wholly or even partially unfulfilled. Among some caregivers, it was necessary to reconsider their perspective—to adapt and overcome the potentially precarious situation of a dwindling self.

One would assume that the nature of the relationship one has had with the elder *before* caregiving undoubtedly plays a role in the woman's willingness to take on caregiving responsibilities, as well as her ability to adapt to negative conditions. The interviews substantiate this for many caregivers—a loving connection lightens the load considerably. On the other hand, many women confronted parents, grandparents and husbands without a burning necessity to serve. Out of duty, perhaps, or social pressure, one is willing to give on a "sort-of" basis. Such a mindset leads only to "maintenance" or minimum giving, "and that ain't much," as one caregiver put it.

In a significant sense, we have oversimplified the self-concept, treating inner and outer aspects as though they were one. A more elaborate view entails three components of self: what others see, who we think we are and who we really are (the so-called authentic self). Without moving into a detailed metaphysical description, the idea of an authentic self versus a "false self" deserves attention. The authentic self survives the vicissitudes of loss and change.[6]

By contrast, the "false self" appears motivated by attempts to present the self in a manner that will impress or win the acceptance of others.[7] When a caregiver presents herself as the "loyal wife" to physicians and institutional staff, but lacks genuine identification with the role, the effects can be quite negative: depression, low self-esteem and declining energy. Again, who we think we are may be like a "will of the wisp," an ever-changing self that appears and disappears depending on the situation. But the more an individual can tap into their "authentic self," their inner self, recognizing and accepting their life's purpose (which only the individual can know) the greater strength she can summon. Inner resources, unlike a pat on the shoulder or even a good movie, sustain one over time and space. A crisis situation often brings the authentic self into consciousness—not what others think and say about us, but what our own inner voice commands.

To what extent do some women take on the arduous caregiving role as an escape from self? I had strong hints that a few of our caregivers did just that. Roy F. Baumeister, a psychologist from Case Western Reserve University, posits that in Western society, people are presented with a "remarkable opportunity to become autonomous, self-determined, unique and fulfilled, but the pressure to be all those things can be daunting."[8] For women in postmodern society, the demands can be overwhelming. Trying to appear attractive, feminine, charming, successful and thin often requires considerable and sustained effort. If the burden of self is stressful, one can take on a demanding role, such as caregiving, which facilitates minimal self-awareness and a sense of self as merely a physical entity existing in the immediate present. This self view is strongly opposed to understanding the self in all its complexity. The minimal self, of course, is simply another version of the false self, with its accompanying negative consequences.

The variations in self-concepts we found among this group illuminates the reality that for an enhanced sense of self, each caregiver might summon the heroic, highly evolved self from existing life resources, including the authentic self. And, in many instances, once they have listened to the inner self, they may recognize that, whether minimum or maximum, giving one's self with intention is a profound undertaking.

Chapter 5

The Ever-Widening Circle
of Co-Dependency

I lost myself in this experience… I didn't take care of my-self. I forgot to value myself. I feel I could have done better. I gave up things I shouldn't have. Those things would have made me feel better about taking care of him…. I felt I owed him. The most difficult part was trying to always be there for him—always, always, always.

~ Renae

A Starting Point

Your brother John calls you Monday from California and tells you that Mom fell down and broke her hip. He explains that she's recuperating nicely in the hospital, but will need extensive time to get back on her feet. After you recover from the shock, you ask: "What can I do to help?" You had in mind sending a card, or maybe paying a visit to the hospital or recovery center. Your job has just kicked into high gear, and you won't have much time to devote to Mom. But John makes it clear: "Mom needs to be in a safe and comfortable environment. You know how she hates hospitals and other confining places. I can't take her in because I just signed a contract for a new job, and will be leaving town within the month. I'll be driving her up to Washington State next weekend, so you'd better get ready for her."

John couldn't hear you gasp at the unwelcome news, as you said, "Umm, sure, I'll do what I can. See you soon. Give my love to Mom." Now, I'm in for it, you thought. Where do we go from here, Mom and I? We've never gotten along. She's always preferred my brother. What will

I do about my job? What about the financial costs? What will this do to my marriage? How will my children react to taking in their often difficult grandmother? What kind of space can I find in the house that will fit "her majesty?" How can I pull this off?

These questions haunt a soon-to-be caregiver, who confronts an unknown situation—one fraught with fear, anxiety and a sinking sense that one's life is about to become undone. Such a situation sets the stage for a condition, popularly known in the recovery literature as "co-dependency."

Co-dependency describes a relationship that begins when one person, the care receiver, relies upon or is sustained by another, the caregiver, and who adopts a subordinate role, simply by virtue of her physical, mental and emotional needs.[1] The "co" in dependency occurs when the facilitating partner—in this case, the caregiver, loses herself in the process. Her identity, her very sense of self, becomes wrapped up in the elder's survival ("He'd be dead without me"), not for an episode or for a day, but often for years.

Whereas society extols specific kinds of human dependencies, such as infants and young children on their parents, or traditional wives on their husbands, the reverse is not the case. Society frowns upon parents becoming dependent upon their children, or husbands losing their independence and leaning on their wives. Yet, this is precisely what happens in most of the caregiving cases we studied.

Caregivers become the operative adult, making executive decisions for their dependent parents or spouses. But not without a struggle on both the caregiver and care receiver's part, I should add. The most unpredictable part of this role will be to create a discourse and a set of routines that will let the caregiver endure the interaction with as much grace and humor as possible.

In theory, illness and dying cancel out the old rules. After all, we owe a huge debt to our parents, and the marriage vows explicitly dictate, "for better or for worse." Yet, the culture of care remains exceedingly poorly developed in Western societies. No one knows for certain how to create new rules to guide one through the maze of long-term care. And whatever advice is sometimes given—"just act like his 'wife' or ('daughter') and everything will be all right"—doesn't work when normal roles have been turned inside out. The strong, assertive husband, the independent, competent parent are no more. Instead, they have been replaced by a re-constituted being: more dark shadow than substance.

The next three sections explore the unforeseen consequences for some women who have taken on the caregiver's task and exhibit signs of co-dependent patterns. Unfortunate childhood experiences with parents may set the stage for co-dependency, which then undermines or negates the adult child's efforts to negotiate difficult interactions successfully. More typically, long-term caregiving itself generates vulnerabilities: a sense of being overwhelmed and lacking adequate resources, a loss of confidence, and in the extreme, one's integrity. First, we explore the "de-valued self," linked to a consciousness of "never being good enough," or "failing at the task," a condition characterizing a fairly large proportion of our caregivers (more than one-third) at least some of the time. Next, we examine the loss of self—a sense of being rudderless and even emp-tied out. Finally, we take up the broader set of issues of co-dependency articulated by scholars and clarified by caregivers' experiences.

The Devalued Self

In the social psychological process of taking on the caregiver role, the newly vulnerable woman acquires: (1) a host of new duties and activi-ties that requires special knowledge and training (e.g. administration of medications, wound care); (2) a potentially unlimited time commit-ment; (3) a morally altered self, as she adjusts to her losses, and those of her loved one, adjusting her world around ever-changing circumstances of care; (4) an entirely new set of "experts" that dictate how the elder must be managed to promote survivability; (5) an attitude that denies her own fears and limitations; and (6) a muddied self-concept that struggles between "selfless helper" and "selfish child"—"why does it have to be me?" For more vulnerable, ill or overwhelmed women, this process sets the stage for redefining the self as "morally unworthy."

In many instances, a flawed relationship with the loved one in the past now re-emerges as a daunting obstacle to caring effectively for that per-son. Especially discouraging is the continuous emotional bombardment against the caregiver by both family members and sick elder, a situation experienced by Jill, a highly competent university professor in her "other life." After she moved into her dying mother's home, she discovered how little she was cherished.

> *I think I did a good job, although I felt overwhelmed when my brother came. He didn't want to be there. He came in and started bossing me around. No compassion there at all. But my mother's insults and lack of appreciation were the hardest. Every chance she had she told me I was too fat. She didn't like my* [care] *work either… I got to a place where I felt that I couldn't do a good job—it was my mother knocking me.*

Even where a parent appreciates the caregiver's efforts, and many do, the seemingly unending responsibility of looking after another person undermines the sense of self. Jean admits to feeling devalued by the demands of caregiving required for her 90-year old mother over the last eight years. Rather than question the non-stop demands, Jean focused on what she perceives are her own physical and mental shortcomings. She said:

> *I'm duty-bound. That's the pattern in my family, and I'm tired of the fact that it's* [caregiving] *gone on as long as it has. I'm just not smart enough to work out the financial. Financial things make me feel desperate. I do worry about my level of intelligence.*

Jean's main worry is that she cannot confront her mother about what is on her mind—to have an honest and open relationship.

> *I feel guilt and angry. I need to work on my procrastination. I'm trying not to beat myself up too much… but I can't help it.*

Eva, an Hispanic woman, now disabled because of a car accident, had always sought her mother's approval. Even with very limited means, she brought her mother into her home, pleasing her with small gifts and clothes, as well as total care. Yet, her mother and brothers had regularly abused her as a child. She commented:

> *I used to have nightmares about her. My mother and two brothers— all abusive. I was punished daily. I was fearful of being killed by my mother and two big brothers. I was so overwhelmed* [interacting with mother]. *I shook and cried all the time. My mother played so many*

head trips. I spent my whole life trying to please her. I wish my mother would die. The sicker she gets, the happier she is.

Eva feels she owes her mother for bringing her into the world, but also feels guilty about not spending enough personal time with her. *I feel I can't do enough, and I can't express it.* Her inability to communicate with her rapidly deteriorating mother causes her daily grief, for which, she believes, death is the only resolution.

Loss of Self

Although some caregivers admit to being unable to make choices and prefer to leave decisions to others, a significant number of caregivers we interviewed experienced periods of literally losing themselves to the caregiving process. Caring for another begins in the context of a multi-dimensional self. Over time, however, that self gets engulfed—all of their time, energy and social contacts are focused on their caregiving duties. A young woman talked about the two years she provided care for her grandmother, who had Parkinson's disease.

I tried to have a social life, tried to have a life of my own. It was hard to break strings—going out to get a job, and needing something instead of being here 24/7.

As the demands of the caregiving role expand, a few women real-ize that something is not right. Their entire life has been thrown out of balance. Most women are able to recognize this before they lose their capacity for self care. Others abandon nearly everything else to serve the elder. For this caregiver, giving her all to her stepfather left little energy for her own family.

I promised my stepdad he could die in his home. I understand the need for respect and dignity during this passage in life. I moved into my stepfather's home during the week, then back to my family on week-ends—there was no balance. I had to miss my son's baseball games. For six months, I minimized my own medical crises, and made it clear to my stepdad that he was calling the shots.

For many women caregiving duties arise at an inappropriate time

—when other priorities take center stage. For newly married Natalie, the caregiving of both parents was nearly heartbreaking.

Right after I got married, my father became ill, then my mother had a stroke. I took care of them for ten years. For six months I lived with them. I did the best I could. I felt overwhelmed at times—dealing with the insurance companies and all the health issues. I missed the time with my husband and put off dealing with my problems. I felt lost and guilty. When I started [caregiving], I was a newly married homemaker with a job; after a year of caregiving, I was a married woman and a daughter. [Now] I had become the parent, handling everything for my parents—financial, health—everything. I put my mom first in every-thing, causing problems with other relationships in my life. My husband listened while I ranted and raved.

At the outset of caregiving, women often report a sense of rising to the challenge, combined with commitment to the care of their loved one. As the difficulties of giving care accumulate, the caregiver discovers her inability to deal with the situation beyond an obligatory response. In her sixties, Joyce took on a commuter role of caregiver to her mother, who was in her eighties and suffering from heart disease, deafness and arthritis. For 14 years, she traveled 150 miles round trip each month or more to look after a steadily declining loved one. Joyce commented:

I'm always involved since I'm her daughter. I guess since Dad died (1976), she's been alone, but she's totally independent. She's very gull-ible, lost every penny to a nephew, who ripped her off for thousands of dollars [he was on drugs]. She was totally in denial.

Conditions of care went from bad to worse.

Mother had a house fire one week before Christmas. Unfortunately, it was winter. She had an oil stove and flames were up to the ceiling. It was terrible smoke damage. After this, she became so angry. She had no judgment. She was out of control, and that was the issue. My mother took it out on me, blaming me for things I shouldn't be blamed for.

Perhaps the greatest indignity was her mother's lack of affection toward her.

She hugs and kisses her friends, but not me. She doesn't show her feel-ings. She was hard-hearted to me. She doesn't believe in sympathy. It makes it worse she was hurt so badly. My biological father left when we were little. She never showed me love when I was growing up.

Anne, who left her home, family, job, and social network to care for her husband, described her fighting spirit when he received the diagno-sis of Parkinson's disease. She refers to the diagnosis as her own—stating that in a very real sense she has Parkinson's too because her thoughts, reactions, and decisions are considered and measured in the context of what a Parkinson's disease patient can handle and absorb. The "I" merges into the "we."

Carrie is a wife and mother who is caring for her elderly father after a recent return to college. As she explains it, she doesn't know where her father "ends" and she begins.

His habits have become part of my habits. Part of me feels as if I've never known anything else. Part of me hopes for a time that I can con-centrate on my own life.

Some women were surprised to discover, along the way, their dimin-ishing selves. Jean felt "duty-bound" to care for her 90-year-old mother, who suffered from dementia, osteoporosis and Parkinson's disease.

I have been doing this since I was 44—I need to focus, but can't. I finally abandoned the dream of going back to school. I quit looking for oppor-tunities. It's just easier to do what you're doing. After all these years, I am resigned. She has lived so long and I no longer feel this is a stage of my life, but this is my life. I don't see an end to it.

Sociologists refer to this condition as "role engulfment" or "role en-trenchment." It occurs when one role predominately encompasses the time and energy of a person. Women who have lost themselves to the caregiving process describes themselves as "sinking into an ocean," "falling into space" or having the sensation that their bodies are disinte-grating. The loss of self can be highly problematic, as it can contribute to disassociation and breakdown of physical and emotional maintenance for both caregiver and care receiver.

When individual identity is swallowed up, what can replace it? For a few women, the loss was irreparable, leading to severe depression and an inability to cope with even the most mundane household tasks.

Renae's entire life was thrown completely out of balance when she faced the demands of caring for three loved ones. Her only child, born with Down's syndrome, still needed her close attention. Her 90-year-old mother, suffering from Alzheimer's disease, was rapidly deteriorating. David, her 61-year-old male companion had been diagnosed with pancreatic cancer. Rather than taking charge of the situation, she "gave up" and collapsed into passivity. Renae's story clarifies the caregiver's reality of sacrificing too much for the sick beloved.

> *I haven't kept in touch with neighbors. I used to play in a music group, but I had to drop that and nearly everything else. When David got sick, he didn't want me out of his sight. He didn't want me gardening. It made me kind of give up any kind of life I might have had.*
>
> *While I was caring for David, I suffered from 'mental health problems.' [Renae said,] 'There you go, losing it.' I had a hysterectomy. I got lazy. I never had that problem before. I just got fat and lazy. David wanted to eat all the high calorie foods he could. I kept him company sitting around watching TV. I think my health deteriorated because of age, worse diet, [being] more sedentary and depression.*
>
> *I don't think my health problems affected my caregiving. He wanted me there all the time. He had been a very independent person. He didn't want to be a burden. He was in charge of the bills until the last three months. He was never bedridden—trying to keep up his morale and spirits. I helped him with that. We shared the costs. I should have moved into his house. He had a number of properties.*
>
> *I told him, 'Just because you're sick, I'm not going to take you out [to a hospital]. You can stay here.'*
>
> *When I met David, I tried rescuing him, but I fell into the pattern. Once he got sick, I never had confidence in myself. I just always wanted to help him. He felt bad that he caused me all this trouble.*
>
> *David wasn't anxious to have Hospice. He had chemotherapy and developed cataracts. He was going to beat his cancer. No other family members helped with David's care. His kids were grieving the death of*

their mother, who had died of cancer. The kid thing gets sticky. It mud-
dies things up. For care, I was pretty much it. I felt overwhelmed toward
the end. I started not being able to sleep. I felt guilty because I wasn't
seeing my son enough. I said I needed to get out, but he didn't like that
very much.

I started out as an independent woman, enthusiastic, [a] workahol-
ic, good friend to David and a good mother. I became more concerned
about him and became a person who dealt only with sickness and death
everyday. I think doing that 24 hours a day, seven days a week is just too
much: treatments and sickness all the time—also death, death, death.
It gets you down.

Renae is re-evaluating her main source of self-respect, which comes from
taking care of others.

[I] don't know anymore—changing in this area. I felt like I owed him.
I wanted him to stay here, just because I would feel awful if I had no-
where to go. My life was disrupted. I gained weight. I forgot to value
myself. I lost myself and I gave up friends and family… After he died, I
painted my toenails.

Lack of outside activities, isolation, inability to relate to family members or other potentially supportive persons, a chronic sense of doom,
the absence of a religious community, and a feeling that "nothing really
matters," may all be the ultimate consequences of role totality. All of one's
consciousness becomes wrapped up in giving care. At the extreme, this
is part of a co-dependency pattern in which the self has collapsed into a
"blended system," not an interdependent relationship, but one in which
caregiver and care receiver merge into a single psychological unit.

Certainly, this merging experience may be more pronounced for a
highly traditional woman, whose sense of self is completely bound up
with giving to others. Additionally, the feeling of not having control either over the loved one's disease or one's own life further contributes to
a sense of fatalism and sorrow.

Patricia, an Hispanic woman who fully embraced her cultural and religious values, emphasized how important it was to focus on her sick
husband, whose multiple heart attacks required her total attention and

devotion. At the same time, she was unable to assume household management and bill paying, because "my husband takes care of the money." Patricia commented:

> I want my husband to be happy and have good health, but he's stubborn (smiles). I want to give [him] my breath to get well. I never thought before that in my life I was going to have this experience [caregiving]. God gave this to me to prove my love for Him and all humans.

Patricia admitted to the difficulty of receiving sustained family support, because of traditional arrangements—women look after their male family members first, and only after this duty is accomplished can they consider the needs of their female relatives. With her mother gone, her surviving aunts and sisters are busy with their own families, and could not help her out with her husband.

> All my family take care of our brothers down to the last minute [of death]— that's our commitment in our culture for humans—it doesn't matter who they are.

Patricia expresses a sense of ongoing anguish and grief. Not only did her mother recently pass away, leaving her alone to cope with her husband, but also her work in a nursing home leaves her saddened when patients die—"it was a struggle for me because I loved them." Above all, Patricia wishes to be reunited with her family in Mexico City, an impossible dream because of her full-time caregiving commitment at home.

Co-Dependency

Most caregivers exhibit some elements of co-dependency. Melody Beattie, author of *Co-dependent No More*, defines co-dependency as: "One who has let another person's behavior affect him or her, and who is obsessed with controlling that person's behavior."[2] Beattie says that some women have been taught that co-dependent behaviors are desirable feminine attributes. Beattie proposes that the loss of self and the accompanying dysfunctional behaviors arise out of necessity to "protect ourselves and meet our needs." In an effort to cope, the individual performs, feels and thinks in erroneous ways, believing that survival itself is at stake.

Originally the word **co-dependency** referred to people whose lives had become unmanageable as a result of living in a committed relationship with an alcoholic. However, the concept of co-dependency also describes relationships with people who are chronically ill and emotionally or mentally disturbed, who are adult children of alcoholics or who are engaged in other types of distorted psychosocial relationships.

Two common denominators of co-dependency are: (1) having a relationship with troubled, needy or dependent people: and (2) strictly following a number of unwritten, silent rules. Among them: **no** discussion of problems or open expression of feelings; **no** direct, honest communication; **no** realistic expectations of self, such as being human, vulnerable or imperfect; **never** any selfishness nor trust in oneself and other people; **no** playing and having fun; and, certainly **never** rocking the delicately balanced family canoe through growth and change. For many caregivers we spoke with, it is the inability to speak out that is most difficult.

In the later stages of co-dependency, a caregiver may feel lethargic, depressed, withdrawn, hopeless and isolated, and may not be able to maintain even the most basic of routines. They may also become violent or ill—emotionally, mentally or physically.[3]

Mary Beth described her relationship with her husband of nearly 50 years before and during the early stages of her caregiving.

> *Before caretaking, we were both independent. After a few months of caregiving I was just unhappy. I felt tied to my husband in an unhealthy way. I was his wife. I was his wife. I was his wife (emphasis). He wouldn't accept respite care. He became totally attached to me. I got tired, impatient and nothing I could do would change the situation. I lived the 36-hour day.*

The National Mental Health Association (NMHA) describes co-dependency as a learned behavior that can be passed down from one generation to another—an emotional and behavioral condition that affects an individual's ability to have a healthy, mutually satisfying relationship. Co-dependents often take on a martyr's role and become "benefactors" to an individual in need. NMHA lists some typical attributes of co-dependent persons, such as exaggerated sense of responsibility, taking on more than their share, lack of trust in self and others, difficulty in adjusting to change, problems with boundaries, chronic anger, poor communications and difficulty making decisions.[4]

The following characteristics were frequently observed among our caregivers. We can rephrase these in more personal terms as the "caregivers' perspective," one I certainly share. The caregiver speaks to her loved one, and I paraphrase, as though it were a single voice.

Characteristics of Caregiver Co-dependency

- My good feelings about who I am stem from receiving approval from you and others—our children, my siblings, relatives, friends, employer, etc.
- My struggle affects my serenity.
- My mental attention is focused on you.
- My fear of your anger, disappointment and regret determines what I say or do.
- My social circle diminishes as I involve myself with you.
- My self-esteem is bolstered by relieving your pain.
- My own hobbies/interests are put to one side. My time is spent sharing your hobbies/interests.
- I am not aware of how I feel. I am only aware of how you feel.
- I am not aware of what I want. I ask what you want.
- The dreams I have for my future are linked to you.
- The quality of my life is in relation to the quality of yours.

For some women, the increased reliance on the caregiving role develops a sense of reward and satisfaction simply from being needed. Some have expressed the fear of "losing their job." Kathy, 61, cared for both her very aged parents in their home. "I worry about the time when they will not be here. What will I do? I'm so nurturing."

NMHA clarifies the problem of the rescue attempts of the co-dependent in that the needy person continues on the destructive course of passivity, becoming ever more dependent on the unhealthy caregiving of the "benefactor." As this reliance increases, the co-dependent feels that *she alone* can carry out the necessary physical, emotional and medical tasks required. Caregiving becomes who the person is, but not without ambivalence and a sense of powerlessness.

Carrie, a 39-year-old university student, has been a caregiver since preschool and now looks after her blind father. She reflects on the caregiver role as one without an end.

> *Although most of the time I feel grateful that I can 'be there' for the various people I have been able to assist, there is a part of me that sometimes wishes that I had a 'break.' Perhaps, at some point in my life, there will be a time that no one around me will need me to be a caregiver. I do not see that happening. Part of me sees others in my family needing assistance as soon as my father no longer needs me. I suppose I will step up, again and again.*

Burn-out characterizes many caregivers at this stage, despite their assertion of being happy. Carrie goes on to say:

> *It is sometimes difficult to cope after I am done with a 'session' of helping. I sometimes 'crash' when I go home. I'll stay 'up' when I'm with my dad, then later I am mentally, emotionally and physically exhausted. Again, at the same time, I have gotten to spend much more time with my dad than I probably would have… I see him much more often now. I am happy that I can be there for my dad.*

When caretaking becomes compulsive, the co-dependent feels choiceless and helpless in the relationship, but remains unable to break away from the cycle of behavior that causes it. Faith, whom we met earlier, describes her adolescent years taking care of her alcoholic mother as a role reversal. Even though her mother told her frequently that she was no good, Faith felt a lifetime commitment to her mother's care.

> *I was the designated caregiver. I was nine years old, on crutches from polio and was sent to take care of my grandmother. From childhood, I knew I would be responsible for my mother. I didn't look for any other way.*

Co-dependents view themselves as victims and are attracted to that same weakness in their love and friendship relationships—they do not know when or how to stop. Sandra lamented:

> *My husband was negative and unappreciative and expected I would provide care, regardless. I was the only one he had.*
>
> *Over the one year-plus, the situation got to be overwhelming. I guess it was my intention to be his caretaker—for better or worse, sickness and health—but I didn't know what it would be like. Intentions are there, but it takes a lot out of you. He had a bag and needed help with [his] colostomy.*
>
> *The most difficult was the financial stuff. I didn't know about any of it till it happened. I was overwhelmed and helpless. I broke down and cried a lot in private, went on autopilot—do it (now) and think about it later. I lost my husband and I felt guilty about feeling bad.*
>
> *I was really committed in the beginning, but the sicker he got, I couldn't deal with his feelings. Instead of speaking up to the doctors about their lack of care, I got short with my sick husband instead. We took things out on each other—heat of the moment. He's dead because of the medical system. After one year of giving care I'm an emotional wreck, disorganized, not a good friend and I'm moody.*

Co-dependency becomes a familiar pattern for women who have been abused or neglected in childhood, and been forced to perform as a parent to their parents. When they move into adulthood, they continue the pattern, assuming the role of caretaker for the abusive parent. Additionally, childhood abuse often generates post-traumatic stress syndrome. This is a condition whereby a person who has suffered deep trauma may continue to experience the same disordered emotions and thinking years later, feeling as though they were still in the midst of the abuse.

As a child, Jane had been abused by her father and mother. Now, as an adult, Jane has been diagnosed with bipolar disorder, depression, post-traumatic stress syndrome and anxiety, as well as stomach and intestinal problems. Additionally, Jane's two sons both have chronic medical conditions, and require close supervision and care. Yet, when Jane's mother was ill, Jane left her husband and children, and flew across the country to take care of her mother. After her mother's death, she felt called to act as caregiver for her father, who had Alzheimer's disease. Prior to caretaking, their relationship was "stressed and tense."

To facilitate care, she transported her father across the country to be closer to her home. Once her father was ensconced nearby, Jane reported feeling very stressed, out of control, finding it difficult to divide herself between two sick boys and a demanding, mentally incompetent father. During the entire 18 months of caregiving her dad, Jane saw a doctor for depression, but apparently did not respond to treatment. She described herself as her father's lifeline.

> *I moved my father cross-country to be in a home near me. The job of caregiver was stressful. My life was out of control. I found it difficult to divide myself between two sick children and a father dying with Alzheimer's.*
>
> *But my method of operation has always been to address the immediate concern. I'm good at rescuing. I felt helpless on the plane—they need to make adult diapers available in airports. I had a stressed relationship with my dad, and in the end I made choices for him that he was unable to disapprove of. I wanted him to be happy with the choices I made.*

After one year of caregiving, Jane described herself as simply "a very tired daughter." After her father died, and without warning, she left her husband and children and moved away to care for a man who had cancer, whom she had only known for four months. Caregiving situations like Jane's—of sinking into the role and excluding all other options—are certainly not common. But hers is a story of co-dependency at its most obsessive.

Reflections

This chapter continues the theme of the caregiver burden by considering how an emotionally charged situation, inherent in caregiving, generates unhealthy or maladaptive behavior. Part of the problem may be traced to early childhood experiences, including being devalued or abused by parents or other significant persons in one's life. Another part may be connected to gender; for example, the need for approval related to female socialization into deference and self-deprecating behavior.

Women who have been devalued may respond to crisis situations by withdrawal, a strong sense of inadequacy, and a sense of their own unworthiness, no matter how hard they try to "do it all." For caregivers, taking on the semi-medical, semi-social work, invariably maternal role for another adult often appears to necessitate their all-consuming attention. When they fail to measure up to their own impossibly high standards, they may collapse into anger, passivity or tears. In more extreme situations, a feeling of no-self occurs. This entails a disembodied sense of self, a sense of being adrift, of having lost one's way in the world.

Finally, I clarified co-dependence as a matter of deep concern from a mental health point of view. Many of these caregivers' responses show that the co-dependence issue I have described here is not simply their isolated response to the situation. Rather, it becomes an intrinsic part of the caregiving role itself—a role that requires a level of sacrifice they perceive to be total; a sacrifice that disrupts their personal goals, drains their serenity and tears away at their very selfhood.

Chapter 6

Oh, For a Caring Medical System

When it comes to the healing professions, wisdom means knowing what it takes, and understanding all the factors that are involved in the healing process. It is not limited to making the correct diagnosis and applying the proper medication or surgical procedure. Wisdom incorporates the attitude of caring along with all of one's training, experience and knowledge of disease. It is the combination of all these factors that we can call wisdom.
~ Chokyi Nyima Rinpoche and David R. Shlim, M.D.,
Medicine and Compassion[1]

No problem can be solved with the same level of consciousness that created it.
~ Albert Einstein

Health Care: A Broken System

Elders and their families confronting terminal illness turn to their medical providers as lifelines in a shattered world. They seek not only medical "treatment," but compassion and understanding, as well. Hope and inexperience fuel their efforts to locate the most effective and caring treatment for what appears to be an unknown medical problem—one, most seekers assume, that is easily remedied by the multitude of new medical technologies spawned over the last thirty years. Their belief is that medical support comes in tidy packages, or at least a reassuring safety net, containing the prerequisite providers and their professional acumen and wisdom: originating physician, medical specialists, nurses, hospital, recovery center, followed by home care. Above all, these seekers believe that the physician plays an enlightened, indeed critical, role guiding and facilitating the patient and his/her family through the health care labyrinth.

"Today, the medical care system resembles more of a tightrope than a safety net," says Nicholas D. Kristof in a *New York Times* editorial, "Medicine's Sticker Shock."[2] In a sign of the growing disenchantment with our health system, Kristof says, 13,000 doctors have joined Physicians for a National Health Program, an organization that lobbies for a single-payer government-financed health program. It is not merely the exorbitant and growing costs of our existing system—we have the most expensive in the world—but our medical care system also leaves out 45 million Americans. This translates into higher mortality rates: Americans' life expectancy has been steadily slipping and now ranks lower than Costa Rica's. Additionally, Kristof writes, the entire system is grossly inefficient. The emphasis on curative medicine, rather than public health and prevention, further contributes to runaway costs.

Other critics support Kristof's critique of the costs of America's medical system.[3] Defibrillators, which jump-start the heart if it enters an arrhythmic pattern, cost about $1,800 to $ 2,000 each. Institutional models fetch even more. "Miracle" drugs to treat cancer are so expensive, consumers often must weigh the value of extending their life for a few months for a lifetime of debt for their survivors. *Avastin*, which can add an average of 20 months to the life of a colon cancer patient, costs more than $4,000 a month. Current trials of *Avastin* are underway for breast and lung cancer patients. If approved, the drug could cost as much as $100,000 per annum for each patient. And, Bristol-Meyer-Squibb's new colorectal cancer drug, *Erbitux*, which was recently approved for treating head and neck cancer, will cost $16,800 to $26,400 for one course of therapy. In contrast, many popular, brand-name drugs can be purchased for 30 to 80 percent less in Canada, due to government price controls.[4]

What's more, medical providers must confront patients about end-of-life care as reasonable assistance and not heroic interventions that circumvent the course of nature. Treatment, such as Hospice, focuses on palliative or comfort care and comes replete with compassionate and supportive medical staff to assist the patient and family in accepting the coming death for a smooth transition. In addition, Hospice provides a better alternative than risky treatments for prolonging life, which fail to extend the most important component: **quality of life**.[5]

Medicalization of Old Age

Sociologists have long observed how a variety of deviant and troublesome behaviors and social groups become targets of special social control.[6] One group, hyperactive children, also fall under special social control. Prescriptions and regimented school systems ultimately force these youngsters into a single mold.[7]

On the other end of the age spectrum, older persons disconnected from the world of work and professional power tend to be treated as a surplus population—unneeded and unwanted in a highly productive culture.[8] Our society demands a transformation for elders to be part of the mainstream: look young, feel young, act young and you may be accepted. Deepak Chopra, the guru of New Age enlightenment, has created a 10-step program to reverse biological age —a process that, he claims, is not only possible, but ultimately necessary.[9] Whereas many of his "steps" involve sound health practices, the negative sentiment remains: biological aging is never to be embraced, but only avoided. Anti-aging medicine, a growing segment of American health care, sets the beauty bar high, and affluent customers flock to practitioners' doors.

For some, excessive medical intervention for extension of life and bodily beautification has become a way of life.[10] Anti-aging medicine has become a multi-billion dollar industry. People can rejuvenate their skin with injectable fillers to eliminate wrinkles, reshape their body with cosmetic surgery and austere diet programs, as well as restore their lost hair with transplant procedures.

Yet, for all of the money spent on looking young and "aging successfully," the average older citizen often lacks information about the rudiments of a reasonably healthy lifestyle, including getting proper nutrition and moderate exercise, as well as following the no-smoking rule. These low-cost, natural approaches provide a better chance of having good health into old age.[11]

For millions of elderly, who lack the resources or choose not to reverse their aging and who now or will have bodily and emotional ailments, the issue is social management. The question of managing elders lies in the realm of *social control*, or the study of society's strategies and methods for directing human behavior. The logical institution for coping with the avalanche of elders pouring into retirement has been the medical system.

You may ask: Why is medical care a system of social control? The answer is simple: A high proportion of elderly—certainly those in their 70s and older—have some form of chronic disease or physical/mental ailment. Black and Hispanic elders are most likely to report fair or poor health.[12] Our modern ethic demands youthful vigor and good health. Doctors appear to have the answers—sometimes, the only answers in our "you-can-do-it" culture. And what the doctor says becomes gospel—take this medication, follow this regimen, and do as I say. Oldsters imbedded in this system develop identities around their latest surgery, compare notes about their pacemakers and brag or lament about their proliferating medications. Changing disease-producing lifestyles is rarely part of the prescription. The medical model has only a truncated idea of the social good. Cut, cure and drug is the short-hand recipe for intervention. For elders facing terminal disease and death, the system appears wholly out of sync.[13]

Another facet of the medicalization of the aged involves the power to label. Groups in powerful positions have not only the capacity, but also the will to label and stereotype subordinates or those dependent on them as inherently "different" from themselves.[14] Thus, teachers judge and label their students (bright, dumb, ambitious, etc.), social workers label their clients (lazy, disorganized, a problem, etc.) and doctors label their elderly patients (chronic, hopeless, troublesome, and so forth). The labeling process is often so effective that the individual unconsciously takes on the stigma—the belief that they are morally inferior and a burden to themselves, their families and society.

Stereotyping the Elderly and Caregivers

Cultural stereotypes of the elderly abound. On one side, traditional models of aging focus on physical and cognitive deterioration; aging implies decrepitude. On the other, a novel form of ageism has emerged generated by the "successful aging" ideology—the sophisticated, successful, beautiful senior. These new images of aging contribute to a new form of ageism—the ageless self. Katz and Marshall note that in our consumer society, these new images promote an impossible ideal, one that ignores other ways to age. Moreover, many of these images marginalize the very old, elders with disabilities and older people with different perspectives on aging.[15]

Clearly, the medical system did not invent stereotypes. Such stereotypes are very current in society and involve all that constitutes "differences" between the old and the not so old, a perception that varies by social class, ethnicity and other social divisions. The elderly are, indeed, different from younger, ideal-type populations by a number of criteria, which strike us as common sense, but certainly worth the mention (see Sidebar 1).

Overcoming negative stereotypes requires that the non-elderly and those who assist them pay attention to the uniqueness of elderly persons—not merely as patients or oldsters, but as remarkable survivors who have much to teach us.

Caregivers, too, experience the stigma of their role as mediators between the outside world and the elderly care receiver. First, since 80 percent of caregivers are women, gender inequalities plague negotiations with medical practitioners and institutional staff.[16] Patronizing attitudes are only too common—a pat on the back for a harassed caregiver, rather than a clear diagnosis and treatment plan. Again, women caregivers differ from their male cohorts in both caring ethics and caring styles. Women tend to "give their all"—an emotional brimming over. Men tend to take a pragmatic stance, setting aside their feelings to deal with matters at hand. Conversely, women caring for parents and spouses are more likely to expose their vulnerability, responding to excess demands with compliance or appeasing the elder and other family members. The result: increased stress and a sense of powerlessness.

Men, perhaps by virtue of traditional socialization, take on an authoritative role with parents or partners in similarly stressful situations. Another approach we have observed among many male family members of care receivers in our study is their physical and emotional withdrawal from both decision-making and caring.

Sidebar 1: Elder Stereotypes

1. *Physical appearance.* The elderly typically have gray hair and their skin has lost its elasticity. They may also look bent over. Clothing, shoes and other indicators of "being out of style" additionally reveal the aged as "poles apart" from the young.

2. *Motor skills.* Aging bodies demonstrate the "wear and tear" factor—body parts give out. Visible indicators include shuffling gait, slow responses, stiffness and an inability to negotiate steps and sitting positions easily. Such signs denote human limitations. However, some younger observers equate loss of motor skills with decrepitude.

3. *Voice.* Quavering, shifting timbre, low volume or speaking in a near-whisper are frequent traits found among the very old and frail. For hard-of-hearing elders, voice quality is often distorted.

4. *Memory gaps and losses.* The phrase "senior moment" summarizes the delayed or non-response many elders experience over choice of words. In the case of dementia, the losses are profound, eventually silencing the patient as brain function is lost.

5. *Health.* Illness stalks the aging person. Most folks 70 and older have one or more chronic health conditions, such as obesity, heart disease or diabetes.

6. *Psychologically dependent.* The elderly demonstrate neediness for others' attention, clinging to their children and grandchildren or other supportive persons. The visible loss of independence marks them as inferior.

7. *Old-fashioned.* In a global culture, with vast social changes occurring in the blink of an eye, the elderly reveal how out of touch they are with the world. Their very language appears obsolete, as do their stories of "old times," which appear irrelevant to younger generations. Their observations of contemporary life—gleaned through sensational media portrayals—contribute to elders' "gloom and doom" reactions to the world around them.

8. *Useless.* Rarely said aloud, but intrinsic to a culture of intense productivity, workers resent the idle. The elderly are not work-oriented, are slower to complete tasks, have surplus time and lack current job skills. Their visible failure to make a contribution to society through work or even steady volunteer activity constitutes their "otherness," making them social outsiders.

Second, caregivers experience a type of "guilt by association," rendering them a deviant class in the eyes of many observers.[17] Identifying with the illness and dying of a loved one implies their inability to interact or participate in normal ways. Chronic fear, fatigue, stress, anxiety and lack of humor characterize the overwrought state of many caregivers, contributing further to their marginality. Because they represent and attend to a sick elderly person—the latter seen as a morally inferior being—caregivers receive some of the same negative evaluations as their elderly charges. Many caregivers, of course, are elderly or aging, as well—another strike against them. When caregivers happen to demonstrate competence, assuming a take-charge attitude, they may be treated as an onerous and unwelcome presence by medical providers.

Third, caregivers are often perceived by medical staff and even by themselves as ineffectual, bumbling and overwhelmed as they take on a role that does not fit their background, personality or level of expertise. At the same time, the average lay person looks up to members of the medical profession. They often feel a sense of inadequacy because the gap in knowledge is so great. Having to confront a highly impersonal and bureaucratic medical system only compounds the problem. Thus, caregivers may feel reluctant to communicate their ignorance or express their own needs to medical staff.

A fourth consideration, the tendency for micro-managing their loved one's life, a highly time consuming task, creates further estrangement from friends, family and the health care community. Initially, friends may offer open arms of support and nurturing. However, the nature of long-term care means that old, comfortable habits and friends often die along with the decline of the sick elder.

The Problem of Medical Treatment of Elderly Patients

The first step to system reform is recognition within the various medical professions that care delivery is seriously flawed. Before we present our caregivers' experiences coping with the medical system, we need a context to understand the essential limitations surrounding medical care for the elderly *from the perspectives of physicians themselves.* I have summarized some major considerations from three professional groups: the American Medical Student Association, American College of Osteopathic Family Physicians and American College of Emergency Physicians.[18]

- Lack of medical-psychological knowledge of the aging process, as well as failure to train specialists for the geriatric population. Only 10 percent of teaching universities require students to complete at least one course in geriatrics.
- Severe shortages of geriatric physicians throughout the country, leading to the assertion that the elderly are "patients in peril" by the American Academy of Medical Colleges.
- A health care system that cannot respond to the growing numbers of older people. Americans 85 and older are the fastest growing segment of our population.
- Fifty percent of hospital beds are occupied by patients 65 years and older, a percentage that will substantially increase over the next 20 years as baby boomers enter retirement age.
- False ideology about elderly patients as physically and cognitively disabled across the board contributes to physicians' discomfort with primary care of elders.
- The "heroic model" of American medicine emphasizes high technology and skills, appropriate for acute care and younger patients, rather than care and compassion to deal with elderly patients, who have chronic diseases and face death.
- The cure orientation of American training runs counter to the reality of sick elderly patients, who often have more than one chronic illness requiring the attention of various health care workers.
- Many physicians suffer from an ageist bias that contributes to discrimination against elderly patients, resulting in an "elderly care gap"—too few services, especially for minorities and the poor.
- Bureaucratic obstacles to care confound the system, and discourage the elderly from pursuing treatment. In a study of five Boston hospitals by the American Geriatric Society (1996), people 80 or older received less care in hospitals than did patients younger than 50 by as much as $7,000 per patient.
- Poor and unsatisfactory communication between physicians and elderly patients hinders effective health care. In a study of elderly

emergency department patients 65 and older, only 15 percent of elderly persons could list all their medications, dosage schedules and indications. No medical provider had ever spelled out this information to them, or they were too cognitively impaired to understand the directives.

- A patchwork system of financing health care for the elderly leads to excessive or inadequate treatment, and invariably higher costs for elders and their families.
- Health care providers are typically between 25 and 60 years old, and show little interest in caring for the frail elderly on an age basis alone.
- Managed care complicates treatment for the elderly, and most poor elderly patients do worse in this system than do younger and more affluent individuals.

Medical Demoralization

The problem of medical treatment of elderly patients, then, depends upon the nature of medical knowledge and the medical profession itself, as well as the type of diseases— many of them incurable and untreatable. Above all, the medical profession, as currently organized, contributes to patients' dissatisfaction. Negative encounters with medical and institutional staff and hospital situations contribute further to the burden of care. Caregivers articulated widespread frustration with the treatment they received. Some complained that their doctor failed to take charge or clearly avoided direct contact. Others were deeply upset over the hostile nursing home staff they encountered. The following brief statements summarize caregivers' more frequently expressed concerns:

- *My medical background made me feel very positive. Even so, when it was time for my husband to quit driving, we went to a very good neurologist, but he wouldn't say 'no' to his driving.*
- *My husband had mesothelioma, a cancer that attaches to the nerves in the chest. The most difficult part of caring for him was having to take charge of medications and not knowing anything about it— doctor's appointments, day-to-day care, writing everything down. [There were] too few answers from medical professionals, especially in the year-and-a-half before he was properly diagnosed. They*

weren't persistent enough to get the right diagnosis.

- *I took my dad to his neurologist. They did an MRI that showed spinal cancer. The doctor never said a word. I read it off the chart.*
- *We experienced four different doctors, four different evaluations before they could tell her she had cancer. They were very evasive.*
- *My mother had mini-strokes, heart problems and osteoporosis... she really was not receiving adequate care. I didn't think the medical professionals were forthcoming about my mother's condition. Doctors and nurses were vague* [about pain management]—*morphine was too high a dose.*
- *I was sorry that the primary care doctor couldn't visit in our home, where I provided round-the-clock care. Doctor didn't visit in the hospital, either.*
- *I didn't know. The doctors didn't know either. I got a lot from reading—the doctor never explained anything to me.*

Drawing on my own experience, I felt great apprehension after Jim had his second heart attack. Because he needed to spend a long time in the hospital with follow-up in the nursing home, we had to limit the number of family visitors for any one time. But I discovered in the nursing facility that the nurses didn't like *any* family members hovering around the patient's bedside for more than 10 minutes One nurse in particular was very hostile, no matter how much I tried to accommodate her demands. At one point, she said to me, "We could give a lot better care if you and your family would stay out of the patient's room.'" I felt devastated, but decided we all needed to be there for him. And besides, my family of six children, their partners and my 12 grandchildren refused to stay away.

Failing to inform the patient of a terminal diagnosis was another leading complaint among caregivers. Another major issue was a lack of communication with hospital and institutional staff. As a result, a sense of frustration and powerlessness typically dominated caregivers' interactions with doctors and medical personnel in hospitals and nursing homes.

Teri, the young woman who took on the job of caregiving her grandparents, said:

Grandma had Parkinson's disease and dementia. The doctors didn't talk to each other and consequently, she was over-medicated. She suffered from dopamine-induced schizoid behavior because of the over-medication. I had five gals handling Grandma around-the-clock. One of them was using [dirty] needles under the sink. [The] facility was a horrendous experience: no bed, Grandma was sleeping on the floor. The rooms were hot, hot.

Grandma fell a lot and was sad and depressed. She had trouble keeping all those medications going—just too much. She was always so positive and appreciative. I was amazed at how she was treated by the hospital. She had arrhythmia and they released her at 3 a.m.

In the nursing home, my grandfather rejected the feeding tube. He was combative and boycotted his pills and in the end, they didn't give him enough morphine. He went screaming into death.

The most unfair experience I had in the 6 years, 31 to 40 hours a week, of caregiving for my grandparents was dealing with the medical professionals and how they handled it—keeping my grandma in a room for one hour and then misdiagnosing and sending us on our way. It really made me distrust doctors.

Despite such setbacks, Teri, like so many of these caregivers, expresses gratitude for the opportunity to care for her beloved grandparents.

I was pretty much alone in their care and grateful that I had the good sense to step forward at the right time, put myself out for them. I am appreciative of the opportunity to care for them. I try to make a difference and I realize how short life is. It felt good to give back to people who were good to me—instead of taking from them.

Over-reliance on the medical system and on the "correct" medical diagnosis reduces patients and their families to a state of childlike dependency. Their entire sense of reality becomes centered around the doctor's understanding of their loved one's symptoms and his or her ability to reduce or eliminate them. In many cases, they are disappointed. In an interview, Anne, who is featured in "The Face of Parkinson's Disease" (a section that follows), expressed her profound frustration around the lack of knowledge and caring, especially at the higher level of medical expertise. Initially, Mike self-diagnosed his symptoms, Anne observed:

> *his changing and stooped posture, his stiffness and inability to smile and his dark moods, but finally he knew he had Parkinson's when his hand-writing went to a flat undecipherable line.*

Still, he wanted to have a medical confirmation of his suspicions. Their first encounter shocked them both.

> *In the spring of 1993 we made an appointment to see a neurologist at [the clinic] to either verify Mike's own diagnosis or worse, to determine whether his symptoms were something more frightening: a brain tumor. The first time my husband was examined, the doctor asked him to do a few simple finger and hand coordination exercises. Mike tried to repeat what the doctor had demonstrated but couldn't quite match the coor-dination. The doctor slapped his hand. 'No, that's not right. Do it this way.' We were stunned and saddened and immediately left the doctor's office to request a transfer to a different neurologist.*

This couple concluded that the problem was not the physician's off-putting behavior, but rather the "assembly line" treatment that was so dehumanizing.

> *The expertise is, without question, at the [distinguished] clinic, but the assembly-line process of morning registration, conveyer-belt to next waiting room, more waiting, conveyer-belt and waiting, and finally be-ing called for an afternoon appointment was dehumanizing and the doctor's brusque and impatient treatment added something sour to our already wrenching situation. In spite of our disappointment, we decided to stay with the experts and had to wait another two months for the clinic machine to reach a diagnosis of Parkinson's disease.*

Although the clinic doctors' visits improved, Anne and her husband needed much more.

> *Our future visits to the clinic were more pleasant, but too short. Mike and I would prepare our lists of questions to ask the doctor, but after a half hour of interview and hand exercises, the doctor had no time*

for questions. He explained his expertise or specialty in neurology. 'My work is really in the area of Parkinson's Disease research.' And while it seems a common practice for doctors to tape record the present condition of the patient after the check-up, this doctor taped his observations in front of us, referring to Mike as a number and summarizing his current physical appearance and condition on a machine rather than talking directly to us. There are too many machines in medicine! We found an independent neurologist, whose manner was compassionate and kind. He gave us the time we needed to vent our worries. However, he admitted his lack of expertise in the area of Parkinson's disease. 'That's really not my specialty and everyone is so specialized today. You're better off doing your own research.'

During our family's efforts to get a diagnosis for Jim, I experienced a similar sense of futility dealing with specialists. At one point, during my most agonizing experience as a caregiver, I confronted the cardiologist's resident nurse practitioner about Jim's prognosis and asked: "What can we expect? What can I do to ease the pain? What does the future hold for Jim?" Other patients must have asked these same questions innumerable times, because his answer was short and glib. As he patted me on the back, he murmured, 'Don't worry, dear. In a year it will all be over.' I wanted information and consolation. I received only a death sentence for my loved one.

We returned home to resume the difficult and lonely path of congestive heart disease patient and overwrought caregiver. I remained deeply angry for months. I was furious with what I perceived to be an indifferent medical system, upset over Jim's apparent passivity and concerned about the spiraling costs and bungling of home care. Above all, I was disappointed with myself for lacking the knowledge to know the 'right' course of action and for succumbing to anger and a sense of futility, instead of following my normal pattern of taking a clear, positive course of action. In the meantime, my personal and social life began to shrink and eventually disappear. There seemed little time for anything, aside from teaching and caregiving. I felt trapped and helpless—and incredibly alone.

Like Anne and I did, most caregivers eventually confront the reality that their care receiver's disease will never get better, and the best course of action is to accept this fact and muddle through the medical system as well as they can.

Long-Term Care
Unlike death and dying in an earlier age when patients lingered only a few weeks or months, today's terminally ill elder is likely to languish for years, too weak and listless to undertake a normal life, yet too wedded to the idea of living to envision stopping the medicines and moving toward a willful and deliberate death. A protracted dying process, with no end in sight, challenges even the most well-intentioned caregiver. As Anne told me in a moment of frustration:

No matter what I do, how much positive or up-ness I conjure, squeeze or drag from within, these diseases absolutely will not get better tomorrow or next week—or ever. There will be no reversal. This thought occurs frequently to some caregivers, once in a surprising while to others, but can never be allowed to escape in the presence of the person who is really suffering.

Long-term or chronic care taking place over years is wholly unlike acute care. Childhood illnesses, adult colds and flus may interfere with life's routines, but they don't stop the flow of normal life. Long-term care turns inside out one's deepest expectations and sense of personal and domestic order. My own experience with the problems and hazards of long-term care demonstrates the frustration many caregivers have in coping with a reluctant medical system. Many caregivers observed that once Hospice stepped into the picture, care became both more predictable and humane. The turmoil until that point can be extraordinarily challenging. From my husband's first heart attack until he needed to make a life or death decision, I carefully tracked his medical encounters.

Jim returned from the hospital after treatment for his first heart attack. I made sure I could help with medications at home—follow-up care. Four months later, he had the second heart attack—more heavy care. I fully intended to take care of Jim, but with a cardiologist, a personal physician and a psychiatrist, I found the medical structure confusing. I simply could not find a single doctor to treat him as a whole person.

Certainly, of all the activities I performed as a caregiver, the most demanding was interacting face-to-face with medical providers. I had the sense that they had no clue as to my feelings or Jim's needs; they never seemed to answer my questions. Quality of life was not their bailiwick.

My deepest values are independence, self-management, a spiritual component to personality, being kind, family and friendships, but after a few months of caregiving, I was frightened, disorganized, panicky, out-of-control and a reluctant caregiver. I felt hopeless and overwhelmed. I couldn't see that what I was doing had any point. It seemed he was just getting worse, as he ingested more and more different medicines.

The medical professionals were dodging my questions and patronizing. I experienced a cavalier, and in some cases abusive, treatment by physicians and medical people, even facility administrators. After a period of frequent episodes of hospitalizations, Jim's personal physician was "right on." He said to my husband, "You're not dying right now, but you will need a lot of care. You have a choice—live or die." He couldn't walk and could barely speak, because he was so weak, and the doctor knew this. So if Jim chose to die, the doctor carefully pointed out he would need to stop his medication and stop eating. But if he chose to live—and the doctor emphasized this was *his* choice—he would need round-the-clock care. Jim chose to continue his struggle for life.

The most difficult decision, the one I worried about most, was putting Jim in institutional care. I couldn't believe I could put a dearly beloved in a home and walk out the door. In one of the many nursing homes Jim was in over a three-year period, the NACs shouting made us both cringe. No one was on the floor to supervise the workers. It was utterly frustrating. I was devastated—tormented by a place that couldn't provide proper care or enough staff. I wondered about the honesty of the word 'skilled' in skilled nursing facility—that was not my experience most of the time. Thankfully, the Hospice volunteer stepped in for the last 18 months. But segmented medical care for Jim made the choice to live incredibly difficult, as I indicated in the interview I had with Traci Harpine, the student who interviewed me for the study. I said:

The medical system is fragmented and many of its practitioners are incompetent. I suggest that caregivers find physicians/medical people with whom they feel comfortable and leave behind practices that don't work.

Those who must cope with institutional placement of their loved ones confront equally formidable problems, as described by Sally, who had two parents who required supervised care. According to Sally, her father's Crohn's disease led to episodes where he could no longer leave his home, while her mother's Alzheimer's condition required a special unit in the facility. She reports of her difficulties in coping with their care.

> *My father had progressed to the point where his bowels were completely out of control and he was almost a skeleton, really. He had all his mental faculties, but couldn't leave the house. So I felt that they needed to come to assisted living. They were admitted to assisted living here, only on the basis of my father, because my mother's confusion was so great by that point, that she absolutely needed a full-time caregiving facility.*

Once Sally located the facility, she thought her problems were over. But this was not the case.

> *The facility was very lovely, a new facility, but I felt that the staff was not satisfactory. They didn't hire the higher level professionals and the Alzheimer's unit was absolutely a nightmare. They were absolutely incompetent. They hired people who had no training and no skills and who would work at the lowest wage possible, and the people in that unit did not receive any of the type of care that was necessary... even to the point that they had one LPN for the whole building and the only way that they could control many of the patients was to overmedicate them.*
>
> *My mother had three very serious accidents because of being overly medicated and trying to walk. One time she fell into the nurse's station and just bashed in one side of her head... They didn't even keep her clean. Every time I picked her up in the ER, she was soaked up to her armpits in urine, because they couldn't even diaper her correctly or keep her clean... or wouldn't do it.*

Sally regrets she never reported these incidents, but the precarious state of her own health under the stress of caring for her parents created impossible obstacles for following up on the matter. At least her doctor's intervention made it possible to place her mother in a safe, if far less attractive, environment, which was uncarpeted and extremely noisy.

> *They* [accidents] *probably should have been reported. I shouldn't have blown it off. Once the doctor recommended I take her to another* [less] *pretentious facility—but with more expansive service. Once I did that, she got the care. They kept her clean and they kept her dry and they fed her well.*

Sally was fortunate in having medical assistance in locating a different facility, even if the environment was less than ideal. She was also fortunate in being on-site to supervise her parent's care, and intervene before the situation became disastrous. Sally felt she had triumphed over the situation because "my mother lived three-and-a-half years there with lots of social contact and lots of stimulation."

Costs of Care

Technological and pharmaceutical innovations have improved people's health and extended their lives—but at horrendous costs to individuals and society. The rising tide of spending stems from demographic and health trends, as well as from medical technologies that older Americans need and demand. According to the RAND Corporation, if half of the patients who had recently suffered a heart attack or been diagnosed with heart failure were to get defibrillators (automatically correcting the heart beat), health care spending on the elderly would increase $14 billion, or four percent, over the next ten years.[19] Add to these costs the ever-rising expense of health insurance and we readily see how health care costs are spiraling out of control. Most of our caregivers were managing fairly well with their current health care insurance policies. However, for a significant minority, financial costs for self and care receiver were overwhelming.

While in her fifties, Laura assumed care of both parents located in two different settings. Her mother was living in a nursing home and her dad was in his own home some distance away. Whereas her parents were able to pay for their health insurance, many of their incidental costs fell to her. Add to this her own personal difficulties—health insurance costs, living expenses, cancer relapses, death of a beloved parent—and the results are predictable: Laura experienced deep exhaustion and inability to cope.

My yearly income was $28,000. I didn't balance my checkbook for a couple of years—just do the necessities and keep going—that's about it. I [relocated] to care, for ten years, for my mother who had Alzheimer's, diabetes and dementia, and my father, who had a stroke, depression, arthritis, lung problems and chronic problems with asbestos poisoning. The most frustrating time was getting them through the initial part of their illnesses—just getting the diagnoses.

For ten years, I ran back and forth between Mom's care facility and Dad at home. Go see Mom, then Dad, drive home, do errands, then cook and take meals to Dad, then visit Mom again. Dad had an eating disorder; he called two or three times a day. Mom tried to feed me and fix my clothes, very physically and emotionally draining. I didn't know how pooped I was till it was all over. The most difficult decision I made was at the end [of life] with Dad. They didn't want feeding tubes [for him] and he was saying, 'I'm starving.' But I didn't give him food.

The largest item in my budget was medical insurance, plus eight to nine times a year [treatment] by the chiropractors. During the time I cared for my parent, I was diagnosed with colon cancer one year and ovarian cancer the next. It was a horrendous time! Sad, but not tragic. Financially, we had some pretty tough months—mainly paying for health insurance. And still, I felt the medical professionals were being evasive. Not once did we talk to the doctor regarding Alzheimer's—we need to clue the doctor in, but he doesn't listen anyway.

The middle class are not alone in their concern over elder care costs or medical competence. Billie Mae, a wealthy caregiver in her eighties, reflects on the frustrations of hiring competent help to provide home care during the extended dying period of her 95-year-old husband, John. Agency-trained staff did not appear to have adequate patient training, insight or compassion.

I had a 24-hour care force, six caregivers from the agency, and four caregivers from Hospice over the course of the day-night shift. And all this *help costs us a total of $12,000 a month. But the agency help just stood by, physically and emotionally. They kept misplacing our things. I could do a better job without training. As it was, I was caring for him over 80 hours a week. I just got tired of being captive [to the professional caregivers]. I had to supervise everything. I even had to cook for the work force. Six persons coming in and out, all day, every day, was just too much.*

Billie Mae's greatest concern was a lack of patient drug monitoring on the part of the staff, which contributed significantly to her husband's cognitive decline.

When I reviewed the care force notes, I realized that John experienced medicine-induced confusion and restlessness. There were very few notes from home care workers. This meant they weren't keeping score of what they were doing: no indication of tasks completed. I think they must have been talking to each other and neglecting John.

Elder Care: A New Direction?

Because elder care is embedded in a system both unprepared and unwilling to deal with chronic illness and death—especially among the aging population—caregivers experience a host of unremitting challenges in their efforts to cope with medical care. Among them: financial pressures, physical and emotional overload, lack of information and an overly bureaucratized system, which appears inherently indifferent to the needs and suffering of sick and dying elders, and those who look after them. Part of the problem resides in the sheer number of frail and infirm elderly patients flocking into doctors' offices, hospitals and nursing homes.

At the same time, the medical profession has not stepped up to the plate to train physicians for elder care practices. Recommendations have been put on the table to alter the current gap in elder care training. The American Academy of Medical Colleges urges medical schools to: (1) institute healthy senior mentors as part of the medical team; (2) recognize elder patients as having special needs (e.g. multiple illnesses, impaired cognitive ability, limited communication skills, reluctance to complain, etc.); and (3) push the federal government to increase payment for primary care of the elderly for geriatric physicians, as well as to expand loans and grants for medical students to encourage geriatric careers. Such recommendations would go a long way to ease the current medical situation of elders as "patients in peril."[20]

But there is more to elder care than highly trained physicians and nurses. The lack of overt compassion in medicine comes at a time when medical science can do more for a patient than at any time in history. Chokyi Nyima Rinpoche and David R. Shlim point out that "major advances of the past fifty years include antibiotics, anti-inflammatories, sophisticated non-invasive diagnostic capabilities, minimally invasive surgical techniques, immunization against a wide variety of diseases, kidney dialysis, open-heart surgery and organ transplantation."[21] These are only some of the more utilized and miraculous achievements of modern medical science.

Yet, few people are happy with the way that medicine is practiced—and this includes the doctors. Many of those who manage health care systems throw up their hands at making medicine either affordable or universally available. Additionally, the over-treatment for terminally ill patients both raises costs and severely diminishes quality of life. And, ultimately, two components are missing from this picture: humanism and care (see Sidebar 2).

The fault is not the doctors alone. We need to also implicate our medical and legal culture, as well as doctors' assumptions about the family's wishes. Pauline W. Chen writes in *Final Exam: A Surgeon's Reflections on Mortality*[22] that "hope can hurt." When doctors push for greater intervention for older patients, they reflect not only the family's hope to keep their loved one alive, but also the medical belief that dying represents failure. When asked what doctors would request for themselves if diagnosed with a terminal illness, the overwhelming majority of doctors choose to limit or withdraw life-sustaining therapy. And while they are likely to support those patients who ask them to withdraw care, they may feel obligated to continue treatment for others, for fear of legal repercussions. Chen says that in a recent study, a third of attending physicians and almost three quarters of residents felt they had acted against their conscience while caring for the terminally ill.

Sidebar 2: What Your Physician Needs to Know

Caregivers could contribute to their "physician's handbook on elder care" by requesting their doctors to consider this alternative remedy for terminally ill care: develop a compassionate attitude and work style based on the principle of *lovingkindness*.

Shlim, a medical doctor and Rinpoche, a Tibetan Lama, believe that the power of "lovingkindness" eases elderly patients' fears and anxieties, as well as lightens the load for the practitioner. Moreover, *patient-centered care* enhances the medical interaction, and contributes to positive feelings, attitudes and actions for all persons involved. The authors offer a five-point program of wisdom and compassionate care for medical practitioners and nursing home staff:

- Pay full attention to the patient and the patient's illness. Let the sick elder know that he/she is, for that moment, the practitioner's only center of focus. Actually care and *want* to help, rather than seeing the patient as a problem to be solved. This raises the patient's trust level and aids in the healing process.
- When caring for sick people, who may be in deep pain and suffering or be short-tempered and irritable, "extend infinite tolerance and patience." The greater the practitioner's patience, the more likely the patient can be eased.
- Compassion is the wish to alleviate suffering. This attitude should be foremost in the practitioner's toolbox of skills. The way to compassion entails the recognition that suffering and illness is the lot of every human being, including oneself. Thus, compassion is "to suffer with" the patient, rather than disengage from the patient emotionally.
- Compassion cannot be generated from outside sources. Rather, compassion is a natural outpouring of our humanness. Illness, death and dying are universally relieved with the tender mercies of compassionate care.

Finally, a *patient-centered* approach means more than just embracing wisdom and compassionate care for others. It asks that we all remind ourselves of our own limitations—our attachment to results, concern about the opinions of others and need for social approval—and adopt a truly "healing attitude" toward ourselves and others in our care.

Chokyi Nyima Rinpoche and David R. Shlim. *Medicine and Compassion*. Boston: Wisdom Publications, 2004.

The Face of
Parkinson's Disease

Parkinson's disease is a degenerative nerve disorder of later life that significantly affects both body and mind functioning. The disease is characterized by rhythmic tremor, muscular rigidity and slow movement, masked facial expressions, slurry speech, depression, anxiety and stress—conditions caused by degeneration in the basal ganglia of the brain. According to the National Parkinson's Foundation, 1.5 million Americans have the disease. About 60,000 are diagnosed with the condition each year. No known cure exists for Parkinson's disease, but various medications can delay or help reduce certain symptoms.

Anne Mikkelsen, my research assistant for this book, is an active caregiver for her husband, Mike, who was diagnosed with Parkinson's disease more than 10 years ago. Her observations about the difficulties of caring for her husband clarify the special problems associated with this disease type. Other diseases present equally challenging agendas, but in this instance, the difference is that both Anne and Mike have made a pact to mindfully monitor both the disease and each other as they move together through their travail. Mike retains his lively mental ability, but confronts the erosive effects of the disease on a daily basis. Anne's narrative contains elements of many of the stories provided by our 61 caregivers, who sometimes found hope even when surrounded by despair.

Let's begin with Anne. Following Anne's story, we shift to Mike's experience with Parkinson's disease to provide the only extended self-reflection by a care receiver in the book. Although the book focuses on the caregivers' perspective, bear in mind that both parties—caregiver and care receiver alike—must cope with the disease, and for some, old age and ultimately, death.

Anne's Story

We've been living with Parkinson's since 1990. Mike and I had been married for ten years, when I first noticed his posture changing. Mike is an artist and always had been a resourceful, brilliant problem-solver. Together, we built our earth-bermed home on 40 acres in the country. We built stone walls and graceful stairways around and through the gardens we planted. Every year, we planted trees to commemorate our anniversaries, our birthdays and to honor people who died. Together we could conquer anything.

Mike began walking from the house to his studio with his head down. Over the months, from my office window at home, I watched as his shoulders gradually slumped forward, his walking becoming more difficult. He looked beaten, wounded and sad. I felt guilty because I was happy with my job, my children and our home in the Minnesota countryside—and he was miserable. Then in 1992, Mike became seriously depressed and angry. We couldn't talk rationally about the problem. But what I didn't know was that for more than a year, Mike had been following his symptoms in [a] patient handbook. In 1993, when his handwriting deteriorated to a flat line, he made an appointment at [a clinic]. He self-diagnosed either Parkinson's—or worse—a brain tumor. The neurologist at [the clinic] concurred; it was Parkinson's. So, this was our time of celebration—it was not a brain tumor. We could live with Parkinson's. How little we knew then.

Mike asked for a prognosis. The doctor told him that he could go an average of ten years before he'd need serious care. The celebration did not last long and the reality of end-of-life and end-of-identity took center stage for Mike. His depression worsened and he chose not to take medications. As a couple, we were in crisis and not at all mindful of the physical or emotional stages of terminal illness. We were not ready to let go of anything. Yet, simultaneously, we were more than willing and ready to let go of everything to ease our pain. In the meantime, I resigned myself to the seemingly endless rounds of his deterioration and depression.

The positive changes began in 2001, when Mike declared that he could not stay in Minnesota another winter. This was the time when

I would have to make some serious changes in my life. I would have to leave my job, my children and grandchildren, sisters and friends to move to a more temperate climate. I was conflicted, angry and anxious. I did not completely trust that our situation would improve even after making such a radical change and another significant commitment on his behalf.

After some soul searching, I decided to view the move as an adventure for myself as well as for Mike, what I termed—'getting down and wrestling in the mud together.' Now, as I look out my kitchen window in Bellingham, Washington to our hillside garden, I am constantly thrilled by the accumulating generations of euphorbia, heather, artichoke, rosemary and lavender, as well as the cedar, cypress, fir, ceanothus, Asian pear, Rainier cherry, fig, apple and plum trees we've planted, most of which would not grow in Minnesota. Mike's lyrical sculptures are permanently displayed in our new yard and he is designing and creating more than we ever dreamed was possible or even likely.

In 2005, I made a decision to go to school full-time at Western Washington University's Fairhaven College, where I created my own concentration of study in Creative Writing and the Science of Social Relations. There, I met extraordinarily generous professors, as well as smart and compassionate writing friends. My son, Andy, and his wife, Juliana, moved to Bellingham from California three years ago. They have two children, one-year-old Teddy, born in Bellingham, and three-year-old CharlaAnne. All of these unplanned gifts ease the rough edges of change; they increase my joy and give me hope. I know we did the right thing. I am fully accepting of the path we are on, including my caregiving responsibilities and the traumas brought on by this ever-changing disease. I am at one with the cultural anthropologist, Angeles Arrien, who described the second half of life in terms that resonate today in each and every moment. Arrien writes:

> *A chance to resurrect the dream we were entrusted with at birth, to make the 'great crossing' and create our legacy. It is a time for reparations and humility, for mercy and grace. So often we associate the second half of life with illness and depression and giving up and waiting for death to come. But the truth is that midlife is a threshold*

where creativity can burst you wide open, and real intimacy finally comes into your life.[1]

Less than a year after we made the decision to leave Minnesota, I was walking on the beach in Bahia d'Kino, Mexico. I was alone on the wide, warm sand with the sun on my back and the seagulls gathered in noisy conventions. I focused on Tiburon Island ahead of me and I thought I heard my father talking into my left ear. 'So that's how she turned out.' I knew he must be talking to my mother. He made it clear by his intonation that he'd left early and appreciated the fact that Mother finished the job. Then I heard Mother answer, 'Yes, it is.' I interpreted the encounter as a message from my parents, who would be proud of the decisions I've made.

Along with this vision, I've been uplifted by Mike's ongoing awareness of his own suffering and losses. His experience touches me deeply, because he has managed to transcend the pain and loss by holding on to a double reality—as both the sufferer and the observer of one who suffers. And thus, he has found a measure of salvation. His story follows.

Mike's Story

I am a lifelong artist. I began in 1956 in the ceramics department at Montana State University, where Frances Senska 'gave me legs.' For years, I had no limitations of size or scope or time or endurance. I taught pottery, drawing, painting and jewelry making. I could keep five plates in the air at once and still answer the phone.

After 40 years of wedging and throwing the 25-pound balls of clay into over-sized platters and colossal bowls, decorating, glazing and firing thousands of pieces of pottery, I began to notice the loss of small motor control. Gradually and reluctantly, I accepted that I had to give up clay. With the aid of an assistant, I began a short career of sculpting and welding four by eight-foot sheets of stainless steel into lyrical, life-sized lawn sculptures. But soon my endurance and muscular ability dwindled and I could no longer participate in big or heavy work anymore.

As Parkinson's disease gained ground in my muscles, I explored less physically demanding methods of pursuing my art. After another seven years, I could not lift or move heavy objects. Sometimes, I could not move myself. I could not safely walk to or around my studio without the fear of 'freezing' and falling. I sat on a stool and looked out the window. What can I do now?

My wife and I spent winters in Kino Bay, Mexico, where the seagulls noisily convened in straight lines on the beach or bobbed and rolled on the azure waves of the Sea of Cortez. I sat on my chair and watched them move. Graceful, buoyant and free. Anton Chekov's play, 'The Seagull,' used that bird as a symbol of Konstantin's broken dreams. I thought about that.

My speech deteriorated to the point that I was forced to repeat every statement three times, but I overcame my insecurities and was able to communicate with two Mexican welders in their dusty, rusty, dirt-floored shop in Old Kino. They understood my desire, my need to create the images of the seagulls. We formed the birds of bits and pieces of scrap metal and made them to fly freely over and even through obstacles.

Today: the strength in my legs is almost gone, but I am still an artist—in my mind and in my soul. That is exactly what I have left and I will use my mind the best way I am able.

I'm reminded of a Chris Isaak song about a bird who longs to fly, yet cannot.

Big, bold and colossal statements have been replaced in my life with the simplicity and power of symbols. For me, it has become more critical to convey essence and meaning. My yellow seagull symbolizes the freedom that eludes people with Parkinson's disease. There is an adjustable nut on the back of the yellow bird that allows for dependable and graceful movement. The color yellow symbolizes hope, courage and perseverance, all of which have been critical for me in recognizing and embracing the continuing and exciting possibilities for the creation of art in my life.

I am the orange gull—different from the others, but still standing. There is something I can do.

~ Eduard Alden (Mike) Mikkelsen, August 23, 2005

Chapter 7

Family Support:
Hopes, Dreams and Crashes

Family caregiving, however noble and essential, is an act done largely in private, invisible to the world. Perhaps for that reason, it's a subject often confined to private conversations.

~ Marilyn Gardner, *Christian Science Monitor*[1]

The Care Network

Medical care is only one part of the caregiving circle. Support by trusted family members and friends plays the central role in sustaining caregivers. But family elder caregiving patterns have long been sustained by silence. Employees hesitate to discuss it with their employers or even fellow workers. Friends may be sympathetic, but no one really wants to hear the details. Even family members sharing the care burden may not talk to each other about their feelings of anger or resentment. For a variety of reasons—embarrassment, pride, disgust, fear, trauma or grief—caregivers have remained out of public view, their caregiving labors ignored, unappreciated or simply taken for granted.

But caregivers are not alone when confronting the burden of long-term care for their elderly spouse, relative or friend. Instead, they participate in what Karen Hansen refers to as "overlapping circles of interdependency."[2] Ideally, caregivers are connected, at varying levels of closeness or distance with a network of persons: immediate family, extended kin, friends and neighbors, local public and private agencies, and beyond these, medical insurance companies, as well as state and federal governments. The medical community, we found, assumes a dominant role at certain stages of caregiving, but other agencies exert profound influences, as well. Federal agencies on aging with local offices offer a plethora of information, as well as advisors for guiding elders and their family members to various resources. Hospice care for the dying is a lifesaver for a caregiver during the terminal stage of her loved one's life. Medicaid or Medicare programs can make a difference in the quality of care provided to the sick or dying elder.

Unfortunately, many caregivers have poorly developed personal networks or fragmented family relationships. Additionally, they may be unaware of outside resources, believing themselves to be alone or completely dependent on family or close friends. Moreover, being anxious, fatigued and often in a state of grieving or illness, they may feel incapable of making the effort to seek out a more extended set of relationships to sustain them. Especially among those with limited financial and personal resources, the idea of sharing their load appears improbable or unworkable.[3]

In most cases, caregivers expect their family to take on the crucial role of directly supporting their care efforts. Elders turn to sons and daughters, daughters-in-law, female grandchildren and occasionally siblings for day-to-day support. Those middle-aged or younger caring for their elderly parents expect spouses, siblings and friends to come to the rescue. But what do we know about these family care networks?

True, in stable and supportive families, caregiving can produce unexpected rewards, strengthening ties between those who give care and those who receive it. But what happens in troubled families, where relationships are strained and normal bonds of affection are frayed?[4] What about those families where the adult child has been the victim of sexual, physical or emotional abuse, or the wife has been a battering victim of the now-aging husband? This raises an entire series of questions about the nature of relationships in caregiving networks.

How stable and resourceful are family networks during good and bad times, especially when the going gets tough? What kinds of support can family members realistically provide—financial, practical or emotional? Do such persons share the caregivers' values? Are they willing and able to serve elder care needs? What expectations does the caregiver have about family and friends' contributions? Are these expectations commensurate with the kind of relationships the caregiver has had with individual family members? How are caregivers expected to "pay back" intimate others when they step into the circle of care? What circumstances contribute to caregivers seeking non-family and paid services, rather than depending on family members? How consciously and cautiously do caregivers construct and maintain their care networks? I will explore these and other issues as we develop characteristic network patterns among elder caregivers.

The Network Anchor

Karen Hansen, who writes about networks of care, takes up child care issues by identifying distinct networks of interdependence. She asserts that these networks are loosely correlated with social class differences. Here, the child's mother serves as the "network anchor." The networks include: (1) "an absorbent safety net;" (2) "a family foundation;" (3) "a loose association of advisors;" and (4) "a warm web of people."[5]

These ideal types correlate with our elder caregivers' network patterns. In addition, two more network types emerged among our elder caregivers: (5) "an empty network;" and (6) "a loose, brittle network." Resources are another significant feature of network building, and these will be investigated, as well. First, we consider the caregiver's social class—a partial predictor of her material resources: upper, professional, middle and working class. Then, we discuss how individual caregivers exemplify different network types, working out the details of their care management with available human, financial and personal resources.

The chapter also includes a discussion of specific topics that place the caregivers in their social context, including: caregivers' and care receivers' age and relationship; level of resources; potential and actual network members; social class location; level of family solidarity; ethos of helping; sources of satisfaction; and sources of unresolved tension. For example, potential network members include those who feasibly *could* provide financial, practical or emotional support. Here, our caregivers' networks or memberships averaged 10.19 persons who had the capacity (but not necessarily the willingness) to participate. I contrast this with the *real* average of persons, including kin, friends, neighbors, colleagues or others, who actually showed up to provide help. For our caregivers, that average number was 4.24—a significant gap between the potential number and the actual availability of supporters.

I conclude with a brief overview of caregivers' current lives, sometimes based on a projection of their existing situation, but more commonly on follow-up interviews. Before we turn to actual cases, we must first identify similarities and differences in the day-to-day care of young children and the special problems of sick or dying elders.

Child Care and Elder Care

A paramount feature of child care is its universality. Every viable culture promotes procreation, and couples without children are often perceived as deficient or "selfish." By contrast, long-term elder care is a recent phenomenon among developed countries, and is specifically related to technological, communication and medical advances.

Another salient feature of child care and elder care is the primacy of gender. An assumption among the general public is that taking care of anyone—child or adult—is a gender-specific activity, regardless of age. This belief is part of the cultural bias that presumes women to be maternal; therefore, they can handle childrearing or sick elder care as a natural and normal activity.

Regardless of social circumstances—career, family, vocational, professional or creative commitments—these women were uniformly expected by family members to take on the responsibility of caring for their elderly relative. True, many of our caregivers have raised children or are in the process of doing so. Like most middle-class and upper income parents, they sought information about child care needs through their pediatrician, or later adolescent medical specialist, as well as through the media, friends, school sources, their children's peer groups and the larger environment. Children are a central focus of most social groups, and for most parents, sharing information about the "stages," problems, joys and stresses of childhood/adolescence with friends and strangers alike is a common experience. If a parent is in doubt about a child's behavior, tune in to Dr. Phil or pick up a favorite self-help book. Knowledge and cultural sharing about children, then, characterize most parents' lives.

But these same adept women who managed to negotiate jobs, family and community activities while raising their children may find themselves baffled with the problems of their mother's Alzheimer's disease or their husband's congestive heart failure and the attendant depression.

Another feature of childrearing and family ties involves grandparents' expectations that their adult children will "allow" them to baby sit or help with child care. Many grandparents relish the opportunity to enjoy the children with or without their parents around, rekindling the maternal and paternal warmth and love that sustained them throughout their own children's growing up. Aunts and uncles often get involved, as well—playing ball with energetic nieces and nephews and going on outings together. Hansen discovered repeatedly that looking after children was "fun"—allowing adults to be playful and "young again," reliving their own childhoods.[6]

By no stretch of the imagination can we say that elder care is "fun," nor can most caregivers turn over elder care to peripheral relatives, casual friends and helpful neighbors. The demands of care are frequently too exacting or difficult. An immobile elder may need assistance using the toilet, while another may need help with the morning routine of washing, dressing, shaving and hair combing. Each may require medications to be dispensed at specific intervals. Clearly, caring for a sick, often confused or depressed elder, is fraught with complexity.

Moreover, healthy children follow an upward track: growth and development over time is inspiring to behold. Each child has his/her own special destiny, and wise parents intend to promote the best attributes of their offspring: first steps, first words, first day of school, graduation from eighth grade, high school, college or even graduate school, first regular job, and thence into full adulthood with marriage and family. The parent role mainly has a steady and predictable pacing along a well-established cultural groove.

None of these positive conditions prevail for elder care or parents whose children have illnesses like terminal cancer or inoperable brain tumors. Here, the spiral slopes downward and out. It is only a matter of time before the loved one is gone.

Networks of Interdependency

Whereas two caregivers in this group had lifestyles that happily can be described as "it takes a village"—to care for a sick elder, all other 59 caregivers indicated more typical network arrangements: reliance on family, close friends and agency or institutional support. Being embedded in a small village has definite advantages available to only a few persons living in Western societies. Most of us who live in cities, suburbs or larger towns have limited access to spontaneous support persons or groups. Work and careers, family obligations and community commitments prevent most of us from the free give-and-take of traditional kin and neighbors. Instead, the majority of us are under continuous pressure to be clock watchers and schedule keepers. At the same time, individual "anchors" can create a strong support network to be mobilized during periods of family crisis. Such is the case with Rachel, a vibrant high school teacher and mother of adult children, who, in caring for her ill spouse, developed her own "absorbent safety net."

An Absorbent Safety Net

An *absorbent safety net* is a network that remains in place for times of need. Unlike the *warm web of people net* I will be discussing later, it is neither local nor pervasive. Network members maintain their independence, but can be summoned during critical family episodes. Members are willing and able to absorb the shocks of a family crisis, and even stand in for the caregiver.

Close family and friends dominated the milieu in which Rachel turned over the responsibilities of the last three months of her husband's caregiving to their children. The network could be easily mobilized for crisis periods, because Rachel's relationships with network members— her children and friends—were strong and resilient at the start, and actually strengthened over the period of caregiving. Calling herself a "traffic director," Rachel summoned her children and close friends to her aid. She recognized her own severe limitations in providing the level of care Philip needed in his valiant struggle with colon cancer, which now had metastasized to his liver. Rachel admitted she "wasn't up for taking care of Philip herself," but was fortunate to have children who not only embraced their father's illness, but also became an integral part of the process.

> My husband knew I was burned out on caregiving. My mother had been trying to commit suicide since I was five years old. I couldn't go to the

prom because she had overdosed. I couldn't sleep at night, afraid my mother wasn't breathing. I just shut down. I was an adult when she finally succeeded. She left a suicide note saying that it was my fault.

Instead of feeling besieged, Rachel turned to her children for help.

The feeling of incompetence overwhelmed me and when Philip was diagnosed with liver cancer, I asked for help. Our adult children moved in to help with his care. We knew it was going to go fast and I knew I would be a terrible caregiver by myself, just unable to cope. I really was afraid of doing it wrong again. Philip and I went to Europe in July and he died at home in October.

With the family network in place, Rachel continued her active life.

With our children there to help, I was able to keep my job, go for walks every day, keep my husband at home and remain detached enough so I didn't lose it. The children loved him and we shared the load for 81 or more hours a week. The family support was the best part of caretaking. I leaned on everyone I could. My advice is to minimize the impact of caregiving.

Rachel and her husband, both in their sixties, were professionally established in their local university and high school communities. Both had extensive friendships and community connections. Rachel's network structure thus involved a large number of potential members, and had three levels. The inner circle was comprised of her two children, a son and daughter, as well as a stepson and his daughter, an "adopted" daughter (her son's best friend), a daughter-in-law and one grandchild. This constituted an immediate practical and emotional support group of seven persons. Within that inner circle, her son emerged as the anchor, coordinating practical tasks and providing emotional support to his dad.

In the next circle, long-term friends, teaching associates and a religious mentor offered primarily emotional support. Later, Hospice entered the scene to take over many of the more onerous medical tasks, as well as grief counseling for the family.

And finally, in the outer circle, we would place professional and religious associations, not necessarily as individuals, but as group sources of knowledge and strength when the family must confront the myriad of details associated with end-of-life issues.

Rachel's network is among the strongest of these caregivers. Part of the reason is that she could let go of the burden, and have the strength and energy to devote herself emotionally to her husband. By absolving herself of the practical details of care, and focusing on keeping her life together with job, community and athletic activities, Rachel had energy left over to fortify the care team by shopping, cooking and leisurely enjoying her family. Rachel felt unburdened because the safety net she had created over the lifetime of her family was a remarkable success. Her husband contributed to this positive outcome by "making it so no one had any feelings of being burdened." After her husband's death, she showed her appreciation for her children's efforts and took them on a three-month vacation, which included swimming and scuba diving in the Caribbean.

A number of other caregivers created networks that could be depicted as "safety nets." In Rachel's case, clearly the network members acknowledged specific obligations and responsibilities toward one another, as well as shared the expectation that the assistance they provided would be "repaid" at some time in the future. For Rachel's children, a relaxing vacation followed the rigors of shared caregiving. Among friends, Rachel remains a hospitable, delightful companion.

Loose Association of Advisors

Not all caregivers have the luxury of a well-established and highly supportive network when the need arises. Yet, many manage to meet the care crisis by mobilizing support, wherever they can find it. Such a temporary network requires a solid anchor, one who intuitively recognizes that a *loose association of advisors* has a makeshift quality, but can fill in the gap when family bonds are weak.

I earlier introduced Kendra, a 23-year old college student, as a special example of an overburdened caregiver, because of her vulnerability as a teenage girl struggling with her father's care without additional family support. Now, we examine her role as "anchor" in a disrupted family situation. Kendra was raised in a middle-class family where high achievement was a standard expectation—and Kendra had not disappointed her family. An outstanding athlete and honor student throughout her high school years, Kendra suddenly confronted another challenge—the task of caring for a terminally ill father with lung cancer, heart disease and kidney failure. The task was "almost too much to bear."

I was forced into caregiving. Mom had to take care of her ailing father… [she] *left me with my dad through my high school years.*

In her mother's absence, Kendra was responsible for shopping, cooking, running the house, arranging medical appointments, transporting her father to his various doctors and dialysis treatments, administering his 25-plus medications over the course of the day and still managing to keep her head above water as an honor student and student athlete playing high school basketball, softball and volleyball. Her immediate family could not come to her rescue. Kendra expressed a sense of desperation. On the one hand, she had an absentee mother, who had moved into her ailing parents' home, and on the other, a younger brother, who limited his contribution to yardwork and occasional handyman duties. Otherwise, she was bereft of other willing or able relatives. Where was Kendra to turn for help with her dad?

At first, she felt "hopeless," wishing there was "something more I could do." Then, she swung into action. First, she identified a family friend to assist with day-to-day household chores. Next, she succeeded in shifting the dialysis care from hospital to home with a nurse, who could also answer her medical questions, as well as spend time with her father. In a final stroke, she turned to her school teammates—girls her own age—who came forward with an outpouring of emotional support and practical help with shopping and keeping house. Low family solidarity was balanced with high friendship bonding.

Once Kendra had her "team" assembled, she felt more able to share her feelings with "trusted friends, cry and take alone time at a beach near my house." She also discovered the "gift" of caregiving—loving and sharing with her father.

Not all was drudgery, she found, as their time together evolved into a deep and unspoken level of understanding Kendra described as "unspeakable trust." In this sense, caregiving for Kendra became another "accomplishment." She said, "I felt so much more mature than my peers and more knowledgeable." Another plus was that her father was both positive and appreciative, lightening her load considerably.

Certain sources of unresolved tension remained, however. One was her mother's surprisingly negative reaction to the father-daughter bonding during her husband's illness, as well as Kendra's own feelings of loss about the degraded mother-daughter relationship during her adolescence.

Since her father's death, Kendra has tried to make every effort to assuage her mother's anger. Although busy with college, she visits regularly, but her mother is insistent she return home after graduating and look after her. Kendra has both resentment and regrets about her caregiving experience.

I'm still dealing with my mother's anger and resentment. I continue to go home once a week to assist her around her house and visit. But the majority of the time, she is verbally abusive.

Tragically, Kendra's dreams for an athletic scholarship had to be abandoned.

I wanted to play softball in college, and planned to go to California [for] college. I was accepted to my first choice school, but turned it down to stay closer to my father. I think if I hadn't taken on the caregiving role I would have a better relationship with my mother, and maybe a better degree.

At this point, Kendra remains caught between family expectations—her mother's pull to remain a faithful caregiver—and her own push into independent adulthood.

A Family Foundation

Wealthy and well-connected individuals are most fortunate in tapping into a large pool of financial and human resources for managing caregiving tasks. At the same time, very old age often brings many physical complaints, regardless of status. We first met 85-year-old Billie Mae earlier, as a well-connected, upper-income caregiver. At this point, we discuss her role as the network anchor for her 95-year-old, now deceased husband, John, who was afflicted with multiple ailments, including blindness, mental confusion, eating problems, chronic pain and prolonged physical dependency.

Together, they have been a force in their local community. The creation of a family foundation made it possible to support large community projects, such as major reconstruction of the local opera house, as well as commitment to a myriad of child-centered charities. Having a disposable income of more than $200,000 annually, this "independent" woman, as she enjoys calling herself, has maintained her active life over 10 years of caregiving—exercising, reading, listening to tapes, travel and dining out. During the period of John's dying, she supervised three shifts of home care workers over a 24-hour period, plus Hospice staff during the last six months of John's life.

Day-to-day help was also provided by Jim, a full-time paid home assistant, and two daughters, one of whom was an executive director at the nearby hospital, and the other, a school psychologist located an hour away. Paid and unpaid family help, including her husband's son from a former marriage, as well as other children and grandchildren, provided additional assistance. Add to their combined family of seven children, an abundant collection of friends and fellow board members from their various charitable trusts, and you get a picture of an abundant, bustling, well-supported household.

Billie Mae embraced the caregiving role with enthusiasm and profound love. When I asked her if she had made a "conscious choice to be the primary caregiver," she answered, "Yes, I just did it. That was my role; that was my man." The downside of the home-care situation was the questionable quality of the six-member daily agency team, who appeared to be less than stellar medical or domestic assistants. They rarely initiated services and failed to write adequate drug and medical notes, which led to John's medicine-induced confusion and restlessness. What was most challenging for Billie Mae, though, was providing meals for the workers three times a day. None of the agency workers contributed to household management or domestic tasks, which tended to pile up over the course of the week. And, turnover was high. Over a three-month period during October through December, Billie Mae hired 12 different nursing assistants, a dizzying number when you consider she was also juggling a daily housecleaner, weekly chaplain visits and maintaining her presence on various community boards.

Because of her background of owning and managing three successful companies, Billie Mae had high expectations for her professional caregiving staff. But the reality was very different. Instead of being physically and emotionally supported by their presence, she needed to pay very close attention to John's care: "I was on call every minute." As her husband's medical condition worsened—frequent hospitalizations, and when home, either bedridden or limited to a wheelchair—this highly capable caregiver admitted to struggling with "patience." Still, it was their long, loving relationship, her husband's appreciative attitude toward her efforts, and the fact that "John could be in our home" that sustained her. A deeply religious person, Billie Mae now welcomes the peace and tranquility of her home and has taken up an active life once again, having only one regret: "I don't have John to share it."

Warm Web of People

Flourishing non-family networks can alleviate not only the scarce family labor supply in caring for elders, but also the sense that one is not alone in the struggle. We first met Anne in Interlude 2, "The Face of Parkinson's Disease." Here we continue her story as the anchor for her care network. Anne, at 61 years old, is a unique kind of a caregiver who, first, moved away from her all-embracing network, and then, had to kick start an entirely new support group in a different state. In Minnesota, Anne managed to raise four children, work full-time at various creative jobs, including head chef, and later, as an executive director of a nonprofit organization. Once the children were raised, Anne readily made the shift from child care to elder care when her husband was diagnosed with Parkinson's disease. What made it all possible is Anne's extensive network of family, friends, co-workers and community supporters. She had no choice but to begin anew—to create new networks.

> My husband was diagnosed in 1993. As the disease progressed, so did my attention to it. In 2001, he felt he had to leave Minnesota [and said], 'or I'll just die.'

As for Anne, losing her network was tantamount to tearing a huge chunk out of her life, requiring her to make a fresh start. She admitted to feeling ambivalent about it.

> *I left my home state of 55 years, my children and grandchildren, my job, my network and my history. But all of that is also positive! I didn't mind being a caregiver. It seemed a natural part of my life. I was, however, extremely anxious about leaving my family, friends and huge support network.*

Anne recounted her list of "misses"—those irrevocable losses in her life.

> *I gave up a lot when Mike got sick, and we moved. I am missing pieces of my partner; I am missing my friends, I am missing my good job, I am missing my home.*

In a real sense, Anne is walking the walk of Parkinson's, as she struggles with adjusting to her 73-year-old husband's deteriorating physical and mental state, a decline that severely limits his life's work as an artist/sculptor.

> *In a very real sense, I have Parkinson's too. My thoughts, reactions and decisions are considered and measured in the context of what Parkinson's can handle and absorb. My husband's gradual loss of strength and speed have challenged my patience and 'alert' level, as if I had a young child in my care again.*

Now more than six years after the move, Anne has a beautiful new home in a park-like setting, and serves as a round-the-clock caregiver, while attending the nearby university as a full-time student. Anne's newly created network continues to expand. Frequent trips to Minnesota allow her to stay connected with children, grandchildren and dear friends. Now that her son and his family have moved into her home community, she receives practical help on a daily basis. One daughter, a therapist, serves as a constant source of wisdom for weekly chats over the phone, where Anne can unburden herself and be consoled and restored. Mike's outpouring of appreciation renews her self-confidence to carry on with the tasks at hand. Furthermore, Anne understands the necessity to take care of herself, and treats herself to an energizing regime.

*I walk fast to keep my brain balanced and I write everyday. I read won-
derful books, garden and eat good food. I am gradually developing a
satisfying routine of daily activities, some with my husband and some
alone.*

Anne's capacity for flexibility attracts friends, neighbors and fellow
students alike, who are attracted to her positive energy and outgoing
manner. As one of her network members said, "To know Anne is to love
her."

With ample resources—Mike can still sell some of his artwork, and
continues to receive inheritance money and Social Security—this upper
middle-class couple has considerable economic advantages over most
American families facing long-term illness. Additionally, Anne continues to seek information about the disease to better equip her for dealing
with the limitations she must confront in caring for her husband. Mike is
actively involved in both national and local Parkinson's associations, and
attends annual conferences as a participant. Anne supports Mike's autonomy, facilitating solo trips to visit his own children, which keeps family
ties strong. As part of self-care, Anne has consciously made a decision
to "turn lemons into lemonade" in her struggle with the disease. Anne
reviews the ways she benefits from her commitment to caregiving.

*Today, I am accomplishing a new adventure. I am adjusting to pulling
more of the wagon. I am a more patient person as a result of caregiving.
I am stronger than I was 12 years ago* [when this began].

Her care burden lifted once her husband recognized her dedication.

*I feel much better about myself now that Mike admits to me that he
needs my assistance. This has empowered me and made my presence
valuable and gratifying. Mike now believes that I will take care of him,
advocate on his behalf, and knows that we have productive and valuable time left.*

Caregiving has ultimately opened her to a new way of being in a
relationship.

*Caregiving has been a healing experience for me, in that I've been forced
to slow the pace of my life, and that has been healing. I have the rare*

opportunity to know my husband as a child. I especially cherish the quiet times with Mike, where he spends sweet moments recollecting and reflecting out loud.

Change has been a mutually gratifying experience.

But the best part about caring for him is living with the evolution of Parkinson's, and the gradual release of Mike's normal 'power over' [others] behavior to a gentle acceptance of help.

Unresolved tensions persist, however. Some are part of the nature of the disease. Others are an inevitable part of a family coping with a loved one's severely crippling illness. Anne remains worried that in this blended family, her efforts and intentions will not be accurately represented to all of Mike's family. She explains her solution:

I initiated a more regular and complete dialogue with my husband's family, informing them of the positive events and the reality of Parkinson's.

Anne still feels conflicted about the way people react on first meeting her husband.

I noticed years ago that people just meeting my husband (and even our very close friends) have a hard time looking at him, and so they didn't. It was because his facial muscles don't move and he appears at least incoherent, and at most, hostile. People would talk to him and look at me. He gradually realized that he needed me beside him at most social occasions, and he resented it.

To offset this reaction, Anne now explains to their closest friends the reason for Mike's lack of facial expressions. And, she adds, "I ask them to make eye contact with him."

As for the future, Anne remains uncertain. Her plans to attend graduate school may not be feasible, she recognizes, because Mike is "so dependent on me." At the same time, she lives with a chronic health problem (cutaneous T-cell lymphoma) that drains her energies and spirits. As a result, she fears a diminished capacity to carry on her current level of care without making drastic changes. Anne has indicated a willingness to put "some of those potential support people to work on a more active basis" if either Mike's health or her own health take a sudden downward shift. Already, neighbors have shown their willingness to help ease the burden in Anne's absence, such as checking on Mike or picking up groceries. She remains ambivalent about planning for recuperation time after her upcoming surgery, but undoubtedly, family and friends will be at her bedside, as well as helping out with Mike.

Having a strong relationship with her husband before his illness—when he was "passionate, spontaneous, independent, brave and creative"—helps smooth those rocky periods that are bound to come. Anne's self-concept remains intact. She continues to feel and act as a loyal and dependable person, which are important self-attributions. She explains how carefully she maneuvers in her situation.

My freedom of thought and movement are definitely restricted, but new freedoms have appeared. Loyalty was simple before; now, I must consider and carefully weigh statements to and about my husband and his condition. I am trying to be sensitive to new messages and messengers every day!

Like her mother before her, who was widowed in her forties and raised eight children on her own, Anne is an intrepid survivor. She will undoubtedly continue to be adept at generating creative solutions to cope with the inexorable progression of her husband's degenerative disease.

Loose, Brittle Network

A network in which human, financial and practical resources appear to break away or disintegrate may result from an inability or failure to build a strong support network, lack of personal and monetary resources, limited education or a set of beliefs that undermine one's own place in the world. Our next story focuses on a caregiver, Fran, who never really had an opportunity to create a new network before she was hurled into full-time service as a "worker bee in my husband's business." Not only was she providing care for her long-ailing husband, but also for his mother, who was sickly and required her assistance. Subordinate to her husband's demands, Fran could not overcome her feelings of unworthiness, which she said came from her limited education and lack of formal training.

Her inability to visit friends because of constraints of family and work commitments completed the picture of a caregiver who felt bereft and isolated. (These sentiments were underscored by Fran's frequent outbursts of crying during both interviews. Yet, she said, it was "important to tell my story.")

An attractive, but exhausted, 61-year-old caregiver, Fran has been nursing her husband since their marriage in 1993. Married late in life, Fran knew at the outset that Pete had Crohn's disease, and it would be her "duty" to take care of him—"Doing what I know I have to do for the duration." Now, at 72, Pete moves between care sites: home, hospital and nursing home, with little or no assistance from his two sons from an earlier marriage. Fran's own two sons are unavailable for assisting their mother. One son, who lives in the same state, is "too busy" with his job, while the other son is mentally ill. Her husband's two sons, both professional pharmacists, "don't do anything" to help their dad. Fran often expressed anger and frustration during our conversations.

I find it most unfair that his children have no feeling of responsibility to help along the way. I left it up to Pete. We took care of their grandmother. That's how they grew up—'family takes care of family.' I told them to visit their father now that he's at home.

When I probed further about Pete's sons' response to their father's illness, she replied:

Until the last three months, they didn't respond very well. Both sons are pharmacists. The doctor spoke to his sons. They didn't seem to care— they didn't have any realization of how sick Pete is: his kidneys, his ileostomy. They seem to be visiting better when he's in the hospital or nursing home. How they'll do once he gets home? I can't say. But it's not with helping.

In earlier years, Pete's pharmaceutical skills helped build a flourishing drug store. After marrying Fran and appointing her as store assistant, they were able to make sound investments and accrue wealth. But these arrangements rarely favored Fran, whose care assignment extended to both her husband and his aging mother.

I also had his mother, who lived behind the store. Since I married him, I was chosen to take care of Grandma. Living at the lake, I worked all the way through Grandma's illness—made lunches for both Grandma and Pete. His boys said: 'You married him, so you take what you can get.' Eventually, we got to the point where we got someone else to cook for Grandma, and then I cooked only dinner. I was constantly working and taking antidepressants. My schedule? I made Grandma breakfast, then I went to work, went back and made her and Pete's lunch, cleaned up and served, then more work, and then cooked dinner. Pete had his knees replaced—but no one came forward. The sons' attitude was: 'you married our dad, so you married the job.' They called me their dad's wife. They had a 'I don't care attitude' toward me. I've cried myself to sleep many times. I was supposed to prove myself.

Grandma's care proved to be far easier than her husband's.

She was a very appreciative, loving person. Taking care of her was much easier than [taking care of] her son. Pete can be very demanding. I have a baby monitor, so I thought the situation would improve. But there's just too much work and physical stress.

I asked Fran how she manages all of the work.

So, how do I deal with this? Sometimes with anger and complaints, other times with organizing more help for us.

Fran's sister-in-law, once a strong supporter, backed out after Fran ignored her advice not to bring Pete back home, because of the intensity of his medical needs. And, while Fran's sister could be counted upon for an occasional lunch, friends have worked out best, even though she doesn't have much opportunity to make the 90-mile trip to Seattle to see them in person.

Friends have been better than my relatives. They keep calling me—my dearest friend keeps in touch with me all the time [by phone].

At the time of the interview, Fran was struggling to apply for COPES, a statewide program that provides medical and household support for at-home elderly patients. This has necessitated hiring a lawyer to avoid the worst repercussions of the "spending down" requirement, a condition that would have left them with greatly reduced assets. Fran prides herself on successfully negotiating this process, and indicated that rather than losing $50,000 to the state, they have been able to hold on to the rest of their nest egg of $90,000. Despite a weak network, Fran's community outreach efforts resulted in excellent financial advice, as well as respite care through the auspices of the Northwest Regional Council on Aging. Help in negotiating the state system from her attorney and visits with a counselor have taught her both the virtue and necessity of speaking up for herself.

Fran experiences the all-too-common plight of women who believe they have an obligation to care for others before themselves. "I know I should take care of myself in order to take care of others, but it's hard," she said. At the same time, she faces failing health, especially back problems, and serious questions over whether she will be able to continue her current responsibilities without a great deal more help. With few close friends, none of whom live nearby, and no family allies or neighbors to carry out the day-to-day care and home maintenance, Fran feels incapable of handling the job of caregiving. She says she once "loved her wifely role," and cherished time together with her husband. Now, Fran's current strategy involves seeking outside kin and friendship circles for assistance, as well as relying on state and local agencies, doctors and professional counselors to get her through her days.

Fran treads a lonely and difficult path. As expectations about her stepsons dissolve and she comes to accept their non-involvement, and instead, relies on government and professional assistance, some of the tension of her situation may lessen. Until she releases herself from her overburdened sense of "duty," reclaims former friends and reaches out for new experiences and friendships, her life may continue on a dangerous course—one of exhaustion, illness and despair.

An Empty Network

The sheer absence of day-to-day support plagues a number of caregivers. In some instances, having entered into the task without giving it thoughtful intention, the caregiver has devoted little or no time to building a support network. An *empty network* is more than a lack of people,

however. It also involves a state of mind in which "doing it alone" is part
of a lifestyle. Such is the case with Toni, a fifty-two-year old, self-em-
ployed woman who never married.

Toni has been forced to reinvent herself—admittedly without much
success—after she brought her mother to live in her home. Not only is
Toni accustomed to living alone, she cherishes her solitary life. Now, she
has been confronted with the full-time care of an 81-year-old mother
with multiple maladies: diabetes, peripheral neuropathy, mild dementia and depression. A highly successful designer, Toni anticipated taking
care of her mother, but expressed her resignation in the face of how long
the responsibility would last.

> *She is my mother, and it is my job as her only daughter, I guess. It is
> very wearing and can be frustrating. I can't seem to come up with a 'best
> part' in this situation.*

Toni has a brother and an aunt, her mother's sister, who potentially could
have helped with the care, but they both live a great distance away. The
aunt offered to let Toni's mother move in with her, a plan her mother
rejected. Her brother was a different story; he has been fairly unresponsive in helpful ways, preferring to make jokes about it. Her brother's
childhood "mean behavior" toward her now extends to his disinterest in
being a support person for their mother.

> *Mother didn't want to live with my aunt as they had just finished taking
> care of their own mother who lived with my aunt. My brother won't do
> it, he doesn't even want her to visit. I don't feel like I can leave her alone
> for long. She [mother] wants me to make all the decisions. I am expect-
> ed to take care of everything, and I wasn't prepared to be a 'mom.'*

Toni deeply resented losing both her freedom *and* privacy. To accommodate Toni's desire for privacy, she closed off one of the doors that
separated her mother's living area from her own, but it fails to give her
the privacy she prefers. In addition, Toni has experienced a number
of health issues. Her multiple symptoms, including mood swings and
chronic pain, were somewhat relieved recently by two surgeries—a hys-
terectomy and colon surgery. Although her physical health has improved,
the strain of her mother's constant presence provokes her into frequent

outbreaks of frustration and anger. Losing control further deepens her sense of failure, and beyond that, of feeling overloaded.

I expected to help with Mom's care, but I did not expect to be in charge of everything. I am overworked. I have no privacy. I feel trapped and angry. There is twice as much work to do—repeating everything over and over because of Mom's hearing loss and mild dementia. I've remodeled parts of the house to suit our needs, and did a lot of the work myself.

Aside from friends, who once listened to Toni's self-admitted "whining," she had no practical or financial support for four years. After a medical emergency, she placed her mother into skilled nursing to recover, then decided to place her in an assisted living facility. Toni managed to convince her brother to contribute some money to nursing home costs; still, she had to remind him.

I was very direct about my frustration and anger when I asked him for help. I told him, 'You will have to take care of her if this kills me.'

When her mother demanded that she be moved back home, Toni suggested a senior retirement facility. That situation lasted a couple of years, but her mother was depressed, getting bladder infections, and falling a lot. She found it actually took more of her own free time to have her there than having her at home. She brought her back home to save money. Now her Social Security income covers her expenses.

The daily irritations resumed. From Toni's perspective, her mother appears quite capable of carrying out ordinary tasks, but acts reluctant or simply doesn't think of doing them. Toni has little sense of reciprocity with grace. Being responsible is an important value for her, but the spirit of giving does not come easily. Friends have dropped by the wayside because of her unavailability, leaving her even more vulnerable. Toni buries herself in her creative work, but cannot seem to strike a balance between care for the other and care for self. Toni recognizes her predicament only too well.

Having to deal with the frustration, overwork and anger makes me realize it's probably just a character flaw that hadn't surfaced yet, because

I never married and had kids. After talking with friends, social worker, doctor, etc., I'm accepting that I'm not really caregiver material.

Perhaps the irony is that Toni—like thousands of other women who feel trapped and angry in their caregiving role—cannot seem to find a satisfactory strategy to resolve the tension of having their lives turned inside-out for years at a time.

Networks Are Not "Native Plants"

In my part of the country—Northwest Washington State—the hardy, self-propagating native plants like Douglas fir, Oregon grape and rhododendrons, as well as a host of others, seem to thrive almost anywhere. River banks, mountain tops, meadows and valleys, each have their special habitat with distinct flora and fauna. They require no cultivation or special tending.

Social networks are a different species altogether. Although one is born into a family, a life-sustaining circle does not necessarily emerge. As siblings grow up and leave home, they often lose track of one another, or move into adulthood without resolving the pains and anxieties of childhood. When the time comes to care for elderly parents, adult children have probably cultivated very distinct interests and lifestyles, far removed from the life their parents lived. Given the constraints of independent lifestyles and heavy work/family loads, a care commitment has not been part of the unspoken contract for most contemporary Western people.

Conditions of estrangement are even more likely to occur among married partners. Separations, divorces and staying together "for the sake of the children" mark a high proportion of modern marriages. Care of older parents as a cultural expectation for adult children may still occur, but the likelihood of practical follow-through is poor, unless older couples have explicitly indicated their personal preferences to their children.

Among caregivers in our study, almost all have made a strong commitment to care, and most have maintained solid, flexible networks that could adapt to life's inevitable changes. At the same time, we have a few cases in which friends or neighbors are the primary caregivers, in the complete absence of on-site family involvement. In other instances, we have very reluctant caregivers who are physically carrying out the job, but mentally and emotionally are distant from the care receiver, and suffering from the effort.

Members of family and friendship networks, then, must have a high level of awareness as to their rights, responsibilities and rewards, as well as the ability to draw boundaries. But the reciprocity issue looms large. The sense of obligation often remains below the threshold of consciousness. We normally do not keep careful records of what we owe someone, or what someone owes us. But reciprocity entails a kind of spiritual indebtedness that may or may not involve material transactions, such as money, gifts or services. It could involve something as simple as *recognition* of the gift of service.

So, what does nurturance of network members involve? Let us place ourselves in the role of caregiver for a moment. It involves a mindset, so that you, the caregiver, situate yourself in the fullness of each relationship. Recognize, applaud, acknowledge specific offerings, value each contribution and honor the donor's presence. This network cultivation may not be possible for everyone. Some young adults, never-married persons, couples without children, persons isolated by work or excessive family demands, those with few social skills, those handicapped by negative childhood experiences, illness or various deprivations may have to rely on the charity of others, including the state for caregiving help. For the rest of us, building and maintaining viable social networks for caring for our elders demand our creativity and persistent attention.

Chapter 8

The Costs of Altruism

You can die of a broken heart, not just when your partner dies, but also when your partner falls ill.
~ Dr. Nicholas Christakis, Harvard Medical School[1]

Scientific observations point to a response system that is hardwired in the human brain—no doubt involving mirror neuron 00 that acts when we see someone else suffering, making us instantly feel with them. The more we feel with them, the more we want to help them… empathy is the prelude to compassionate action.
~ Daniel Goleman, *Social Intelligence*[2]

Altruism Reconsidered

In introducing the caregivers and their stories in the early part of the book, I argued that their roles as family caregivers grew out of altruistic leanings. They gave service out of love. Let us now reconsider altruism as both a type of action, as well as a social role.

In its simplest rendering, *altruism* involves unselfish regard for others. The altruist is one who has a concern for other people, and whose sacrificial beliefs motivate their actions on behalf of others. Daniel Goleman writes in *Social Intelligence* that in today's psychology, the word empathy carries these distinct meanings: (1) *knowing* another person's feelings; (2) *feeling* what that person feels; and (3) *responding compassionately* to another's distress.[3] The altruist may act out of compassion or a strong sense of duty, and altruism ultimately depends upon empathy, a "feeling into." Goleman argues that in an important sense, "We experience the other person's emotions in our own body."[4]

Regardless of the initial motivation, the altruist is a person of action.

Deeds invariably speak louder than words. Rescuers, heroes, saints, martyrs and generous benefactors are all versions of altruists, admired for their larger-than-life qualities of nobility, courage or achievement. In Greek antiquity, the *hero* embodied superhuman qualities, and was favored by the gods. Typically, the hero story stops with the courageous rescue or outstanding exploit. Rarely, do we have a look behind the scenes to discern the losses, sacrifices, penalties or disadvantages that accrue from such selfless giving for others.

By any definition, these family caregivers are altruists. They have given time, money, strength, attention, love and devotion to the elderly loved ones in their care. While their efforts usually remain invisible, except to family members or immediate friends, they play an incredibly significant role in managing periodic crises and relieving the burden of elder care for other family members. But such sacrificial giving involves more than heroic measures. Giving selflessly comes at considerable cost. Sometimes, it can result in a loss of sympathy and compassion, which was what originally served to motivate and energize the caregiving act.

This chapter explores the underside of giving care by showing the suggestive connection between caregivers' negative beliefs about their role and subsequent negative outcomes in increased levels of stress, medical and psychiatric disease and poor coping skills. At the same time, stress, illness and poor coping skills reinforce these negative beliefs—a hard cycle to break.

Environmental Stressors

Environmental stressors or demands are at the very core of the caregiver burden, as are complications from social, financial, medical and other outside pressures faced by caregivers. I have collected a variety of environmental stressors reported by caregivers. Some of them have to do with excessive hours of work, others with the medical condition of their loved one, still others with lack of family assistance, costs of care and the like. What stands out is the high proportion of women giving care for 85 hours or more weekly (51 percent), as well as those who have given care for four years or more (63 percent). Many were wholly responsible for the entirety of the home-based medical and personal care their loved one received, with little or no respite for most of the women. While no single activity is likely to send a person over the brink, consider what a full-time schedule of services to a frail, dying or demented person could do to anyone courageous enough to take on such tasks.

The Stress Management Model (Graph 8.1) allows us to discern some possible connections between several variables: self-regarding attitudes, perception of the caregiving role, emotional responses, behavioral responses and type of outcome. The model, created by Sheldon Cohen and his associates, shows two *opposing* ways of responding to environmental demands and pressures. When stressors appear, persons can either appraise or evaluate them as burdensome, and react with a variety of negative emotional responses, including pessimistic attitudes, downbeat emotions, poor bodily care and behavior that may be harmful to self and others. Higher risk of physical and mental diseases, the model presumes, follow from the negative perspective and failure to adapt to stressful demands.

Or, a person confronting unexpected demands and pressures may have an adaptive orientation or bring more personal resources to bear. Rather than sinking under the load, the individual assumes a benevolent attitude, looking for positive features of the experience. According to this model, the positive appraisal generates a series of affirmative outcomes: positive attitudes, emotions, self-care and productive behavior. The risk of becoming seriously ill or having a mental breakdown substantially declines. Most importantly, the model assumes that not all persons respond equally to the same environmental demands.[5] (See Graph 8.1)

Among caregivers, unremitting environmental stressors, coupled with a weak or inadequate network, a perception of being overwhelmed by demands and a sense of not measuring up to the role appear to contribute heavily to a negative outlook toward caregiving. How can one begin to assess or measure stress levels these caregivers have experienced? Physiological tests exist that can accurately measure an individual's accelerated heart rate or blood pressure. One can also observe stress first-hand: people talk faster, they may hyperventilate, or they may appear distracted or overwhelmed. Or, one can simply ask a person to describe their beliefs and experiences, which I did, inviting them to indicate their various responses (e.g. stress) on a scale of one to 10. (Table 8.1) Here are several verbal observations from our caregivers.

Graph 8.1 Caregiver Burden And Stress Management Model

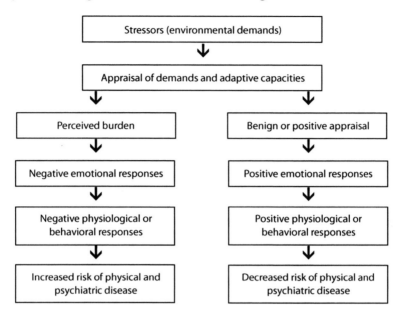

(Adapted from *Measuring Stress: A Guide for Health and Social Scientists*, edited by Sheldon Cohen et al. Oxford: Oxford University Press, 1995.)

Renae

I got tired of it, 24 hours a day, seven days a week—sickness, treatments all the time, also death. I've given up friends and family. I just wanted to get out, but I couldn't, so I gave up things that would have helped me.

Faith

My stress level was 8 out of 10. I never looked for any other way of doing this and as a result I exacerbated my back problems. I still wake up thinking about Mother falling out of her wheelchair. I felt overwhelmed and lost my temper.

Mary Beth

I had very high blood pressure and exhaustion, mini-stroke and I couldn't write, couldn't speak. I got to the end of my wits and just screamed, 'I'll leave you.' Toward the end, my stress level was at 10.

Cindy

I didn't stay in touch with neighbors; no reason to be in touch. I was confused and frustrated in the responsible role struggling with multiple decisions every single day, and failing at any level of control and comfort in the decisions I did make. I had high blood pressure and essential hypertension. There was just no relief.

Mary Ellen

I was always exhausted. I was angry but I knew it had to be done. I cried a lot—depression, frustration and anger. So I fought with him and yelled a lot and today I am lonely [after his death].

First, our interviews reveal that many environmental stressors are common for caregivers. Deep losses, lack of boundaries, grueling hours, confronting the death of a loved one, gender strain, inadequate medical services and other stressors generate frustration, anger, despair and a host of other negative emotions. Second, high stress levels, anxiety and exhaustion are *normal* and frequent experiences for caregivers, not extraordinary or occasional responses. Third, the caregiver correctly assesses her responsibility as a social and personal fact. But here the situation diverges.

Whereas some caregivers perceive caring as an unrelieved burden, others focus on the benign or positive aspects, a point we elaborate on in the next chapter. On one side, negative emotions often flood the overburdened caregiver. On the other side, positive perceptions mitigate or reduce the burden to manageable proportions. According to the stress model, those with unabated negative emotional responses are most likely to experience high stress, to become seriously ill, to ignore self-care (e.g., no exercise, poor diet) and develop poor coping responses. For example, the caregiver's behavior is at odds with sensible self-care (e.g., watching television all night, engaging in heavy drinking or drug use). Or, she may withdraw from former friends and organizations, rather than seek outside support. Here, the model predicts an increased risk of physical and psychiatric disease.

Among those who were able to transform their situation from an overall negative experience into a positive or even uplifting experience implies that a shift toward feeling and acting in an upbeat and affirmative

Table 8.1   Stress Reactions Over the Course of Caregiving*

Stress Reactions	Percent
Emotionally drained	82
Strong or very strong stress	53
Tense all of the time	43
Constantly worried	42
Frequently conflicted	38
Feelings of being trapped	37
Having a sinking feeling	32
Anger at family for not being supportive	22
Feeling a sense of desperation	22
Resentful	20
Feeling devalued (in their care work)	12
Anger toward my ill loved one	10
Strong feelings of hostility	8

* Caregivers rated their reactions to stress from one to 10. The figures above reflect those who ranked their stress reactions at seven or above. (Nanette J. Davis, Caregiving Study, 2005.)

manner made them more likely to find workable coping strategies. Instead of withdrawing from friends, they sought them out. Rather than neglecting family celebrations, they welcomed them. They insisted on keeping their jobs (if important to them), which helped them maintain a sense of balance. In these situations, the stress management model predicts a decreased risk of physical and psychiatric disease.

Negative feelings are not necessarily harbored by caregivers all the time. Mitigating influences, such as a strong network with supportive relationships, engaging outside activities and accomplishments and good self-care practices can reduce the stress reactions, and contribute to positive beliefs about oneself and the caregiving experience.[6]

Warning Signs of Caregiver Stress

In earlier chapters, I documented some of the hazards and risks of caregiving in a highly medicalized and technologically sophisticated milieu. Drawing on a larger body of data from the Alzheimer's Society, we can further expand on the leading *warning signs* of caregiver stress.[7]

According to the organization, the extent to which caregivers manage these stresses indicates successful versus unsuccessful coping. In our caregivers' experiences, such warning signs were only too clear. As the narratives show, some women suffered from multiple stress responses, including: (1) denial; (2) anger; (3) social withdrawal; (4) anxiety; (5) depression; (6) emotional exhaustion; (7) sleeplessness; (8) irritability; (9) lack of concentration; and (10) serious health problems. Table 8.1 includes caregivers' reports of stressful feelings experienced over the course of their caregiving.

Caregivers frequently **denied** both the disease and its effects on the person being diagnosed. Carla, a 50-year-old wife and mother who recently returned to college, willingly took on the responsibilities of caregiver for her friend, but never really considered the medical reality of her friend's illness and death and the impact on her friend's children.

> *It seemed normal, natural, like taking care of kids at home, not really so different. Taking care of my friend with breast cancer gives me satisfaction, knowing I'm helping someone else. I thought it was interesting—gave me a chance to meet people at different stages of their lives. It was a good experience, if it does nothing else but show how you can appreciate people who care for others.*

But after one-and-a-half years, her friend's cancer came back and she died rather abruptly. Carla reflects differently on this phase of the caregiving experience.

> *But thinking back on it, I'm frazzled, tired, trying to finish up school. I'm still married, kids have grown up. I don't think it's something I want to do now. One day I'll probably need someone to look after me. I don't know if it was a healing experience for me. It helped me to know, 'This too shall pass.'*

Many caregivers expressed **anger** at the person with the illness or others when no effective treatment or cures currently existed. They also confessed to feeling obligated to take on the role of caregiver. Cindy, whose voice we first heard in Chapter 6, cared for her father, an alcoholic, who suffered from dementia for 25 years. Because Cindy was the eldest child, she felt duty-bound.

I was haunted by a childhood of morning wake-up calls: my dad vomiting. During the time I was caregiving, I ranted and railed with emotional outbursts. I had no feelings of compassion for him. He got what he deserved, but today I feel guilty. When he was in the care facility, I only saw him once a week.

Today, I am a woman whose husband is 'out of the way.' I have some remorse and lack of contact with my father—big guilt. I am guilty.

Other caregivers withdrew from friends and activities that once brought pleasure. Joanne was told by the doctors that her mother was going to die. Instead, her mother lived with a bad heart and osteoporosis for seven more years. Joanne gave up all outside activities to care for her mother—with devastating results.

I just took care of business [mother's care]*—zero clubs; I quit League of Women Voters, totally lost touch with my friends. I was over there at the nursing home every single day, but Mother was unable to have a conversation. I suffered from mental health problems.*

Countless caregivers described the **anxiety** they felt about facing another day and what the future might hold. Jean had trouble relaxing during her interview. Years of caring for her mother, who had Parkinson's disease, osteoporosis and dementia, had led to her constant sense that something *could* and *would* go wrong.

I worry about money. I just get home [from visiting mother]*, and I start worrying about having to go back and visit her. I worry about the dementia getting worse, which means her needs will increase. I want to do a good job, but my dreams are vanishing the older I get and the longer she lives. I'm running out of time. Will I run out of money? And I'm not taking care of myself.*

Depression about the ability to cope was all too common. Rose, age 75, is a strong-willed woman who feels undone by years of caring for her difficult, aged mother, who has made non-stop demands on her.

My basic value in life is independence. I've lost that through caregiving... I think it's really hard to reclaim your sense of self when you're caregiving. I even get despondent about her loss of self. Mother was always a controller. She always pulled my strings and I'm aware of it, so I can't express sympathy. I've just learned not to blow my own temper. I think if I walked more, I'd be better off. I wonder if the action of [mother's] *temper isn't the action of dementia.*

Caregivers often complained of feeling **emotionally exhausted** over the impossibility of completing necessary daily tasks or coping with unforeseen situations. Sandra, age 42, whom we met earlier, was considerably younger than her dying, elderly husband. She admitted to a sense of overwhelming stress and utter exhaustion. She was especially devastated when she realized her husband had withheld important financial matters from her.

His expectations were always higher than what I could achieve. I didn't know about his financial stuff until after it happened. I cried a lot in private and felt helpless and frustrated—overwhelmed, just overwhelmed. I'd barge through every situation, and only thought about things when it was over. Then I'd break down and feel guilty about feeling bad, and not being able to make him better. The emotions, the high stress, just did us both in, long before he died.

Now, in her mid-eighties, Catherine confesses to feeling tired and exhausted most of the time. Simply maintaining the house and looking after her ill husband and an extended group of relatives was more than she could manage.

I was so tired. I just wanted the day to end, the routine to be over so I could take my Vicodin. I did what needed to be done, and put us both to bed early. I broke both my wrists [lifting her husband], *so I need to manage my pain and make constant compromises. I'm so tense and so tired. I try to rest, so I can do things for other people. The hardest part of the day is getting up in the morning with no energy and being in pain.*

With a seemingly endless list of concerns, **sleeplessness** is a fact of life for numerous caregivers. Faith experienced the 24/7 caregiver consciousness—the sense that everything that happens to your loved one is your responsibility. Sleep seemed out of the question.

I still wake up in the middle of the night reliving the trauma. Caregiving leaves a life imprint. When I was caring for Mother, I would lie awake listening for her to fall down. She was very tall, five foot ten, couldn't walk and hard to pick up after a fall. I managed by drinking coffee and tea—looking for energy. I felt responsible for every bite she took.

For two-and-a-half years, Marsha took care of her father with Alzheimer's and cancer. But it was those last weeks of his life that were the hardest for her.

My whole life was disrupted for three months. Instead of work, I was caring full-time for another person. Toughest time was the middle of the night from two to six a.m.; he was up constantly. As a result, I didn't sleep much. I didn't do very well taking care of myself.

Sleeplessness soon gives way to **irritability**, moodiness and negative responses. True of most caregivers, Mary Beth recognized that her highest intentions could easily be undermined when confronting the daily grind, and invariably contributed to her feelings of irritation. Suffering from dementia, her husband made demands that often seemed unbearable.

The hard parts were bathing him, and his not knowing what was going on. I never had even one minute to myself. He would talk and talk and talk, and every night he would start about 7:00 p.m.: 'Is it time to go to bed yet?' for two hours until finally at nine I would go to bed. I was just unhappy and tied in an unhealthy way to my husband. He wouldn't accept respite care, so I put him in a home, which I regretted.

Caregivers often suffered from a **lack of concentration**, making it difficult to complete even the most familiar tasks. Performing the same routines over and over, along with having no personal time, typified most caregiving in the home setting. Rosanne, who exemplifies the devoted daughter, is a consultant who works out of her home. She exhibited a typical response to the problem of home care in her struggle with concentration.

My husband and I began with enthusiasm taking care of Mother, but with dementia came entitlement feelings, and soon I was on a short leash with little freedom, loss of work, loss of money and an inability to concentrate. I guess I gradually believed there was no time for myself.

Finally, as we discuss in greater detail, a host of **health problems** take their toll on the caregiver, both mentally and physically.

"A Nice Soup of Chaos"

Sally offered the most compelling caregiver statement about becoming ill as a result of stresses associated with caregiving. A divorced mother of seven children, Sally worked full-time as a housekeeper, and frequently commuted to Los Angeles from Washington State to look after both of her parents, and later, her husband's parents. As we will discuss shortly, life for her had truly turned into "a nice soup of chaos."

Undeniably, current medical research findings link protracted high stress levels with illness, and stress has been linked to automobile accidents or other untold events (e.g., breaking dishes, falling off a ladder, being sued, family strife).[8] Table 8.2 shows a list of self-reported caregivers' illnesses and negative events. The generic list does not show causation between negative attitudes and subsequent illnesses—one condition of testing a model. What the list does show, though, is that a fairly high proportion of these women experienced illness, worsening health, and for some, very serious and often multiple medical problems, over the period of time they have been caregiving. In fact, the number of illnesses and negative events per caregiver amounted to an *average* of four different problem areas for each caregiver. This means some caregivers had multiple crises, whereas others had few. (See Table 8.2)

Considering the array of illnesses and negative events these caregivers lived with, one may question whether the sick should be nursing the sick or the old taking care of their even older loved one. In fact, this situation is so grave that a groundbreaking, nine-year research study of 518,240 older couples, published in *The New England Journal of Medicine*, painstakingly documents the "stress of illness" for the partner.[9] The research extends the notion of the "widower effect"—a condition in which spouses die soon after being widowed. The article indicated that while this has been common knowledge as early as 1848, new research also suggests that spouses of people who are hospitalized have a greater risk of dying than the spouses of healthy people. Additionally, care receiver problems

Table 8.2 Self-Reported Caregivers' Illnesses & Negative Events

Condition	Percent
Back problems	44
Exhaustion	40
Arthritis	41
Worsening of health overall	38
High blood pressure	30
High cholesterol	28
Chronic illness	23
Acute illness	22
Death in family	22
Hearing problems	20
Joint problems	20
Mental health problems	20
Failing eyesight	18
Respiratory problems	16
Surgery	15
Accident	12
Cancer	12
Diabetes	10
Circulatory problems	10
Uro-genital tract problems	10
Neurological problems	8
Heart Disease	8

(Average number of illnesses and negative events per caregiver: 4.4.)
(Nanette J. Davis, Caregiving Study, 2005).

that affect physical or mental ability, like dementia or hip fracture, are worse for the partner's health—findings applicable to almost anyone in a close relationship. An afflicted person even affects entire families. In a word, *living with, caring about* or *caring for* a sick person can contribute to illness or even premature death. These findings are clarified by our caregivers' experiences.

During the time Clarice cared for her father, who had heart problems, she suffered from multiple ailments. Negative emotions clearly played a role in Clarice's medical condition.

Caretaking has taken over my life. I had high blood pressure from no exercise, and a bad TV dinner-diet—planned for the times I completely crashed. My back problems were chronic from transferring [lifting] my dad. I felt trapped and depressed and exhausted. I watched Shrek to relax and Valium helped, as well.

Another caregiver, Charlotte, experienced various illnesses throughout the ten-year period in which she cared for her husband of 40 years. Finally, she succumbed to the realization that she could no longer give home care, and moved both of them into an assisted living facility.

I think my poor health is due to… getting older, more stress, more worries, little relaxation. For example, today was a very stressful day. We just got over the stress of moving and now we have the stress of placing him in an Alzheimer's unit—one major adjustment after another. I've had multiple sclerosis for 31 years. During caretaking I've had bladder infections, surgeries, cataract surgery for both eyes, high cholesterol, diabetes, hearing problems, high blood pressure and neurological problems. I finally joined my husband in care.

Sally's story captures the extent of how complicated life can become when juggling too many roles. She describes how personal problems of illness usurped her caregiving role. An only child, Sally believed that *only* she could handle the caregiving, but illness intervened, and prevented her from managing the role.

During the years I was traveling back and forth to help my mother and father in their crisis, I could count the days I was home. If I made it through a whole month not having to fly down, it was a good month. Somewhere in advance of [moving my parents] my large intestine ruptured. I had to have major surgery and they had to remove a foot of my intestine. I had a colostomy bag, and then they did another surgery too… what they called a 'take down,' where they re-connected my intestine. I had so much pain that I was throwing up and throwing up. I couldn't walk. I was dry heaving. I learned, though, that if you're not spurting blood in the emergency room, you're the last one to go in and it doesn't matter. I had a hard time convincing them that I didn't have

some minor problems… they kept sending me home. Finally, they de-
termined that they needed to do surgery. [Doctors] *thought it would*
be a gallbladder surgery—and I did have gallstones—but the major
problem was that my intestine had ruptured. So they took out my ap-
pendix and some intestine. For a year-and-a-half or so, I was in and out
of the hospital with that issue and still not well. Dad did all he could
to keep things together there in California, knowing that I was going
through my situation, but it all created a nice soup of chaos.

Eventually, Sally moved both parents out of California into nursing
homes in her local community, but her life remained "oppressive" until
her parents died.

Coping Strategies

Acknowledging the difficulties and problems of caregiving is one step
toward understanding why caregivers are so susceptible to stress, negative emotions and illness. But the pattern may be more complicated.
Caregivers employed various coping strategies, some of which were highly effective, in their effort to ease the stress. Others used tactics that were
less effective or even destructive. Six *least* successful coping responses
among these caregivers include: (1) **burn-out**—attitudes and behavior
that contribute to exhaustion and feelings of animosity toward caregiving, care receiver or themselves; (2) **drag-on**—strategies that attempt to
maintain a former way of life and relationships before caregiving began
with subsequently poor outcomes; (3) **plow-through**—an orientation
that ignores the here-and-now reality in favor of future hoped-for outcomes; (4) **give-up**—an outlook and set of behaviors that reduce one
to passivity and hopelessness; (5) **fret-at**—emotional and behavioral
response predicated on the belief that "worry" equals action; and (6)
mourn-over—a state of consciousness where one refuses to let go of
one's losses, whether the death of the partner or losses deriving from
social, emotional or financial support.

Burn-Out

Kali, as we observed earlier, lovingly cared for her grandmother, but
was consistently undermined by her grandfather, which dampened her

youthful spirit and led her to question whether she could be a successful caregiver.

> *Every day was an argument with my grandfather. I couldn't do things right for him. I just tried to not give up. I wanted to make Grandma bet-*
> *ter. I tried to please everyone. In the end, I [felt] lost. Maybe this is not what I should be doing, I've been tested too many times.*

As a teenager, Rachel was caring for her alcoholic mother, when her mother committed suicide and left a note blaming Rachel. Fast forward to Rachel at 63, with her husband recently diagnosed with colon cancer. Rachel was so certain she would be a bad caregiver, because of her child-hood traumas with her mother, she did not even want to try to put in the effort.

> *Caring for my mother turned me into my mother. I couldn't handle any-*
> *thing to do with my husband's body. No matter how much I wanted to make things better, I was so afraid of doing it wrong. I was positively unable to cope.*

Cindy, who exhibits the signs of overload, didn't feel any relief during the five-and-a-half years she provided care for her alcoholic father. Her husband pressured her to get family help, but her siblings were unable or unwilling to help because they were also alcoholics.

> *I didn't have a choice. My family could have cared less. I coped by rant-*
> *ing and railing—emotional outbursts. I'm a head-on kind of person, but my father's alcohol and dementia on top of it made him just crazy. Between his bizarre behavior, my husband's lack of support, the lawyer's ineptness and mounting bills, the everyday dread, I lost any capacity for normal emotions and quit visiting my dad in the home. I now live with guilt—big guilt and remorse.*

Drag-On

Toni's "normal" life of working at home and enjoying her privacy grad-ually slipped away right before her eyes, despite her efforts to hold it all together. She plugged along ineffectively, filling holes one at a time. Even when Toni thought she had solved a major problem by placing her mother in a retirement apartment, she was haunted by the knowledge that she might be forced to take her back into her own home. Toni resisted changing her lifestyle to accommodate her mother's needs.

I had no intention of taking care of my mother at all, let alone six years of frustration, lack of privacy, overwork, worry and anger. The dementia was the worst; we go over and over things. Placing her [in care] helped, but now I have to drive way more to do it, which impacts my business and my free time. Run around, run around, solve one problem, another pops up.

Nora cared for her 89-year-old mother with Alzheimer's and heart failure, as well as her father, also 89, with heart problems and depression. Perhaps adding to the complexity and apparent endlessness of caregiving, Nora was designated caregiver for her manic-depressive sister. Nora's way of life was threatened by the sheer volume of caregiver tasks, but she felt unable to change her situation for more capable coping.

No doubt about it, dealing with my emotions is the most physically and emotionally demanding part. I'm depressed when I'm there with Mother, bottling up my feelings and needing to get away from it. We've already gone through the grieving process and they're still alive. They have been dying for four years. The emotional toll is terrible. It's getting harder and harder and I can't find any solutions.

Plough-through

For six years, Teri kept hoping that other family members would respond to her requests to pitch in and help with the care of her grandparents, ages 79 and 82. In the process, Teri became resentful and angry at her father and aunt. She was unable to express her feelings of frustration, and frequently broke down. She now lives with some mistrust of others.

I was angry with my dad and aunt for not getting involved in the care of their own parents. I wrote letters to my aunt; she was worthless. I think my frustration level would have been lower, my long-term health better, if I'd had some family involvement. The hospital treated Grandma terribly. I still distrust doctors. I believe it's good karma—that somewhere, somehow, it's good to do good deeds.

Kathy lived with her 90-year-old parents for four years. The cumulative effect was both physically and emotionally demanding. Sometimes Kathy was overwhelmed by her parents being old and sick. Although she knew she should appreciate the time with them, she wasn't able to relax. She resisted total engagement with the caregiving process, felt stuck, hired elder-friendly help and waited for her life to change.

> *I have to force myself to sit with them. I pray every day they will go at the right time. I try to believe that whatever you believe will happen— intentionality. It's a paradox for me, though; as long as my parents are alive, I'm tied down, not free, there's a weight on me. This guy could live to be 120. I wonder, why am I doing this? What happened to my life? And when they are gone, what will I do then?*

Give-Up

Renae was caring for three loved ones simultaneously: her mother with Alzheimer's, her son with Down's syndrome and her boyfriend, who was diagnosed with pancreatic cancer shortly after he moved in with her. Renae's story should be well-known by now. But her despair was so profound, her words bear repeating.

> *I guess I gave up on any life I might have for myself. I sat around watching TV, eating too much. Once he got sick, I fell into a depressive pattern and lost confidence in myself. Then Mom would bring her teddy bear in and treat it like a baby. I was around sickness and death all the time. I've given up on me, friendships and even family.*

Marianne began her caretaking experience by looking after a friend's husband. But when he was taken to a nursing home, Marianne stayed on with his wife as companion. She was content to be with her for a while and to "have everything paid for and a cocktail party every night." But life became far more tenuous when her friend developed cancer. Eventually, she felt that her friend's family had abandoned their mother, leaving her with all of the responsibility.

> *It was either her or me. I was there except for weekends. It really was someone else's life. I planned on three weeks and stayed for two-and-a-half years. But the last six months, it just got to be too much. Eventually,*

I got tired of it. I was vegetarian; she was not. I was very impatient, sit-ting there watching baseball games, [with] no support from her family. I just took an intermission. A time out—time to get out.

Fret-at

Joyce admitted that even before taking care of her mother, she worried a great deal. And life simply became more complicated after she took over the responsibility of looking after her mother.

Before I began taking care of Mother I was happily married, upbeat, active, [a] healthy woman, who does not like conflict… and I am a worrier.

Maybe I wouldn't have so many low feelings if I weren't so angry at Mother. We were close until my father died, then she became angry because she didn't grieve. I worry that she will fall. I worry about peo-ple taking advantage of her. She allowed things to happen to her that shouldn't have happened. I worry about her judgment; she's totally gullible. I'm on anti-depressants to try to cope.

Claire, now in her eighties, had many sources of worry: her husband's multiple illnesses, her own declining health and the fact that she now had to make the significant decisions for both of them.

My husband had prostate cancer, which I downplayed. The diagnosis that really horrified me and changed our lives dramatically was macu-lar degeneration—[a] very tough row [to hoe]. He couldn't drive, so I drove after my stroke. Finally, we hired a driver, very lucky that we could manage that cost. It was hard to watch a professor not be able to read. Life was so restricted. We hunted for resources that would help him have a better quality of life. Talking books were a lifesaver. I also worried about my decision to put a pacemaker in [for myself].

Mourn-Over

Mourning refers to the "outward expression of grieving (often cultur-ally patterned) or to the continuing process of reorientation after loss."[10] Almost all caregivers in this study spoke of their deeply felt losses, even while their care receiver was still alive. Among them:

- Losing an emotionally important image of themselves, their family, work and life.
- Losing emotional, social, financial and personal control over their lives.
- Losing the possibilities of "what might have been."
- Abandoning their plans for a particular future.
- Seeing their cherished dreams die. This could include visions of achievements, retiring together, that everything will work out, that the family can withstand this and other challenges, that time for self will be available, that financial security is assured, that the relationship can still flourish or that wounds between family members will heal.

Some Hospice workers observe that "anticipatory grieving" is an integral part of caregiving, as current and future losses accumulate over time, and caregivers feel they must prepare themselves for the death of their loved one. For long-term caregiving, the mourning process can seem endless, as their loved ones disintegrate from wholeness into increasing disability and cognitive loss. Additionally, Daniel Goleman's work recognizes that we also experience the emotional pain of our loved one as they struggle with disease and their own losses.[11]

These caregivers expressed their anticipatory grieving in a variety of ways, but almost always in strong emotional terms: "I am sad … exhausted … depressed … overwhelmed … sick to death … on stress overload … wrung out … collapsing … ill in mind and body … agonized … at the end of my rope." Most caregivers found ways to cope with unending sadness and grief. Yet, some may seemingly carry their sense of loss and futility to their graves. Certainly, chronic mourning undermines both the capacity for empathy and, ultimately, the commitment to another.

Perhaps the most significant maladaptation experienced by the caregivers in this study was denial—of one's own needs, serious medical conditions, simple joys, such as visits with grandchildren, and even the time required to grieve the loss of loved ones. In such instances, the presumed needs of the care receiver assumed dominance over all aspects of life.

Denial of One's Own Needs

At the time of her mother's death, Jane had three daughters (two of them with chronic illness), a house and a husband to care for. Jane promised her mother she would "put on her big boots and march into action" to take care of her father with Alzheimer's. Jane's approach was to jump totally into battle with one constant, frantic focus and no balance.

> *My life was already stressful. It became out of control. I drove back and forth to the nursing home, feeding him, taking him out for walks, staking out the lobby to catch his doctors so I could communicate in person. I was very tired, very sad and considered myself primarily a daughter—just a daughter, a very responsible daughter. I believed I didn't have any time to take care of myself. I promised my mother when she was dying that I would take care of Dad and I did it. I coped by just doing it and doing more of it... [such as] address immediate concerns and keep moving.*
>
> *Two years after my father died: I'm not well and I realize I could have taken better advantage of respite care and it would have been all right to do a few things for myself. A break from caregiving is paramount to your own mental and physical health.*

Denial of Medical Problems

Laura took care of both her parents in two separate locations. She drove between them with hot meals and good intentions because she was a "good daughter." During her ten years of caregiving, Laura had a few medical problems of her own—one she almost forgot to mention during her interview.

> *Yes, I had a medical crisis myself. It was sad but not tragic, even so, a horrendous experience in 1995—colon cancer, then in 1996—ovarian cancer. Oh yeah, I had carpal tunnel syndrome and skin problems, too. I'd go see Mom, then Dad, then drive home, do errands, cook meals and take [them] to Dad, then visit Mom. The longest vacation I had in ten years was four days. I coped with caretaking by being a master food preserver and by just doing it.*

Denial of Simple Joys

Martha used to see her two grandchildren regularly, but while she cared for her husband with Alzheimer's, that time dwindled.

> *I'm lucky to get out of the house, but I do visit with my kids on the phone and I e-mail my friends. I'd do a lot more if I had more time. I don't feel as frisky as I did ten years ago. I'd like to spend more time with my grandchildren, but having my husband and a three-year-old doesn't work. I had an interesting reaction to a lecture on stress. I was thinking, 'How can I handle it?'*

Denial of Time for Grieving

While Jean took care of her mother, she was in a car accident and her best friend was killed. Jean never had time to mourn her loss because the demands of her mother's Parkinson's disease and dementia controlled her life, even to the extent that she frequently spent the night at her mother's assisted living facility. She also confided that she was neglecting her husband and two children to care for her mother. Her life felt on hold.

> *I'm not engaging in my life. I miss my friend, she was my walking partner. I want to do a good job with Mother because after my dad had a stroke, I did a couple of things that were unfortunate. I took him to a restaurant that wasn't wheelchair accessible and he had an accident. He also fell off the treadmill because my son played with it, and Dad landed in a hospital bed. I could have talked to my friend, but she died in that car accident.*

Natalie's father died while she was still caring for her mother and her uncle, but Natalie didn't have time to grieve.

> *I put off dealing with things, waiting for the situation to change. Meanwhile, new problems arose with other relationships in my life. I felt guilty over my dad's death, but the guilt diminished as each new crisis was dealt with. My uncle died and my mother's care still came first. I tried to hide my feelings. [Now] I recommend taking breaks from caregiving.*

Why Caregivers Become Ill

The field of gerontology has been enriched by studies of caregivers, their roles, functions and contributions to family life and society.[12] As this study has shown, though, many caregivers experience a wide range of illnesses during their caregiving. Most observers have assumed that the caregiving burden accounts for the greatest proportion of these illnesses. This burden involves extraordinary time commitment, lack of sleep, poor nutrition, self-neglect, injuries (typically from lifting the patient) and, for many caregivers, a sense that they must make a total commitment to the care receiver, whatever the costs. But is this the full story?

Dr. Nicholas Christakis has worked with Hospice patients and their families, and observed how illness, health risks and death in one person can have similar consequences for others in a person's social network. Dr. Christakis and his associates have paid special attention to married couples, observing the high death rate that ensues for the ostensibly well partner when the other partner becomes seriously ill and requires hospitalization.[13] I refer to this process as the "affinity effect," which implies extreme mutuality. After all, close relationships entail special connections. Intimacy involves a process whereby persons are bound to one another through sympathy, mutual attraction and empathy.

Sympathy refers to the sharing or understanding the feelings of another—especially in pity or compassion, while empathy entails a different form of identification altogether. Empathy involves the projection of one's own personality into the personality of another in order to understand the other's emotions, thoughts or feelings. This process can occur at an unconscious level, and helps to account for the frequent statements by caregivers that they were "at one" with their care receiver, that they failed to differentiate themselves from their ill or dying loved one or tended to use the "we" pronoun to describe their activities.[14]

Married couples are not the only ones impacted by this affinity effect. In fact, it can impact any close relationship. A recent call from Rhoda, a caregiver who "simply didn't have the time to devote for an entire interview" is a case in point. A self-professed "professional" caregiver, she has presided over the deaths of her parents, three brothers and a host of fellow church members. Now, she cares for her 55-year-old husband, who suffers from a rare auto-immune disease, and is confined to a wheelchair.

Rhoda and her husband, Andrew, have strong religious beliefs, as well as an abundant social network to sustain them. But recently, their son has taken on "peculiar" behaviors that threaten his well-being, as well as his relationship with his wife.

Rhoda wanted advice about what to do, because her son believes he has a number of dreaded diseases, has been inappropriately self-medicating, acts out deep anxiety in a number of ways and can no longer function as an autonomous adult. The logical question is: how can family members stay well despite being deeply connected and/or giving care to their sick or dying relative? We'll look at strategies for easing the caregiver burden, as well as avoiding the affinity effect in the final chapters.

Reflections

The high incidence of illness among caregivers in this study opens up a number of issues. Is caregiver illness simply a stress-related phenomenon: the greater the stress, the more serious the medical disorder(s)? We could measure this relationship by comparing the responses of highly stressed caregivers versus those of lower or moderately stressed ones. Or, perhaps stress is not really the issue at all. Is it possible that different coping mechanisms account for significant differences in illness outcomes? Again, we can evaluate caregivers with positive versus negative coping capacities.

The affinity effect, the simple equation of mutuality between two or more persons, points to an alternative approach to unlocking the mystery of caregiving and reported high incidence of illness. Loving sentiments of compassion and identification with the suffering of intimates in our social network is a unique human quality. Generally, our social connections sustain us through difficult times, give us a reason for living and provide joy and nurturance in our daily life. When our significant other is joyful, this has a contagious effect, impacting our mood and emanating throughout our social connections. The reverse holds true, as well: illness, despair and the death of a loved one deeply impacts us—and those we are close to—even to the point of illness, despair or death.

Taking on the caregiving role with "ordinary" consciousness—a mental set of "must-do's," "have to's," and "I'm not worthy" mantras—cannot be the answer to effective, sustained caregiving. Feeling guilty or sorrowful over our loved one's medical condition and our own limitations also cannot effectively address the problem of elder illness and death. Instead, let us consider in the chapters ahead how successful caregivers embraced the advocate role, as well as developed positive, even spiritual, approaches toward self-maintenance and competent, loving caregiving.

Chapter 9

Advocating in Institutional Settings

In recent times, there has been a striking 'decasualization' of care for the elderly. This is represented most fully, of course, in the professionalization of caregiving in institutionalized and semi-institutionalized settings: nursing homes, hostels, retirement communities, and so on... [the authors argue that] *there ought to be adequate institutional alternatives for highly dependent people who cannot cope, or who cannot be coped with, in the community.*

~ Robert E. Goodin and Diane Gibson,
"The Decasualization" of Eldercare.[1]

Nursing homes are environments of isolation and disempowerment. They dictate when to get up, when to go to bed, when and what to eat, when to take showers, and who will help, and when and if to leave.

~ Barry Corbet, "Nursing Home
Undercover: Embedded." *AARP Magazine*[2]

The Need for Institutional Settings for Eldercare

Family caregivers eventually confront a time when they can no longer manage the physical or mental care of their elderly loved ones. When the level of care becomes unbearable, putting the loved one into care seems like the only alternative, even if it means having to choose between the lesser of two evils—excessive *care* burden versus excessive *cost* burden.

Gerontologists argue that there *should be* "adequate institutional alternatives." But what constitutes "adequate" is often left unsaid. Yet, few families genuinely have the knowledge, practical experience, support or sense of empowerment to know how to choose an "adequate" placement of their loved one, or what to do if *adequate* is *poor* or even *dangerous*. Placing a frail loved one in an institutional setting represents another phase of caregiving—another distinct extension of ourselves in the spirit of service, generosity and personal transformation. This phase of care is *advocacy*, an entirely new experience for most caregivers.

Experiencing Advocacy

As Jim became increasingly more ill, and my responsibilities expanded to include legal, social and medical needs, as well as managing simple everyday tasks—giving medicine, assisting in showering, preparing meals, doing laundry and shopping—I recognized that I could not maintain both my husband and myself for very much longer, given his deteriorating condition. I found myself increasingly traumatized by the shift in his behavior from a fiercely independent person to a nearly totally dependent one—unable to walk, toilet, dress or manage medications. Thus, my journey into institutional care began.

No warning bells went off when we first placed Jim in care. The members of our family were novices, rank amateurs, who stumbled from one problem of poor care to another. No one offered us a manual or a guide for "good nursing homes." Hospice presented no directive for the best or worst facilities. So, we learned on the job—the hard way—by confronting threatening or damaging situations immediately. Essentially, we operated as crisis managers throughout Jim's three-year stay in a number of different care facilities.

Certainly, bad things happen to patients without good care. But how did we know what good care was? Where should we begin? I started with the legalities and economics of institutional care, and sought our personal lawyer, who provided helpful information to plan for incapacity or disability, which happened in our case. This required three legal directives: (1) a General Durable Power of Attorney for financial purposes; (2) a Durable Power of Attorney for Health Care (I became the legal party that signed off on my husband's medical care); and (3) a Living Will. This last document directed the physician *not* to use extraordinary measures to resuscitate my husband in the event of brain death.

I am not alone in discovering that institutional medicine invariably employs feeding tubes, respirators and other lifesaving equipment on patients who would prefer to die. Heroic measures, as these are called, have become routine in hospitals and nursing homes. Without a personal advocate present to remind medical staff that a signed Living Will indeed exists, medical staff are likely to assume that dying people wish to continue living *indefinitely*.

At one point, I consulted with another, highly knowledgeable lawyer (a professor with a background in welfare law) about Medicaid's state and federal programs, which pay for long-term care in a family group home or nursing home. The attorney clarified that this program had a "spend-down" feature, requiring the married couple to reduce their estate to $80,000 (an amount subject to change), or for a surviving spouse, $2,000 before the government picks up the costs. Medicaid provides low-income elders with months or years of expensive nursing home care. Medicare, the federal program linked to Social Security, has no clause for long-term care, since Medicare payments are linked solely to brief periods of follow-up care after hospital stays.

For our prudent middle-class family, who carefully saved for the rainy day, Medicaid simply did not work. Spending down means the surviving spouse (in this case, me) may experience deprivation, having used up the bulk of savings and pension. Moreover, the significant loss assures no inheritance will remain for the children. The state, as well, can put a lien on one's home, so after the surviving spouse's death, the state claims all monies paid out for medical and nursing care. Lawyers reminded me that assets can be shifted to children or other relations over a few years to achieve the necessary level of income to qualify for state aid. But this abandonment of financial autonomy, I felt, is inherently unethical and probably illegal.

Advocating in Care Facilities

I awoke to the realization that the law, for a variety of reasons, was overly restrictive in its capacity to speak for, defend or support my sick husband. Not every supportive transaction occurs in a court of law. Nursing homes are not likely to face the threat of a lawsuit if poorly trained nursing assistants fail to give the requisite shower or provide a liquid diet after the doctor ordered it. Care involves far more than a formal written care plan or an able body to carry it out. Nursing care is fraught with human error. Even worse, sometimes overworked CNAs (Certified Nursing Assistants) can be cruel, intentionally negligent or indifferent.

Obtaining excellent care requires vigilant oversight by staff and family. My experiences with human error over the years Jim was in a care facility gave me an entirely new appreciation of the need for cultivating awareness, and for staying tuned into the distinct organization of nursing facilities. In my own experience, I found nursing homes to be grossly understaffed, and nursing assistants to be both seriously under-trained and underpaid. Elderly persons with failing physical and mental faculties were often ignored or shunted aside. Fortunately, I also met some marvelous, compassionate people.

Some examples can clarify the "horror stories" our family experienced during Jim's stay in six different care facilities. In one instance, we were moving Jim from the assisted living facility, which required the elder to be reasonably mobile—and preferably continent—to a nursing home. Assisted living facilities resemble an apartment style arrangement, often with a nurse on duty, whereas a nursing home is reminiscent of a hospital, although with a more informal ambience. As we entered the beautifully appointed nursing home, I thought my troubles were over. The facility had a spacious, private room for Jim overlooking a meadow, complete with trees, birds and natural landscape. Contemporary furnishings and easy chairs gave me a sense of comfort and ease. Well-dressed administrators launched into a description of the facility's assets and activities, which appeared ideal. Now, he'll receive the level of care he needs so much, I thought.

Over the course of the next seven months, I learned I had to pay very close attention to his care in this would-be "model" facility. Indifference, incompetence and impersonality pervaded the setting. I learned a patient had been forgotten for 24 hours, left dead in her bed shortly before we arrived. I observed a woman who continuously requested assistance who was ignored because she was "so obnoxious," according to one of the nursing staff. She later died in that nursing home; a formal investigation followed. As a result, the facility was closed down for a time, and then reopened under new management with a new name. But justice was too late for her. I observed a tall, very obese nursing assistant push a small female patient with her entire body out of the doorway of her room, because the patient wouldn't "listen to orders." This same nursing assistant yelled at me a number of times when I requested help for my husband or when I thought he had been neglected too long.

Prior to this nursing home experience, Jim had moved to an available short-term nursing facility for recovery after a four-day hospital visit. This facility offered an entirely different ambience than the genteel but poorly staffed one we later encountered. Instead of soft music piped into rooms and staff speaking in lowered tones, this facility had a *frantic* quality. Resembling the infamous "Bellevue," the public New York City hospital for the indigent, the facility had unremitting noise. The lack of carpeting created a continuous din as loudspeakers transmitted messages from ward to ward, staff to staff, while wheelchairs, pails, trays on cumbersome wheels and other supplies clattered as the staff moved them from one ward to another.

Here, the moaning of patients reminded me of the fourteenth century image of Dante's vision of Hell—*abandon hope all ye who enter here.* This particular facility had a sizeable number of late-stage dementia patients, who required total care, including feeding. As the first seating of patients completed their meal in the dining room, the second seating of cognitively disabled patients was wheeled in and lined up for feeding. Staff fed as many as four patients at one time, many patients with their eyes closed, utterly unaware of who they were, or what they were expected to do.

The perfunctory level of care at many nursing facilities extends to the patients' room arrangements. Few offer private rooms, and when they do, the price can be prohibitive for many families. Elders accustomed to their own space, surrounded by precious mementos and memories, must downsize drastically into a setting smaller than a typical hospital room. Confronted with a roommate they do not know, an illness they cannot control, an impersonal environment they usually did not choose and the loss of any vestige of autonomy, is it any wonder elders have been known to plead with their families: "Never put me in a nursing home!"

Institutional food for the elderly deserves widespread public attention. Food is often unappealing, unattractive, unappetizing, even re-volting and contributes to patients' chronic dissatisfaction. Sometimes, the meals are counterproductive for older digestive systems and dental problems: heavily starchy, meat too tough to chew, copious gravy on cold potatoes and mushy white bread. Where Jim resided I observed the enormous amounts of discarded food left on the plates, as the elders either could not chew or digest what they had swallowed. In some cases, the food was not recognizable because of overcooking or because it had been draped in heavy sauces. I'll never forget Katherine, a 92-year-old woman confined to her wheelchair, whose look of dismay took in the pale canned peas, stiff and jellied pork chops and hardtack rolls, as she commented: "You'd think they'd feed us some decent food, since we're not long for this earth." Katherine often looked forward to her family taking her to restaurants, where she could finally make choices that suited her food preferences.

Sometimes, issues surrounding the food reached a crisis state. Our experience showed us that kitchens were not informed of a patient's change in health status in time to alter the menu. Standard meals were served to a patient who could not swallow or had developed an allergic reaction. Less lethal were rigid feeding schedules, whether in the dining room or in the patient's room, which rarely take into account the patients' changing appetite or taste preferences. What should be one of the livelier and joyous parts of the day—eating and exchanging greetings with table mates—turns into a depressing litany of complaints.

In his displeasure, Jim (or more likely, one of our family members) often led the charge against the food—at least in one facility—and may have encouraged others to loudly lament poorly cooked and monotonous fare. The cook began to hold a grudge against Jim, and started verbally abusing him. Our daughter popped into the dining room just in time to witness the event. The angry young cook was shouting and haranguing Jim, a bent-over elder, because he was too slow in eating his dinner. The young man was summarily dismissed. But we had no idea how long this abuse had been going on. Our family was justified in pressing charges, but after consultation with the director, we agreed to let the matter rest.

In these facilities, I saw how dependent the elderly residents were on institutional benevolence. Most are fearful of complaining about any-thing because they fear retaliation. Remember, this is the generation that endured the Great Depression and fought in World War II. They are accustomed to hard times. Some elders have such severe cognitive disor-ders they cannot find the language to address an institutional grievance. Others who have complained are often ignored, set aside as troublemak-ers or punished through neglect. I experienced many days in which the personal service was so inept, I vowed to bring my husband home again, even at the cost of my health and sanity.

Without doubt, nursing facilities are not hotels catering to customer preference. Alas, they are also not hospitals aiming for highly sterile sur-roundings and low ratio of patients to nursing staff. Our family felt that aside from the visiting area, these facilities exuded an oppressive sad-ness that weighed heavily on staff, visitors and patients alike. The sights, sounds and smells hit the uninitiated like a wall. One can easily be over-come by the tragic faces of demented patients or by the constant moaning and shouting of deranged elders. For the more cognitively aware patient like Jim, the presence of so many mentally disordered peers acted as an added emotional burden to his physical pain. And, many wards emit the unceasing odor of human waste, trapped in rugs, mattresses and floors.

Yet, a heroic quality often flowered from this squalid environment. Where the care facility was truly caring, and where visiting family, friends and volunteers radiated love, concern and positive intention, everyone connected to make a difference. This difference was a shift in sensibility from feeling physically consigned to the lowest underworld, to a reasonable, if physically and emotionally difficult place some elders must accept as their final home.

Consider what institutionalized elders routinely need from staff. I found the list to be extensive: water, feeding (at least at later stages of life), medicine, diaper changing, bed changes and urinals emptied. Then, staff must make transfers for many patients from bed to wheelchair, from wheelchair to toilet, as well as check in every two hours to determine the patient's condition (minimum Washington state requirement for patients confined to their beds). Add to this, nursing aides monitor ma-chines (e.g., oxygen), and for those more highly motivated, drop-in to chat with lonely, and often frightened, patients. So much can go wrong with this picture.

Staff shift changes interrupted service. Over a period of only a few months, I observed a number of instances of exceedingly poor care. A patient was left on the toilet for more than an hour. Nursing notes omitted essential information, including failing to include new orders from the attending physician. Nursing aides had inadequate training for the complexity of the job. For example, washing wounds and monitoring machines were outside their expertise. Some were simply too incompetent or indifferent to handle the work. They had problems at home, came to work intoxicated, experienced chronic fatigue, or worked too many hours the day or week before. In some facilities I observed staff and administrators who were routinely hostile or intimidated certain patients.

Forgetfulness seemed endemic to institutionalized care, as floor staff attempted to answer multiple patient calls, confront emergencies, deal with difficult or hard-to-handle patients, all while simultaneously carrying out their routine duties. Unless the staff person wrote down a patient's request (and few aides did this), they may have forgotten it by the time they reached the end of the hall because of two or three interruptions. This became serious when the elder needed water or had been left in dirty diapers for a couple of hours—a situation we confronted too many times to enumerate throughout Jim's years as a patient.

Without having a specific word—indeed, in the absence of language— I began my personal campaign of advocating for my husband, Jim. My family and I accomplished this by employing a number of strategies:

- Diligently watching staff behavior;
- Immediately intervening on behalf of Jim when inappropriate or poor treatment occurred;
- Speaking out to individual staff and supervisors;
- Complaining about treatment to responsible staff persons;
- Agitating to social workers and supervisory staff for conscious, compassionate care, rather than careless and indifferent treatment;
- Collecting information to better advise hands-on staff on the minutiae of care;
- Defending my loved one's patient's rights, but also other similarly affected elders (with less success);
- Admonishing individual staff for lapses in service;

- Inquiring about other patients' experiences through family members to find out whether I was dealing with an isolated situation or a widespread institutional problem; and
- Connecting with Jim's physician and later, Hospice, to spell out the problem areas.

Intervening on behalf of another, seemingly so simple and humane, evolved into an all-consuming enterprise. Each care facility offered a distinct institutional format, one that had to be meticulously learned. How else would you have known whether you missed the weekly shower unless you knew that the window of opportunity for such care was a brief one hour per week? Some facilities welcomed family. They correctly perceived the positive value that family members brought to the elder's sickbed. Other facilities ignored or constrained visiting because it interfered with institutional routines, purportedly agitated the patient or required a level of social interaction that some nursing staff found difficult.[3]

Few nurses, however, are as bold as the one who told me to keep visitors down to two persons maximum, as it not only interfered with care, but too many people around could be "dangerous" for the patient's health. As I discussed in an earlier chapter, medical staff can be very arbitrary. In this case, my advocating took the form of a non-confrontational nod at her inappropriate request. I then clarified the policy with administrators, who were far less restrictive. Our family of myself and six adult children, their spouses and children, finally resolved this unpleasantness by rallying round the overburdened nurse, and praising her for her nursing skills, kindness and concern about Jim and other patients. Her response: unalloyed joy and an entirely new repertory of interaction that was personal and pleasant.

Not all family members were equally sanguine in dealing with staff transgressions. Our son, Timothy, often flew into momentary rages when his father's care appeared inadequate. On daily visits, Timothy monitored the state of his father's well-being. If it had fallen short, he strode purposefully down the hall to locate the offending staff person who had failed to clean, feed, hydrate or otherwise look after Jim. With

Timothy's tap on the shoulder and direct eye contact, the aide usually jumped into action. But this was not always the case. We all became quite philosophical about developing the capacity to recognize our loved one's immediate needs and our personal ability to meet these needs for the duration of our visit, as well as to understand the constant pressure on staff that contributed to slow or unresponsive service.

Empowering Caregivers: Knowledge About Elder Care Institutions

Personal experiences with elder care institutions serve a crucial role in clarifying what constitutes "adequacy" of care. Additionally, *advocacy* also entails large-scale reform groups who speak out and lobby on behalf of families.

The National Citizen's Coalition for Nursing Home Reform has written a manual, which needs to be on every family's bookshelf: *Nursing Homes: Getting Good Care There*.[4] The manual identifies the seven most common problems in care. The Coalition pinpointed the following cause and effect risks for patients:

1. Not being taken to the bathroom according to individualized needs leads to incontinence (wet and soiled).
2. Not getting enough fluids to drink leads to dehydration (often thirsty and dry skin) compounded by drugs that contribute to excessively dry mouth.
3. Not getting enough to eat leads to malnutrition (weight loss, low energy and cracks in the corner of the mouth).
4. Not being groomed properly leads to poor hygiene (body odors, dirty mouth, dirty clothes).
5. Not receiving preventive skin care or failure to frequently turn bedridden patients leads to pressure sores (holes in the skin, which can penetrate to the muscles underneath the skin).
6. Not being helped with range of motion exercises or physical therapy leads to shorted muscles and chronic joint discomfort.
7. Not encouraged to retain independence leads to loss of ability to eat, dress, walk, bathe and get in and out of bed (increased dependency).

In fact, Jim experienced all of the above during his stays in both assisted living and nursing home facilities. Only after we settled Jim into his last nursing home, a long-standing and respected institution in our community, did we learn about the differences in such measures as patients' rights, quality of care and the role of the family as advocate. Of course, nursing homes typically broadcast patients' rights as fundamental, and cite a litany of features seemingly placing patients first, such as the freedom of association, right to dignity and right to self-discharge, among others.

Nursing facilities also pay lip service to quality of care by involving the resident and family in care planning, and engaging in problem-solving and taking individual needs into account. Nursing homes supposedly welcome the outspoken advocate who steps up and speaks out on behalf of their loved one. In fact, states are now mandated to provide intervention by an ombudsman, should a consumer bring a complaint.[5]

What keeps concerned relatives from bringing formal complaints is related to the same set of issues that contribute to poor care. First, care facilities for elderly and disabled people are typically for-profit corporate structures, invariably removed from the day-to-day supervision of care. Despite strict federal and state standards, resident abuse is widespread in U.S. nursing homes, and largely goes unreported and unpunished.[6]

Since corporations are in the business of making money, shortages or low inventories provide one way of cutting costs. We found a lack of nutritious food, particularly fruits and vegetables, frequent outages of clean bed linens and towels and worker shortages among housekeeping and nursing staff.

Athena McLean's research emphasizes a host of issues.[7] Low pay, poor benefits, difficult working conditions and poor management lead to low morale and high staff turnover, while constant changes in the nursing crew create another litany of problems. This includes an overall lack of staff awareness of individual patient's needs, impersonal treatment, denial of responsibility, as workers "pass the buck," and slow downs, among other problems.

In one facility, I observed staff routinely take their collective dinner during the same time elders needed help with their after-dinner toileting. In such instances, a general sense of abandonment pervaded the environment, as elders in wheelchairs and family members went in search of elusive nursing assistants.

Second, the corporate model, with its bottom line, must be identified as culpable. Absentee ownership also creates a serious disjuncture between a *care facility* and a *caring facility*. Sometimes, this contributed to absurd situations. One nursing home in our temperate Bellingham, Washington community received directives from its central office, located in torrid Phoenix, Arizona. The care facility ran its air conditioning at the same level as in Arizona. However, in Bellingham, 72 degrees is likely to be a normal summer high. The results were predictable: hallways and dining areas of shivering elders wrapped in multiple layers of sweaters or blankets. Over time, I felt the physical coldness was an apt metaphor for the psychological chill that pervaded the entire environment.

A third point: nursing homes are run on a hierarchical model, typical of corporations and hospitals. Administrative supervisors give orders to lower ranking nurses, who in turn give orders to their underlings. This practice undermines team work and joint problem-solving. It also leads to resentment on the part of the nursing assistants, who do the bulk of patient care.

On more than one occasion, I witnessed the frustration and rage of floor staff, who indignantly protested the impossibility of accomplishing the scope of duties they had been ordered to do. But if they failed to follow directions, they were docked wages or even fired. Certainly, having appropriate staff-to-patient ratios could have enhanced staff morale and patient care. And, unless facilities implement different management strategies, staffing shortages will remain endemic to the industry.[8]

Another overlooked issue in nursing home care is the strong bias against the aged held by citizens and the medical profession alike. These negative attitudes may increase, as the number of elderly rise. Today, persons 65 and older account for more than half of all hospital stays and one-third of the nation's health care expenditures. Yet, as I mentioned in Chapter 6, few medical schools train students in geriatric medicine. As of 1993, only eight of the nation's 126 medical schools require separate courses in geriatric medicine.[9] Care for older persons is not reinforced professionally, and professional role models are largely absent. Irreversible physical declines and death may create an intrinsic reluctance among many health professionals to serve this needy population.

A final consideration for understanding the lack of good care in nursing homes involves the residents themselves. Because healthier elders
remain in their homes or choose residential or assisted living facilities,
nursing homes increasingly house the most seriously ill patients, namely
those who are most dependent and most likely to have serious dementia. Patients' problems, especially among those suffering from dementia,
often stem from having to leave a cherished home. Other concerns include patients' lack of knowledge about their medical situation, inability
to communicate, different expectations than staff, conflicts with room-
mates, complaints about food and service, anxiety over their medical
and living circumstances, and only too often, a feeling of hopelessness
that contributes to withdrawal and maladaptive behavior.[10]

The National Citizen's Coalition for Nursing Home Reform stresses,
however, that many of these maladies can be remedied when the environment changes. I found their "Tips to Remember" particularly helpful
for elder advocates.

1. Residents in today's nursing homes have the same needs as anyone else—namely, a need for recognition as an individual—and
   in this case, one who has special needs because of physical and
   mental infirmities.
2. Without individual recognition, residents can feel displaced
   and, without a sense of familiarity, can feel virtually homeless.
   Depression and withdrawal soon follow.
3. Engaging the staff with individual residents remains the best remedy for elder dislocation in an institutional setting. Rather than
   asking the resident to change life-long individual habits, adjustments in routines need to be made by the *facility*. Individualized
   care is the basic tenet of the standards set forth by the federally
   sponsored Nursing Home Reform Law, and it applies to all nursing homes receiving federal money. Although individualized care
   has been lauded as the new standard, it rarely translates into a new
   set of institutional practices.
4. Nursing home staff can accommodate individualized care by carefully assessing each resident, and then developing a plan of care
   to meet that person's needs. The plan must then be publicized

throughout the institution (i.e., kitchen staff, physical therapists, nursing staff) to ensure its implementation.

5. Families play a significant role in nursing home advocacy, as well. They need to share information with the nursing staff, participate in care meetings and expect the facility to make reasonable accommodations for their relative's individual needs and preferences.

6. Nursing homes need to be well-staffed to provide good care—a point that cannot be overemphasized. In addition, federal regulatory agencies must demand sufficient resources to enforce the standards of care.[11]

Before the disabled elder moves into a nursing home, he or she must have an assessment. This assessment is a complex undertaking, in that it clarifies the resident's ability to walk, talk, remember, bathe, see, hear, eat, dress and comprehend, as well as determines the level of assistance required for toileting, wheelchair transfers, physical therapy and the like. The assessment also evaluates personal habits and preferences, such as preferred time for waking up in the morning and favorite television shows. Familiar routines, activities, habits and relationships are precious reminders of our individuality. Nursing homes employing the one-size-fits-all model frequently ignore the "specialness" of each person in their care, which results in inadvertently (we presume) undermining the resident's sense of self.

When Jim was strongly urged to be "more social" with various activities, such as Bible reading, musical performances by volunteers, exercise, movies, popcorn parties or ice cream socials, he strenuously resisted. Jim responded to suggestions that he should be forced to be cordial, even ebullient, when he preferred being alone, by overtly withdrawing. Jim chose the hermit role as his method of coping with illness and depression. The family agonized over his decision, gently encouraging him to participate in at least one or two activities a week. He finally compromised, attending periodic musical events (which often were not very good) or a special dinner (which sometimes were), as long as a family member accompanied him. But this was not always feasible.

The sure-fire way, we found, to integrate a recalcitrant elder in a nursing home was to send an enthusiastic member of the activities team to personally take the resident to the event, which happened a few times with Jim. Focusing on the solitary person's isolation and withdrawal is not effective.[12] The staff at a well-managed nursing home can work wonders to integrate even the most confused and difficult resident with gentle persuasion.

Institutional Care: A Universal Experience for Elders?

Nursing home living is not an isolated experience for the few. One-half of all women and one-third of all men will spend some part of their lives in a nursing home before they die—25 percent for at least one year and nine percent for five years or more. But not all nursing homes are alike; some are downright dangerous. The National Citizens' Coalition for Nursing Home Reform reports 30 percent of nursing homes have regulatory violations that have caused life-threatening harm or death to residents. Another 50 percent of nursing homes do not have enough staff to prevent residents from getting harmed. Nursing home abuses are endemic to the system, as reported by Rand Corporation and the Alliance for Aging Research.

Robert W. DuBois, principle investigator, uncovered medical death records of elderly patients dying in nursing homes, which reveals 27 percent had died because of improper medical care (Rand Corporation). Other finds show that:

- Older persons are either over-or-under prescribed with medications, and drug reactions comprise more than one-half of all deaths (Alliance for Aging Research);
- Persons 75 years or older are much less likely to receive prescriptions for reducing heart attacks compared with younger patients;
- Many elderly diabetics do not get recommended tests for their condition, suffering needlessly;
- For other patients, 20 to 40 percent of all hospital procedures performed on older patients were unnecessary;
- Two of every five of the nation's 1.6 million nursing home residents are malnourished.[13]

Nursing homes and the challenge of long-term care—care which may extend for years—have exploded into national awareness. In 1999, *Time* magazine called conditions in some nursing homes "fatal neglect." Much earlier, Richard Garvin and Robert E. Burger wrote *Where Do They Go To Die: The Tragedy of American Nursing Homes* (1968).[14] The authors wrote that nursing homes are "halfway houses between society and the cemetery," a situation that has continued for decades. The Florida-based Coalition to Protect the Nation's Elders called for congressional hearings on nursing home fraud and abuse. The Coalition argued that residents have been starved, beaten or left to die, while "giant nursing home chains are ripping off taxpayers with phony billing scams." The deep indignation expressed in the Coalition's statement reflects the anguish many advocates feel when addressing elders' unmet needs for safe, nurturing and cost-effective care.[15] A recent legal response to the abuse/neglect problem in nursing homes has been offered by nationwide law firms, which focus on litigation and affixing blame, not simply arranging money settlements.[16]

Nursing home reformers blame the abusive treatment on a severe nursing shortage, low staff salaries and a turnover rate that may exceed 100 percent a year. Nursing aides, who perform most of the hands-on care, are often given only a few weeks training, and paid little more than fast food workers.[17]

During my tenure as an advocate for my husband, I can recount a number of episodes confirming these findings. My husband fell out of his wheelchair *twice* in one day from weakness because of staff failure to secure him to the wheelchair or place him in a bed. This occurred after transitioning him from one facility to another. On another occasion, an elderly dementia patient in the same institution fell out of bed and suffered a concussion, because staff had failed to put up safety rails that prevented falls. In still another preventable situation, one patient, quite demented, physically assaulted another elderly person before staff could intervene. Overworked or forgetful staff may fail to complete rounds, and frail elders, too weak to summon aid, may not be bedded for the night until the late shift comes on. This may be a small matter to a healthy adult, but for an exhausted elder, it can create a major setback.

Fortunately, most negative episodes we encountered were not life-threatening, although some came close. As a family, we mainly appreciated the care, and tried to remain positive and raise morale in the ward. The issue of elder abuse, though, is deeply troubling, because older people, similar to small children, are exceedingly dependent on caregivers and the safety of their immediate environment. My overriding experience over the three years Jim lived in nursing facilities was the pervasive sense of frustration and disappointment, whether as an individual or as a family, to fundamentally change the institutional environment. What the sick elder needs is comfort in a home-like setting; what that elder receives is an uncaring institution. For the 50 percent or more seriously ill elders living in nursing homes without regular visitors and contact with the outside world, life truly looks hopeless.

A Better Way?

Long-term care of elders in the community should really be emphasizing non-institutionalized, long-term care. But lack of adequate public resources to serve elderly clients in a time of perceived scarcity accounts for much of the ethical anguish that care providers and families face.[18] Rethinking basic concepts and practices in long-term care requires moving away from the corporate model to a cooperative one. Liz Taylor, a *Seattle Times* columnist and speaker on aging issues, refers to the "big progress in elder care" as "culture change" or "resident-driven care."[19] Such a model has been available in Sweden for more than 20 years, and can be readily adopted for care centers in the United States.

In 1993, a group from Sweden visited the Lyngblomsten Care Center in St. Paul, Minnesota to compare Swedish nursing homes with their American counterparts.[20] The program was simple. Each year the care center in St. Paul sent two American employees from their center to Sweden for four weeks in the spring, and Sweden would reciprocate by sending two care center employees to St. Paul. Associate Professor, Dr. Leslie Grant, who headed up this innovative research on Swedish care delivery, wanted to learn whether or not the Swedish model could be adopted to improve American nursing home care. Sweden, long known for its generous welfare provisions, assigns responsibility for care of the aged and disabled to local provinces or states.

The Swedes emphasize that what is normal for a person at home should continue to be normal in the congregate setting—an approach emphasizing client autonomy and choice. Consequently, their service houses individual apartments, not semi-private rooms. Each has a full bath, not a bath down the hall. Nursing stations or utility rooms with soiled linens and garbage have been eliminated. Breakfast and dinner are taken into residents' apartments, so they are not forced to have regimented mealtimes according to a predetermined schedule set by staff. They are also allowed to get up and go to bed when they choose.

Since the Swedish system uses a "generalist" type of staffing, the LPNs (Licensed Practical Nurses) in the St. Paul care center initially performed all the nursing and support functions required on a daily basis without the specialization found in standard American nursing homes. This included personal care, medications, administration, treatments, cooking, cleaning, laundry and social activities. By employing an egalitarian approach, the residents more easily developed a rapport with the nurses. Once the program was up and running, the care center added administrators and nursing aides to the mix at the request of the St. Paul staff.

The research showed a significant increase in both autonomy and satisfaction on the part of residents, and many indicated they actually preferred living there. Perhaps, most surprising is that the Swedish model is no more expensive to operate than the standard American nursing home. Ultimately, if the United States were to adapt the Swedish perspective of privacy, dignity and autonomy for giving care in a congregate setting, we would most likely witness a sharp decrease in elder abuse, as well as greatly enhanced care for end-of-life patients.

Reflections

Instead of feeling powerless, caregivers and their families *can* do something: take on an advocacy role. This entails witnessing, speaking out and demanding competent care for their loved ones and similarly situated elders. With one of three nursing homes in America reportedly falling below federal standards or to actually abuse or neglect patients, I believe the time is right for seeking changes in congregate living arrangements for end-of-life care. As a colleague said recently about institutional regimes for his mother-in-law: "If you have a team of advocates, you will be all right."

Sidebar: Nursing Home Care

According to the U.S. House of Representatives, nearly 17,000 nursing homes exist in the United States, which care for 1.6 million residents—a figure expected to quadruple to 6.6 million by 2050. In 1999, the United States spent a mammoth $68 billion to pay for nursing home care for 1.5 million people. Medicaid paid for 60 percent of this total, which accounts for a large chunk of the state health and welfare budget. Private citizens pay anywhere from $40,000 to $80,000 a year or more, depending on region of the country, level of care in the facility and number of people in the room.

National Center on Elder Abuse, 1201 15th Street, N.W., Suite 350, Washington, D.C. 20005.
  ncea@nasua.org

Chapter 10

Affirmations and Spiritual Openings

I want to invite a new use of the word faith; one that is not associated with a dogmatic religious interpretation or divisiveness. I want to encourage delight in the word, to help reclaim faith as fresh, vibrant, intelligent and liberating... that emphasizes a foundation of love and respect for ourselves. It is a faith that uncovers our connections to others, rather than designating anyone as separate and apart.

~ Sharon Salzberg,
Faith: Trusting Your Own Deepest Experience[1]

Our positive and negative beliefs not only impact our health, but also every aspect of our life... Your beliefs act like filters on a camera, changing how you see the world. And your biology adapts to those beliefs.

~ Bruce Lipton, *The Biology of Belief*[2]

A Love Story

Jill, one of our caregivers, endured emotional abuse and rejection during her childhood, knowing her mother didn't love her. But, she rejected her oppressive childhood beliefs and overcame the nearly insurmountable limitations caused by lack of maternal caring and love. Jill succeeded in her life, and beautifully so, as an educator, friend, socially conscious and compassionate woman, as well as a powerful leader in the healing community. Her joy was infectious: she danced in the hallways and brought comfort to the afflicted.

During the final stages of her mother's life, Jill was guided by her capacity to love and by her spiritual connections. She left her home and job for two months to sit patiently beside her mother's bed, to care for all her needs and, finally, to usher her mother through her end-of-life transition. Even on her deathbed, Jill's mother could not relinquish her early attitudes of hostility toward her daughter.

> *I believe in the basic goodness of people. I knew my mother didn't like me. She told me so. I tried to calm her, but she only insulted me. I couldn't make her happy and I abandoned my dream that my mother would have a change of heart—being nice to me. I prayed a lot and wondered why I chose her. She went to her deathbed never saying she loved me.*
>
> *The best part of caring for my mother was that she was allowed to die in peace in her own home, to be surrounded by the people who loved her. She died in a good way and I finally got to see who she really was. I was determined to help her passage. I owed her the best care and I took the experience as a spiritual challenge; it was profound. Healing did happen for me because I came to a much deeper acceptance of who my mother is.*

Love, as the quintessential spiritual value, can be expressed unconditionally in caring for another, as Jill has done. This level of benevolence reflects the highest form of faith: the willingness to sacrifice self by living from the heart—a life practice that turns out to be easier to talk about than to actually achieve.

High Road or Low Road?

Daniel Goleman, writing in *Social Intelligence,* offers an intriguing analysis of the "social brain," by stipulating a spectrum of possibilities for recognizing pattern, social meaning, decoding language and gesture.[3] He simplifies these complex mental functions as a dichotomy: the high road of mental functioning versus the low road of mental functioning.

When on the low road, we are on automatic—outside our awareness—hurrying from one task to another. When on the high road, we are in control, putting forth effort and conscious intent, functioning more slowly and purposefully. Spirituality, the inner component of the self, similarly operates on high and low roads. Perhaps, the low road is, most commonly, the path well-traveled on a day-to-day basis. We operate our spiritual lives on automatic, depending upon "blind faith," early childhood socialization and cultural maxims based on fear as guides for relationships and actions. Taking the high road requires more thought and even inner struggle. It could demand a renunciation of former beliefs and religious practices, and even the creation of new maps to guide the seeker through unfamiliar terrain.

Jill's love story encompasses the essence of taking the high road. Through years of inner struggle, deep empathy, a bout with cancer and a life dedicated to teaching and healing, she overcame her childhood trauma from maternal abuse. Her faith, based on love and self-respect, allowed her to give time, energy and care without reservation to a bitter and unforgiving parent.

High Road 1: Life-Sustaining Attitudes and Practices

Taking the high road requires, above all, the capacity to develop appropriate emotions, beliefs and practices that surmount the day-to-day problems of caregiving. The caregivers in our study developed a number of life-sustaining practices, which helped them have balanced emotional lives, and maintain their social connections and spiritual integrity (See Table 10.1). As Catherine, a highly energetic caregiver, commented:

I think caregiving is a gift if you look at it in a positive way. It enables you to do something for another human being—especially one you love.

Planning involves the use of higher mental functioning. When caregivers indicated that they fully intended to serve their elder *before* the elder's current medical crisis, they needed to have considered the implications of this decision. Intentionality characterizes most successful or even moderately successful caregivers. Apparently, merely having a strong commitment to care *after* the fact or once the person has stepped forward into the caregiving role does not necessarily assure a smooth transition into the role, or a positive course of action during the caregiving years. As such, other methods of coping must be developed. For many women, spirituality and positive attitudes facilitated their sacrificial efforts.

At a glance, we can recognize that attitudes among caregivers reveal clear contradictions. Whereas less than one of three said they had very positive and optimistic attitudes, other emotional indicators suggest an

Table 10.1   Caregivers' Self-Reported Responses to Benign or Positive Appraisal of Caregiving

Appraisal	Percent
Strong commitment to care	98
Compassion (% responding high or very high)	
"I believe loving kindness is the best medicine"	88
Prior intention to serve elder	72
Positive & optimistic attitude (% responding high or very high)	29
Emotions: Feelings of (% responding high or very high)	
Valued	77
"Doing my best"	76
Respected	72
Satisfaction	68
Rewarded	41
Peaceful	32
Rejuvenated	8
Using alternative health providers	33
Visits to Alternative Health Providers	Mean = 4.51
Community Involvement	
1-3 Activities	70
4 or more	30
	Mean = 2.64
Personal Activities (hobbies, exercise, friends, etc.)	
0	23
1-3	46
4 or more	30
	Mean = 2.4 activities
Beliefs	
Care receiver appreciates my effort	85
Family supports and appreciates effort	79
Stated high or very high family support	59
Advocate role	
For loved one	38
For unrelated elders/organizations	23

(Nanette J. Davis, Caregiving Study, 2005)

affirmative set of feelings may have helped them to sustain an upbeat attitude, at least part of the time. More than 75 percent of caregivers reported they felt respected and valued for their work, and derived deep satisfaction from this fact, especially if the caregiver and family appreciated their efforts. "Doing my best" (although most wanted to do significantly better) translated for most caregivers into: "I'm powerless to change what is happening to my loved one, but I'm doing the job to the best of my ability." At one level, then, the phrase, "doing my best," can be interpreted as a positive, self-acknowledging statement. For some women, though, "doing my best," really meant, "I'm no good at this job, and my best is pretty bad," and for a very few caregivers, "I feel sorry for my loved one that I can't do any better than this."

As expected with this highly empathetic caregiving group, compassion ranks high as a motivation for service. Nearly 90 percent responded very positively to the phrase: "I believe loving kindness is the best medicine." For some, compassion extended to advocacy, first, for their own loved one, and among some caregivers, for unrelated elders. Advocacy involved a range of activities, including speaking out to medical staff on behalf of their own or other patients, writing letters supporting particular policies and participating in caregiving support groups or patient-centered activities.

Virginia, an only child, delighted in the fact that her mother, with whom she always had a close, "sisterly" relationship, could join her household of two—her son and herself. Despite friends warning her that bringing her mother to live with her *would never work*, Virginia found her mother's presence comforting during all 15 years of caregiving. Her mother contributed love and good will, as well as funds to keep the household running. When her mother's health broke down at age 85, Virginia confronted the medical system, protesting the poor treatment given her mother to both her doctor and the hospital ombudsman. Virginia admitted that, although she couldn't help her mother medically, she could participate in her care by advocating for her in the system.

As an advocate on behalf of my loved one, I was more aware and determined to get good medical treatment, and insistent on having the right thing that needed to be done.

I also inquired about the level of personal and community activities among caregivers. Since isolation and long hours are most likely to contribute to negative health outcomes, having other activities could serve as an incentive to stay socially connected and mentally active. On both measures—personal and community activities—these caregivers overall demonstrated significant involvement. A word of caution: during the dying process of their loved ones (which could involve months), most caregivers were forced to abandon, first, their community activities, and next, their hobbies, reading and even their most cherished friendships.

A few caregivers turned to alternative health practices, such as acupuncture, massage and chiropractic, to reduce stress and avoid medical intervention. However, only one in three caregivers had ever tried nontraditional medicine, and among this number, use was limited to an average of five visits over the course of their caregiving. Most caregivers pointed out that they either failed to understand the medical value of these approaches, found them too expensive or derived little benefit. For many caregivers, religious or spiritual solutions to personal adversity served as their primary orientation for maintaining balance in their lives.[4]

High Road 2: Religion and its Effect on Health and Well-Being

The core teaching of most religious faiths can be expressed as "Love everybody, serve everybody, always remember God."[5] Mother Teresa, a contemporary spiritual leader, practiced this dictum in her daily life, urging others to do likewise. Religious communities provide ample opportunity for believers to actualize themselves through practicing the virtuous life. Regardless of how believers choose to act upon these "high road" principles, the literature on religion and health suggests that religion may have profound influences on health, shaping our consciousness toward connecting with others and a radical acceptance of our life—its pains, losses and joys.

Social research on religion and health dates back to France at the beginning of the twentieth century. Sociologist Emile Durkheim discovered that the pathways linking religion to health are complex, and emphasized how social support in the form of helping one another through difficult times—a shoulder to lean on—was a major contribution of religious involvement.[6]

Other studies confirm the positive effects of religious identification. Findings by McCullough and Laurenceau found that people who are highly engaged in religious pursuits, or who report that religion is a central aspect of their lives, tend to have a higher subjective well-being, fewer depressive symptoms and live longer lives than do their non-religious counterpoints.[7] Two reasons exist for an increased sense of well-being. First, religion serves to promote adherence to conventional wisdom about engaging in health-promoting behaviors, such as drinking in moderation and getting regular exercise. And, second, religion often integrates people into networks that provide social support.

A study that used a representative community-based sample of men and women born in the San Francisco Bay Area in the 1920s investigated long-term connections between religiousness, spirituality, depression and physical health. Findings emphasize that in late adulthood (i.e., 60s to mid-70s), religion has a salutary effect on depression resulting from personal adversity. Spirituality, conceptualized in terms of adherence to non-institutional religious beliefs and practices, did not have the same benign effect. The researchers proposed that religiousness, unlike spirituality, provides individuals with a stronger and more historically grounded sense of group identity and values, as well as a feeling of support from other church members. Such characteristics are particularly conducive to maintaining positive emotions during stressful times.[8]

A Duke University survey also found that regular attendees of religious services reported larger social networks overall, more frequent telephone and in-person contact, and a strong feeling of support from all members of their social circles.[9]

Religious Beliefs and Affiliations

More than half of these caregivers reported a church affiliation, although some of the churchgoers had a relatively low involvement with their religious community because of caregiving duties. Instead, religiosity was most likely expressed in prayer and service to others, in addition to an acceptance of their life, including caregiving and their loved one's dying process. The most striking responses to the question, "Do you have a religious or spiritual identity," yielded the following: a strong sense of spirituality (88 percent), an active prayer life (72 percent), regular attendance at religious services (56 percent), greater closeness and commitment to a Higher Power as a result of caregiving (50 percent) and high involvement in a religious community (24 percent).

Religious beliefs for most, however, were tempered by recognition that belief in God did not mean immediate or even heavenly solutions to their personal problems. In a response to the question of whether they believed in a "just world," only 26 percent responded positively. Most felt that neither they nor their sick elder deserved to suffer. At the same time, only one in five caregivers felt that they were experiencing a spiritual renewal as a result of their caregiving. This finding seems to indicate that religion may serve as an aid and comfort in difficult times, but by itself, may not necessarily be a transformative experience.

Virginia attributes her positive attitude toward her mother's care to her religious beliefs. Throughout caregiving, Virginia remained active in her church and enjoyed the social life it provided. She was positive and accepting of the care demands, and felt privileged that, as an only child, she could repay her mother for the solicitous care she provided in her childhood. She also reported that the minimal health problems she experienced did not affect her caregiving.

> *Caregiving was not a problem for my emotional health. I have a very strong faith in God and I believe in prayer and in attending church. I get a renewed strength when I go to church. I feel I'm part of serving the church. I believe in enjoying life—all my friends—there's so much to enjoy.*

Another factor is that faith can persist, while other sources of well-being, such as health, independence, social position and connections do not. Many women indicated that religious beliefs gave them a sense of power and control. An abiding faith in God was Virginia's recipe for wholeness.

> *There isn't anything that God and I together can't get through. My strong religious faith pulled me through.*

Virginia was hardly a doomsday type of Christian, despite membership in an evangelical church. Instead, she valued living joyfully and lovingly, and accepted the fact that her values would be tested.

> *People who don't have their values tested are missing out. Caregiving actually strengthened my values. I felt like I was doing my part and it was a job well done.*

Religion, which offers a complex set of beliefs about God, human relationships and the meaning of life and death, can help caregivers make sense of serious illness. More than a few of the women we interviewed echoed the words and attitude of Charlotte, who was raised Presbyterian and remained active in the church while caregiving.

> *I believe in God. I don't believe I've had an unfair experience in caregiving. I was sad that I was losing him but thankful we could be together—accepting the whole gamut.*

For some caregivers, their only social outlet during the caregiving years was church. Religion offered both day-to-day reassurance in a purposeful life, as well as a way to connect with God at the most profound level.

Before being a caregiver to her mother, Rita described herself as angry, troubled and addicted to drugs. Then she became involved with her church.

> *I attend church three times a week and have a high level of involvement. I think you need to turn it over to God. I really do. Spiritual beliefs have given me hope. I was in NA* [Narcotics Anonymous], *but I didn't like it. I feel better about myself because I've grown closer to God. I'll be seeing my mother again* [after death]. *For now, I'm healed and I feel like a good person.*

Carrie, another self-reported, deeply religious caregiver, whom we encountered in earlier chapters, had a profound religious faith that sustained her through her mother's illness as a child, her sister's cancer diagnosis, and now, during the care of her blind father. As a devoted and deeply involved member of her religious congregation, Carrie turned to prayer to relieve stress. She said, "Do not be anxious about anything, but be in prayer and meditation," adding:

This life is temporary. Time seems valuable, but in hindsight, it's very different. It all changes. Don't get so wrapped up in the crisis that you forget the big picture. It all passes—material things, emotions, life—it's all temporary.

Caregiving has not disrupted my life. I just made an unexpected change to do it. My life is going along just like it's supposed to.

Other caregivers specified the normality of their lives because of their beliefs. Here, two caregivers express their religious convictions.

God gave this [caregiving] to me to prove my love for Him. I feel fine because God is with me all the time. I have coped with disruptions by showing my husband that everything is going to be okay, because God is with us. I cope by praying every night on my knees.

Who supported me in caregiving? My faith, absolutely. It's a real blessed feeling that no matter what happens, you can only go down so far. Life is still very interesting, challenging, alive.

Religious individuals can draw on the traditions of their faith to put their own lives in a much larger context, to learn lessons from others who have faced similar troubles, to allay fear or to gain hope for the future. These are all particularly relevant to elder caregivers, who may be facing serious illness while caring for a loved one, who are grieving or who believe they have very little control over the situation. As one caregiver noted, "Don't ever think you have control. Only the illness has control."

Most poignantly, religious belief systems offer resources for understanding tragic or stressful events. Ellen Idler, a researcher who has studied the link between religion and health, observes that religious interpretations of difficult circumstances may have the power to bring individuals to a state of peace, especially when the situation is one that cannot be altered.[10]

Kathy, who has cared for both her very elderly mother and father for four years, acknowledged that while caregiving has tested her values, she remains stronger than before. As a practitioner of the Church of Religious Science, Kathy prays every day, hoping

that they will go at the right time without pain—peacefully—that it will be a joyous experience and we will handle it beautifully. Jesus said, 'whatever you believe will happen.'

Roberta had read that people with dementia, whose Christian faith was an integral part of their lives, are less apt to be ill-tempered or prone to violence. Roberta's faith was her personal buoy that kept her afloat during the seven years of caring for her husband with Alzheimer's.

> *My church friends are important supporters. Prayer is the biggest thing for me and learning from other Christians, friends and the Bible, figuring out how I should behave. I'm so glad God sent me adrift—so many friends He sent to me. I feel in control most of the time because I really know God is in control.*

Spiritual Identification

Whereas research abounds on the impact of religion on health and well-being, the field of unaffiliated spirituality offers, at most, anecdotal, but heartily felt, observations. David James Duncan, a former Seventh Day Adventist and author of *God Laughs and Plays*, emphasizes that personal spirituality can be very grounding, even without having a church. Instead, the emphasis is on our human connections, stewardship of the planet and responsibility in the political and economic arena.[11] "Churchless sermons," as Duncan calls them, can help humanity manage the "epochal challenges of a rapidly globalizing, ecologically compromised world."[12]

For many Americans, this unorthodox line of thinking offers an equally persuasive, secular model of spiritual well-being, but without the judgments and doctrines associated with religiosity.

The 12-step program for recovering addicts is an often overlooked spiritual aid—containing certain elements of Christianity (God's will, forgiveness, contrition for wrongdoing, achieving serenity, service to others)—but offering essentially a secular doctrine for self-improvement.

Theresa, 78 years old, spoke highly of her "happy recovery from alcoholism" many years earlier, which she linked with receiving her mother's care and support over her lifetime. Now, with her 95-year-old mother ill from cancer, she considered her giving not "care, but share." Theresa spoke of her ailing mother in glowing terms.

We're more like teamwork. She gave me the moral support I needed during alcoholic recovery. I've never thought of myself as caregiver—then I would have to admit that she was sick. I've spent 24/7 with her—our lives complemented each other. She has always been so positive and appreciative.

How did Theresa become involved with caregiving? She answered:

It was more a matter of convenience. She was alone and I was alone at that time. It seemed like the thing to do. We shared the expenses together. No, I didn't 'intend' to be a caregiver, but probably yes, I guess I expected to. Still, it was more of an automatic decision. [I said to myself], some day, being an only child, you'll have to take care of your mother. Sure enough, 20 years later, it happened. I feel I gained a lot as a result of caregiving. I came to know mother better, to know what is important to her. It was never a burden. It was more of a privilege.

So, what was the best part of caring for her? Theresa said:

She was always loving, had a heart of gold. She prayed when I had a [drinking] problem. She was always giving. Today, I have more appreciation for life, the importance of others' feelings, sharing with others. [Caregiving] has taught me how to identify with others, to accept responsibility, to do it with love.

Serenity—I achieve this by knowing what the problem is, what I can do about it, what my choices are, and make the best choice possible. I believe in giving till it hurts.

Psychologist Victor Frankl teaches that later life, especially, provides a unique time for inner growth and spirituality.[13] Several caregivers reflected on being spiritually open.

Keep on keeping on and take really good care of yourself. If you never learned to meditate, now is the time.

The first words in 'The Purpose-Driven Life' by Rick Warren: It's not about you. When you give God your day, everything works out....

You need to keep a good attitude because that will affect the patient. You see that it is inevitable, so you might as well do the very best you can. Try it! Rise to the occasion.

I wish I had known from the beginning to live my life every day, so there are no regrets. Thankfully, I learned in time to be a fairly successful caretaker.

Sarah, 90, who has been caring for her husband for more than 10 years, described herself as a "very spiritual person," but not a churchgoer. During a nearly three-hour interview, she stressed the importance of daily prayer and meditation. Despite her heart disease and advanced age, she believes she will enjoy a more bountiful future after the caregiving is over. I asked Sarah about any wisdom she could offer other caregivers in their struggle with eldercare.

Wisdom? I don't know. I think you have to have guts in this life, an inner steel quality. I do believe I will have a better life. I believe that I'll be married again someday. I just know. It happens all the time. But then I've always been a cockeyed optimist.

One of the most moving stories of spiritual strength comes from a woman, who asked to remain anonymous, due to the circumstances surrounding her late husband's assisted suicide. She indicated her source of strength derived from two sources. She cited "The Course in Miracles," which entails a meditative group that regularly meets and focuses on a text of Jesus' wisdom for our own time, as well as her loving and principled mother-in-law.

My husband and I were already into 'The Course of Miracles,' when my son committed suicide. The bedrock for me was 'The Course of Miracles,' which definitely got me through that experience. So, I had an idea of the bigger picture. I had done a lot of reading about past lives—people that die and come back. But I was never involved in church.

I've had two suicide events in my life, first my son and then my husband [who chose assisted suicide]. I couldn't even talk about my husband's suicide because I might implicate the doctor and myself in a criminal act.

Some years back, when Jerry was diagnosed with lung cancer and emphysema, he said to the doctor. 'I want to get out of here.' The doctor said, 'I'll give it some thought and I'll let you know.' Three months later, the doctor gave him the pills. But it wasn't until three to four years later that he actually decided to use them. He smoked to the end. When the doctor told him to stop, he said, 'The smoking is keeping me alive.' His smoking really bothered me.

About two months before he died, I completely lost my voice, I could not talk. This was October or November. I went to my doctor, who referred me to a neurologist. I was diagnosed with myasthenia gravis, they did an MRI, and found an enlarged tumor on my thymus. He said, 'You have a tumor, but there's a 100 percent chance of recovery.' But it took my body a year to recover. I was fragile for about a year.

So, I had the surgery right away in Seattle, right around Christmas. I came back a day or two after that, and Jerry came down with a cold, and the cold went into his lungs. This was his second lung infection, and Jerry recognized that he would no longer be able to take care of himself. He looked at me and said, 'I can't do this anymore.'

That was it. I said I would help him, but I didn't expect to give him the pills. But Jerry said he was too weak to do it by himself. I felt so fearful. There's so much emotion involved in suicide. We used Ensure... and dumped the pills into that. He went in two to three minutes—really fast. I called the doctor as soon as he died, and he called 911. They sent two cops [to investigate a home death].

I asked what happened next.

We didn't want doctors and nurses to get involved, and if the cops had been suspicious, they would have called the coroner. Luckily, they said that because my husband had been under a doctor's care, they would not call in the coroner. Besides, Jerry had been sick a long time. He was a tall man, but he had gotten quite skinny. He looked very sick.

As I reflect on that period, I realize I took care of Jerry, not because we had a strong connection—we did not. We once had a strong connection when we were younger, but not now. I took care of Jerry because I felt that his mother had treated me so well, unlike my mother, who would have nothing to do with us after we married. So I did it [caregiving] *for Jerry's mother.*

Today, five years later, in full health, this woman serves on a number of community boards, has a vibrant social circle and continues her "spiritual journey" with enthusiasm and joy.

Taking the Low Road

Bruce Lipton asserts that the power of beliefs, especially unconscious programming, is so powerful that by the time children reach adolescence, their subconscious minds may be little more than programmed reflexes.[14] Lipton's research concurs with Goleman's work in that self-mastery, using the power of consciousness, can unleash our higher consciousness and problem-solving abilities.[15] As long as the unconscious programming persists, however, (1) the person is captured in the programmed reflexes; and (2) the body and mind shape themselves to the contours of the doctrine.

Among some caregivers, suffering becomes the doctrine that rules their life. Suffering manifests in various ways: the belief that things will never be different; the conviction that they deserve to suffer because of former trespasses; the assurance that suffering is redemptive; and the certainty that God is punishing them and their loved one. And, some simply feel that suffering is the only way to get through an impossible situation. Although this set of beliefs can never set one free, they do contribute to a "grit your teeth and hang on" form of spirituality.

Suffering is deeply inculcated in Western belief systems. At home, children are taught at an early age to silence themselves and endure whatever abuse parents dole out.[16] School offers another oppressive system, a kind of prolonged inmate status where authority prevails, however irrational. Traditional religious education is rarely about discovery of truth, but rather, about paying homage to Truth, a pre-existing set of laws and standards of behavior. Many religions promote the ideology of suffering. Suffering is ingrained deeply into the unconscious as the "right" way to feel. To be the sufferer invites pity and compassion. Consider the legal and public attention to adult victims of childhood abuse by Catholic priests and other institutional agents. Yet, institutional practices rarely change as a result of such humiliating disclosures.

Perhaps, caregivers are especially prone to assimilate the culture of suffering and be bound by its constraints. Caregivers made frequent references to their feelings of pity and "endless sympathy" for the sick elder, a condition that ultimately reinforced a sense of futility. A perception that "there is nothing I can do for this person except suffer with them" reflects a low-road model of mental functioning, doubling the misery. Working with depressed or frail elders, a caregiver may fall into an emotional abyss, saying, in so many words: "Now, I'm as miserable as you are, or maybe even more miserable, because nobody even knows or appreciates the extent of my sacrifice."

Blessed is She has documented the suffering caregivers have experienced in confronting chronic illness and death among their beloved elders. But consider a form of suffering that serves as spiritual armor. Rather than protecting its wearer, it imprisons her inside. Self-blame appears to haunt Kali, as she reflects on her caregiving experiences with her grandmother.

> *I believe it's more important to care for other people. They come before me. I tried everything in my power to make her better. I am Catholic; I believe in heaven. I want everyone to love me unconditionally. I didn't intend to be a caregiver. I'm just a nurturing, caring person. It was emotionally difficult to deal with death, seeing her sick, seeing her on her down days. I had to find distractions to get away from there and I feel like a bad person saying this.*

After years of unresolved conflict over providing care, Kali eventually gave up on any plans she had to be a nursing assistant. She concluded that she had been a *failure,* both as a caregiver and a person.

By contrast, Jean fully intended to serve as her mother's caregiver, but a belief that caregiving is essentially a woman's obligation confounded her sense that she actually made a deliberate choice. Jean could only stammer out her confused beliefs about obligation as a woman's duty.

> *I believe a woman has an obligation to care for others—no—not women as such—but she feels the obligation; men may feel it, too. I think we feel an obligation—not a woman who has the obligation, but me.*

Whether we actually have the freedom to choose in such matters as taking care of an elderly loved one remained an open question for other women, as well. At 65, Wendy took care of her aged mother—who died at 106 years old—for 13 years. Her accepting attitude grew out of "being a Christian." Wendy's testimony emphasized that while the "decision to take care of my mother was forced upon me," she never attempted to do anything differently than to be the sole caregiver for her mother. Besides, she admitted, she does not believe that any significant event in her life was of her own making, but rather God's will.

I'm never in control. You're never in control. Zero control. Whatever happens always has a purpose, which at this moment I don't understand. I never feel in control.

Instead of struggling with control, Wendy determined that caregiving was about

learning an invaluable lesson. I long ago found that the harder something is, the richer the experience.

For Wendy, caregiving has been worth every moment of the struggle.

It's the expansion of the feeling of love and the reality of it—having to show your love. I was very grateful to do something for Mother. She had done so much for me, I was finally able to repay her.

Wendy had a conversion experience in her sixties, and recognized the solace of faith. In response to the question, "What helped you get through the caregiving experience," she replied:

only that the Christian faith helped enormously. It gives you the strength—you can't self-destruct, really.

For a few women, ongoing personal torment plagued their caregiving. These women did not feel redeemed by their suffering. Instead, they experienced a perpetual sense of "feeling bad, like a failure," and blaming themselves for everything. They shared the common thread of "intending" to do good work, yet being "undone" by their efforts. They felt "there was no way out." Transcending suffering requires a shift out of what Goleman refers to as "instinctive compassion," which keeps the brain on automatic response, to the higher level of awareness, which allows self-informed decision-making.[17]

Overcoming Suffering

Although Christianity offers the image of the resurrected Christ, much "popular pietism" remains fixated on suffering as a way of life.[18] This doctrine can be summed up in a few words: Suffering for our sins entails *the* essential path to redemption, since original sin haunts human beings from birth. Among followers of Mary, the Mother of God, penitents are encouraged to pray to "Our Lady of Perpetual Sorrows" when overcome by grief or despair. Michaelangelo's "Pieta," depicts the ever-suffering mother for her crucified son, an image etched into traditional Christian beliefs.

More contemporary Christian versions emphasize the significance of moving through feelings of sorrow, anguish, abandonment and, worse, separation from love itself. [19] Paul Fiorini, a parish theologian, offered guidance about a four-step movement into wholeness, which offers the sufferer renewed hope:

1. Acknowledge suffering without glorifying it;
2. Trust in God through conversations with Him, including lamenting our loss (much like Job);
3. Act by reaching out to others, following the life and ministry of Jesus by working with individuals and communities to overcome and end suffering; and
4. Stand in awe to search for meaning and reasons for our suffering.

This new theology calls attention to the reality that God does not desire suffering, but works with love to overcome it.[20]

Contemporary Christian Theology

Postmodern theologizing, a nonsectarian approach, has rejected such gloomy outcomes as "perpetual suffering" for the human condition, and a few theologians have paid the price for turning suffering on its head. Matthew Fox, a maverick Catholic priest, was excommunicated when he discarded the concept of original sin—as well as other negative versions of Catholicism—and replaced it with an upbeat version he called "Original Blessings."[21]

Buddhism

Contemporary versions of Buddhism offer practical, rather than religious-centered options for grasping our existential unease. Buddha taught awakening by cultivating integrity, meditative stillness and penetrating inquiry. Stephen Batchelor, author of *Four Noble Truths* writes of his own experience that led him to seek Buddha's "middle way."

> At times, I feel hemmed in, inwardly subjected to the vagaries of a fragile body and fickle mind, outwardly overwhelmed by the demands of a suffering world.[22]

To confront the "conflict that seems knit into the very fabric of existence," Batchelor turned to Buddhist doctrines, which are wholly compatible with Christianity's new theology. Principles in Batchelor's book include: **suffering** is an inevitable and never-to-be denied part of human existence. The **origins of suffering** must be understood fully. The **cessation of suffering** banishes the falsehood that the condition is permanent and necessary. Finally, the **path that leads to the cessation of suffering** entails finding solutions for releasing its grip.

The fourth *Noble Truth* may be the most pertinent for caregivers, who have found themselves caught in what Batchelor refers to as "the existential grip... that solidifies our experience in such a way that everything, including ourself, appears inert, opaque and lifeless."[23]

Caregivers' Stories of Overcoming Suffering

The following excerpts are from caregivers who transcended their suffering and moved into a sense of peace and wholeness. Faith's experience, like so many of these caregivers, was embedded in expectations of giving care to others. Faith's story, introduced earlier, offers a more extreme case of an imposed caregiving role, but, as she emphasized, she came to accept her oppressive situation because she learned many valuable lessons in the process.

In her most recent incarnation as a caregiver, Faith devoted herself to her mother, who had Parkinson's disease. Prior to this commitment, Faith had an extended family history of being the "designated caregiver," beginning in childhood.

The practice that made a significant difference for Faith was her commitment to self-reflection. In her early mastery of confronting illness and death as part of life, she could let go of suffering and gratefully follow her inner calling.

> *What supported me was my own self-introspection. I'd been sent away as a child to be cared for, so caregiving was a given role. I really feel a sense of connectedness with all others, a complete sense of democracy; no one is more privileged than the other. It's the rhythm of human life and I have a sense of personal responsibility as an intelligent and responsible woman. This was a healing experience for me: caregiving has a cycle and a clear completion. I can go back to the times of great trauma and remember [them] with peace.*

Another caregiver, Martha, grew up as a Quaker and now pursues a Buddhist path in striving for an open heart. It has permitted her to lead a normal life while caring for her husband on a full-time basis.

> *I swim and paint, attend the Alzheimer's support group and practice yoga and meditate every day. I'd go to church regularly, but I'd have to get respite care for my husband. I'm very careful about my health and I love to walk. I eased into his diagnosis of Alzheimer's, taking one day at a time and learning to appreciate his new language—all his own. We've been married fifty years for better or worse. I look at rough times like the weather—it will pass.*

Martha's way of dealing with the vagaries of human existence is to take everything in stride.

> *Ogden Nash said: 'Which is worse, to have everything going well and know it will get worse or everything going terribly but know it's getting better?' It's the way you feel about it that's the key; there are no magic solutions.*

Gloria monitored her husband's dosage of 15 to 17 prescriptions for heart disease. She needed five different medications for her chronic back pain, much of it related to the strain of caregiving. After ten years of providing care for her parents and then a nephew, she wholeheartedly left work and accepted full-time care of her husband, now going on for five years. Gloria has a gentle peacefulness and new awareness about her situation.

> *It's my whole life and I wouldn't have it any other way. I'm on a new path as a caregiver, with a new awareness of a new experience. There is some ambivalence. I wish it weren't happening, but I know I am becoming a much more patient person. I don't go to church. Rather, I express my spirituality in my beliefs and lifestyle—being kind, supportive of charities, enjoying the world and nature. I try to make the world as good a place as I can.*

Nora literally looked into the face of suffering every day and night as she cared for her 87-year-old sister, who suffered from peripheral neuropathy, a rare nerve disorder that is characterized by chronic and unrelenting pain. Nora tried every resource possible to ease her sister's pain without success. In desperation to provide comfort, Nora finally knelt on the floor beside her sister's bed. She soaked her sister's feet first in hot water, then shifted to cold, after which she massaged them with ointments. Now, her sister, ready at last for bed, hopefully could sleep. Nora admitted the circumstances were often beyond her ministrations, but recognized the significance of her efforts.

> *It was all-consuming and sometimes I couldn't help her at all. Pain pills didn't work, nothing worked. I'd never been so close to someone suffering from pain. I loved my sister, she was my favorite. I just put my intention on the positive; that's how you get positive results. I tried to be more responsible with my actions and follow through on projects. This experience was necessary for my own growth and understanding. Without it, I would have less compassion for others ill or dying. I believe you create your own thoughts and it's important not to let yourself be pulled down into negative thinking.*

Caregivers also reported that they could not surmount the daily tribulations of caregiving—with its vigilance, tight organization of time and activities and the sense that their life was held in suspension—until their loved one died.

As I dealt with my husband's slow, agonizing dying process that lasted for over a year, my personal concern was that I could not bring death into any dialogue with Jim. It seemed as though he carried an invisible, but powerful shield with the words emblazoned, "see no evil, hear no evil, speak no evil," which blocked communication every time I broached the subject of his finality with him.

He seemed to want no part in preparing himself and the family for his demise. I felt so alone in all this. But I believed that everyone should be prepared. Then, I decided to take my own crash course in death and dying, and found a remarkable collection of books and articles that really helped me prepare myself, and hopefully, the family, for his passing.

When the nursing home staff called one morning with the news that Jim had slipped into a coma, I contacted four of my six children who lived nearby, to meet me at the facility. I also contacted our parish priest.

I felt so reassured when Father Frank walked in. My daughters seemed traumatized by their dad's condition. Clearly, Jim was dying. Once my son, Tim, walked into the room with his three children, the priest began administering the sacrament, and then it seemed, everything changed. The tension went out of the room. The room seemed full of light. Jim's labored breathing eased, and we all had the same experience—it was so palpable. Jim had finally let go and was at peace. That was a defining moment for me, because I could finally surrender, and be in harmony with what was happening.

Jim died later that night, as the clock struck midnight.

Taking my caregiving as a whole, I felt I had so much to master. It was like a whole new world. Increasingly, I felt more mastery in my faith, as well. Once I shifted my academic interests to aging, I began writing articles, giving lectures. I felt happy I could transfer my worries and concerns into something positive. I felt a new sense of pride that I could transcend my fears of inadequacy. I overcame the smells of the sickroom, my husband's depression, his dying (but it haunted me for days, weeks, even months).

Today, after Jim's death? I'm a more enlightened person, a writer and researcher of the caregiving experience. I'm far more creative; I'm a friend and partner-centered person, a person who makes strong distinctions among family members, recognizing their capacities and limitations. I am a sociologist, a compassionate person, a spiritual person, an adventuresome person. I feel I have an opportunity to live a full life. I would say I have had a complete renewal.

Reflections

Affirmations come in a variety of forms. The value of positive thinking and continuing one's involvements with family, friends and community served to maintain balance and energy for many caregivers. Religious faith, whether traditional or non-traditional, sustained some caregivers through difficult times. The gift of faith was at the center of many of these women's lives—faith that they were doing the right thing for their loved one; faith that they could stand up to the situation, regardless of how challenging; faith that a positive or healing attitude was essential for their own survival; and faith among some caregivers that suffering was neither permanent nor disabling. Instead, suffering entailed significant meaning for their lives. Above all, they had a belief that suffering could be overcome, given time, patience and trust.

Two important questions arise: Why do some of these women respond to tragedy—terminal illness, infirmity and death—with equanimity, acceptance and even greater strength, while others live in denial or psychological collapse? And, how can caregivers release the "cold, implacable constriction" of suffering to come out the other side with compassion, selfhood and a keen sense of being alive?

Emotional reactions of sorrow, fear, resentment, resistance and anger surround the caregiving act and lend credence to the reality that caring deeply for another puts a person in jeopardy. The loved one's agony becomes your agony; their losses your losses; their pain your pain; their dying your dying, in an endless spiral of negativity. For caregivers, the question is: How to penetrate the closed circle of suffering and break loose into love and acceptance? Certain of these caregivers seemed unable to succeed at releasing themselves from their bonds of perpetual sorrow. Their lives appeared out of control, their relationships unraveling, their daily activities merely repetitive and onerous.

Despite spiritual solace and social support, no "magical solutions" emerged that could extinguish the ache of a loved one's descent into invalidism and death. Some managed to overcome their negative feelings through belief systems, which allowed them to rise above the pain and turmoil associated with the chronic illness and dying process of their loved ones. The path to acceptance entailed other adaptations, as well:

- Perceiving the caregiving experience as a spiritual challenge;
- Believing that caregiving provides an opportunity for personal healing or finding a new path;
- Forming a commitment forged in love; and
- Finding release by acceptance.

These and other approaches enabled caregivers to transcend their suffering, and bring hope, love and peace into their lives.

PART III

THE HEALING PROCESS

Chapter 11

Wisdom of the Heart[1]

The awakened heart is like a luminous sphere—just giving without Thought to any who may come close or gaze at it.
The soul becomes blessedly lost to all but its own holy Being.
    ~ Matthew Fox, *Meditations with Meister Eckhart*[2]

How you respond to tragedy and suffering is one true mea-sure of your strength. You need to see those moments as moments of growth. You need to look upon them as gifts to help you reclaim what is important in your life.
                ~ Kent Nerburn, *Simple Truths*[3]

Discarding Old Versions of Caregiving

With long-term care in the wings for 78 million baby boomers who have passed 60 years of age, and with more millions entering their sixties and seventies over the next few decades, old versions of "care" must and will be abandoned. Our caregivers' narratives clearly spelled out the virtual impossibility of maintaining our current failed system: a frail or dying elderly person must be cared for over many years, often by only one fam-ily member. But first we will need to drastically alter the meaning and delivery of *care.*

Traditional renderings of *care* point to a double-edged meaning. On the one hand, *care* refers to a charge or protection for something or some-one. It involves paying attention to or heeding, to feel concern about, to look after, watch over, attend to. Such meanings capture one significant set of understandings.

But *care* has an underside connotation, as well, for it also points to a weighing down of the mind; a troubled or burdened state of mind—even a mind filled with dread. Certainly, worry, anxiety and dread depict many caregivers' experiences with providing care to their elderly loved one. In fact, it is not an exaggeration to say that most caregivers I spoke with had a careworn manner. They were chronically worried, drained, stressed out and dispirited, tending to count their losses, rarely their gains.

To transform older, outworn versions of *care* into a revitalized version of concern and looking after, let's slightly alter the *care* word into a closely related word, but one that is wholly distinctive—*caring*. Actually, *caring* is what most caregivers seek to achieve, and to do so with an awakened heart. A caring person is kindhearted, tender, concerned, thoughtful, attentive, considerate, altruistic and sympathetic. At its core, *caring* means to be affectionate, loving, understanding and compassionate.

This heartfelt giving of oneself in *caring* is wholly different from the outworn version of *care* with its auxiliary qualities of worry and strain. So, how will this caring approach affect care for the elderly? At the outset, we know that the very basis of elder care must be giving help and assistance, support and concern, thoughtfulness and solicitude. To add *caring* to this mix involves a transformation of the caregiving act. Caregiving now becomes a *gift*, a moral act that invokes a higher level of consciousness than merely "helping" or assisting a dependent older person. As far as scientists can tell us, we are the only known species in which the younger generation cares for the older one. We are thus in the unique position of creating a highly evolved human endeavor. Yet, humans have known about this care legacy from the dawn of civilization.

The Circle of Life

Centuries ago, Christian mystic Meister Eckhart (1260-1328), touched upon what we now see as a crucial feature of elder care—the frequent awareness for caregivers to reach beyond the daily routine to work with an "awakened heart" and "giving without thought," either for our own loved ones, or for those frail elders we meet along the way. This is best conceptualized as an endless round of giving and receiving life's lessons and gifts with others.[4]

So, what do we owe our aging loved ones? This essential question emerges before we surrender ourselves to caregiving as a heartfelt journey. Certainly, at the minimum, we have an obligation to extend respect, empathy, compassion and love. From ancient times, younger generations

were admonished to look after their declining elders. Confucius emphasized that young people must go beyond mere physical care for their
elders:

> *Filial piety today is taken to mean providing nourishment for parents,*
> *but dogs and horses are provided with nourishment. If it is not done*
> *with reverence for parents, what is the difference between men and*
> *animals?*[5]

In many ancient and even contemporary societies, people honor the
circle of life as sacrosanct. Today, a growing desire for ethnic or tribal
identity among Native Americans, for example, has led to a conscious
restoration of ancient traditions, including enhanced status for elders.[6]

Modernization has wreaked havoc with the delicate balance between
generations. The soul virtues of compassion, kindness and tenderness
have been nearly buried by the avalanche of medical technology and the
expanded role of the physician in determining matters of life and death.
"Reclaiming soul" in elder care requires that ordinary people move forward to support their elders during their time of need. In *Blessed is She*,
we have been describing women who took on this responsibility, and
made a protracted commitment to care. As we discussed previously, no
substitutes exist for family, because even in nursing homes, families must
act with diligence and awareness to ensure that the loved one is receiving competent and professional care. Unlike the task-and time-oriented
activities of institutional workers, whose orientation is biomedical and
disease-centered, family members and friends emphasize *personhood,*
and are thus engaged in a *moral enterprise.*

The Moral Practice of Caregiving

When Carol Gilligan published *In a Different Voice* in 1982, she identified
a "distinct moral voice" in the reflections of the women she interviewed
for her research.[7] Gilligan referred to this as the "voice of care"—focusing on compassion and concern. She contrasted this moral voice with
the "voice of justice"—focusing on rights and responsibilities. Her influence on moral development and ethical theory has reached deeply into
psychology and philosophy, as well as having direct implications for the
caregiving role.

Gilligan's "voice of care" discusses the emotional knowledge and imaginative power necessary for entering into the feelings and perspectives of others without taking possession of another's suffering or exploiting this vulnerability to serve one's own psychological or material ends.[8] The caregiver is warned, wisely, not to over-identify with the other or collapse into vicariously experiencing the other's pain. This requires a firm sense of one's own boundaries—clearly, a precondition for the sound caring for others. An ethic of caring has the capacity to transform the caregiver/care receiver relationship from a burdensome duty (the ethic of justice) to a spiritual expression (ethic of caring). What is the one ingredient for lightening the journey toward a pain-free, even emotionally satisfying, caregiving experience? Psychologists tell us it is happiness. Can being happy square with a moral obligation, or are these two entities—morality and happiness—incompatible? Let's find out.

What About Happiness?

But first, what about happiness? Happiness is hardly a simple proposition. The "just be happy" song can make us feel like cringing if everyday emotional reality feels like overwork, misery and pain. Offering nuggets of wisdom, authors Jack Jonathan and Sheelagh G. Manheim propose in their book, *Find More Meaning In Your Life,* that "authentic happiness" requires a strong and good character.[9] The ability to control our moods helps us to develop self-confidence and resilience in the face of difficulties. Lasting happiness is really a habit we build by cultivating our character. People who practice gratitude, altruism, humility, humor and other positive traits develop inner resources and strengths that help us to develop emotional well-being. According to Harvard psychologist Daniel Gilbert, a good life is one that is "meaningful with long-term commitments and projects."[10]

Could happiness be more complicated than simply developing a positive and compassionate character? In fact, Gilbert recommends we think of happiness as three distinct types. The first is what we normally refer to as "being happy," and this is *emotional happiness,* a psychological state, with which caregivers have an especially difficult time. Next is *moral happiness*—many caregivers have an abundant amount of this happiness, because it is action-based on virtue, or "doing the right thing."

And, finally *judgmental happiness*—most caregivers have a plentitude of this happiness as well, as it entails the conscious ethical decision to serve another.[11] The ancient Greeks believed that if one lived life in a proper, moral, meaningful, deep and rich way—in virtuous performance of duties—that person would experience happiness. In other words, we can be happy *about* things, even when *feeling* distraught.

But what if we do not *feel* happy? Then, it appears that no matter how virtuous we are or how total our commitment to serve others, we continue to feel like a failure. In this emotional state, we experience the now-common litany of negative thoughts and emotions, as well as harmful physical symptoms that accompany stress caused by the incessant pressures of caregiving. Spiritual literature suggests three approaches for dramatically raising our emotional happiness quotient from one to ten:

- First, confront and deal with your suffering;
- Second, rethink the situation; and
- Third, practice a kind of wise attention to your body, mind and emotions, a process covered in the final chapter.

Now, let us explore these approaches for overcoming suffering.

Confronting Suffering

Webster's dictionary defines suffering in this way: to feel or endure pain, to bear loss, damage or injury. According to this description, it seems obvious that the person we are caring for is sick and suffering because he or she is experiencing pain. That kind of suffering is easy to understand. But, as caregivers, are we suffering, too? Perhaps our childhood socialization shaped our early memory of what suffering meant. Anne, the co-author of this chapter, said:

> I was brought up in the Catholic Church, with a belief system taught by the priests and the Presentation nuns that suffering was virtuous. When I was eight years old, Grandpa White built a grotto to The Blessed Virgin Mary in a St. Cloud, Minnesota neighborhood garden. The six-foot walls enclosing the statue of Mary were made of carefully placed river rock; the shrine floor was a mosaic of small stones, the edges of every stone purposefully exposed.

Grandma and Grandpa met their friends in the grotto every summer night to pray the rosary to The Blessed Virgin Mary while they knelt on the stone floor and suffered. When I complained about the stones hurting my knees, my Grandpa said, 'Yes, that's a good thing. Think about people who are worse off and offer up your pain for the poor souls suffering in purgatory.'

Today, we understand that pain may not be entirely physical. Instead, as our caregivers told us, their suffering entailed a more complicated set of issues, such as anger, frustration, stress, lack of power or loss of control over a person, situation or illness. Their misery caused them to berate themselves or lash out at others. But as long as the image of suffering confines us to negative thinking, it fractures our intentions to achieve real compassion, and becomes a detriment to a fully compassionate life. As we've seen, the caregiver's suffering is represented in myriad ways. Our first challenge as caregivers is to discover what our own brand of suffering is and how it prevents wholeness and compassion. If we can trust in the mystery of recognizing our own suffering, we may come to realize that the source may be in old conditioning patterns.

"Dread lists"—a second form of suffering—involve catastrophic images we carry in our head that we pull out and dwell on. Caregivers often focus on their worst fears: What if she falls and breaks her hip when I'm not home? Or, what if I have an excruciating migraine and can't take care of him? What if I can't get to the store to pick up her prescription, because my car is old and might break down? Ram Dass calls this fear list the "top ten hits of woeses."[12] The way out is to become sensitive to which negative conditions we are paying attention to, and take additional time to reflect on each condition and allow it to enter our consciousness more deeply. The first step, Ram Dass explains, is to notice and accept the suffering.

Once I had done that, I began to investigate my thoughts and feelings surrounding the condition, and to discover whether the fear could be transformed by shifting my perspective.[13]

The next step is to sink into every aspect of the moment, and embrace the images and feelings of each worrisome condition. Then, Ram Dass advises us to shift our perspective: try thinking of a neighbor you know who is having a similar problem. Think about a family member or friend; the people in your city, state, country; think of all the people around the world and the immense number who suffer. Their suffering may be as great or even greater than your own, and they may have far fewer choices or resources than you have been blessed with. The message is not to identify with suffering and consider it virtuous. Rather, our task is to accept each moment as it arises, and through conscious spiritual practice, welcome whatever comes our way. The ability to live gracefully is our reward.

Retooling Our Thinking

If we, as caretakers, are to exercise imaginative or creative powers of the heart when we attempt to understand the feelings and perspectives of others, we need a fresh approach: let's remind ourselves that we are shifting our behavior, our responses and our reactions. From a caregiver's experience, reactions today will look very different from those of five years ago. For example, when our mother was more able to complete tasks—or for another caregiver—a husband was able to travel.

Anne explains how this works first for her and then her husband.

Today, as I try to develop the skill of creative caregiver, I have to ignore the temptation of previous expectations and respect the evolving illness and the autonomy of the person standing in front of me at this moment.

As Parkinson's disease progresses with Mike, I realize that I take a new tally every day, paying attention to remaining abilities, dwindling skills and changing stress responses. My goal, not always achieved, is to respond with respect to those changes and make it very clear that he has complete ownership of his surviving abilities.

Now, I need to listen to him in a whole different way.

Here is what Mike says:

I can't fit into conversation anymore. No one can understand me and my voice is so soft. I can't seem to hold my own, can't talk fast enough to keep anyone's attention, and it takes too long to put a sentence together.

I can see why some people just don't make the effort to go anywhere, anymore. It's just easier to stay home.

So, I asked, what is the best way to deal with this situation?

Mike answered:

Do not. Do not manipulate or control situations thinking that you're doing me a favor. Don't make excuses for me. I would like the opportunity to make my own choices as long as possible, to explain to people the best way I can, or to ignore them. For example, if the children run to get me, 'Grandpa come and climb in the rock pile with us.' I would like to say for myself, 'I can't play in the rock pile, because I don't have the ability to stand up or balance and I would probably fall.'

Retooling our response systems can help in situations like the one Anne experienced. The strategy is simple and begins with the following understanding. If the care burden is too heavy, it may not be mine. Then, whose problem is it? And how do I extricate myself? The issue may have to do with childhood beliefs or "tapes."

Childhood tapes are memories and beliefs that have been buried in the unconscious, beliefs that as children, we had no control over. As adults, though, we have the power to change them. Retooling these childhood tapes refers to a direct mode of shifting, not only the outmoded perspective, view or belief, but also the actual physical burdens we carry as caregivers. It requires confronting their contents and allowing the images and emotions of the outworn conditioning patterns to arise. After, all, we must acknowledge these patterns before we can change them.

Here's an extended example we have created to illustrate the situation of how we can retool childhood tapes, and show their potential for empowering the caregiver. Mary Pat's story is a hypothetical one, but it expresses some typical experiences among our caregivers, who had damaged relationships with their mothers.

Mary Pat was brought up by her demanding, critical and fault-finding mother. Her adolescent years were emotionally cold and chaotic. Because she lacked love and emotional support as a child, Mary Pat never really established a successful bond or any tenderness with her mother. When her aging mother became ill with heart failure, Mary Pat, at age 58, was the only relative available to take care of her. She moved her mother into her two-bedroom cottage, and even though her mother was still capable of some physical activity and self-care, Mary Pat began waiting on her—as she had since childhood. Only now it had became a heavier burden beyond her strength and capacity.

Eventually, her mother did less and less for herself, and disapproved of everything her daughter did to make her comfortable.

> *Mary Pat, get my soup! The soup's too hot. I don't like this dinner you prepared. I want to go for a walk right now! Why do you live in such a cold climate?*

Mary Pat became impatient. She was physically and psychologically overwhelmed, as well as sick and tired of her mother's demands. Every day as she heard the old childhood "tapes," her anger flared, and she feared there was no end to the situation.

The retooling exercise below demonstrates that even at this late stage of her mother's life, Mary Pat can still establish new healthy boundaries and change responses to her mother's old ways of behaving. Notice the strategy here. The mother complains, and the daughter takes it in stride with empathy, and makes alternative recommendations. The mother has the final choice in what action she will take.

Mother: *The soup's too hot!*

Mary Pat: *Oh, I'm so sorry. Feel free to let it cool before you eat it.*

Mother: *But this whole dinner is terrible! I can't eat a bite of it.*

Mary Pat: *(with empathy) That's too bad. Maybe breakfast tomorrow will taste better to you.*

Mother: *I want to go for a walk now! You have to help me. It's freezing cold out there.*

Mary Pat: *I'd be happy to help you get ready as soon as I finish folding the laundry. Or you could help fold the laundry. Or would you rather get yourself ready for your walk?*

Mother: *I'll just go without my coat.*

Mary Pat: *Oh yikes, how do you think that will turn out?*

Mother: *Well, I suppose I'll get cold and probably catch pneumonia.*

Mary Pat: *(using an empathetic tone) That would be very sad and uncomfortable for you.*

Mother: *Well, you'd better help me then. You are my daughter.*

Mary Pat: *No problem, as soon as I finish folding the laundry.*

In this process, Mary Pat empowers her mother, as well as herself, respects her mother's choices and, above all, her mother's autonomy. At the same time, Mary Pat transfers appropriate control by transferring the responsibility.

Some of our caregivers reported confronting the difficult decisions of money management and automobile driving responsibilities. These are serious issues because they can involve the safety and well-being of many people. In Anne's case, trying new strategies to empower Mike, she asked him recently how he would view giving up driving or turning over the balancing of his checkbook. Mike replied:

> *Sometimes it's easier to let someone finish a job for me, particularly if they're impatient. I have to fumble around for a while before I complete a task, but if there's no reason to rush, I prefer to finish it myself. Once you lose your ability to manage money or drive, you lose self-respect and a certain amount of purpose and understanding of yourself. You lose touch with your own balance sheet of life.*

Mike, who had recently returned from the Northwest Governor's Conference on Parkinson's disease, has learned how to communicate his fears and needs.

Anne further pursued the issue of driving.

> *How are you able to ask me to drive sometimes, when I know how important that is to you?*

Mike answered:

> *There are times, when my medications are wearing off, that I feel we would both be more comfortable, less stressed, with you driving. I trust that you will tell me when you are not comfortable and then I'm done. But until then, I still have a choice. This really is about self-determination, isn't it? If I tell you I'm worried about something, like driving or short-term memory loss, I'm really asking for feedback and I trust you will give it honestly, but I'm not asking for help. There's a big difference.*

Anne shares another recent experience she had with Mike, when they were invited to a reading by graduate students in the English department at the local university.

As usual, Mike took his Sinimet an hour before dinner that night, giving his body at least four hours of maneuverability so he could enjoy the evening. All went well, except that the program started half an hour later than we thought; we had some anxiety finding a parking spot. And, there were more readers than we had anticipated.

By the time the last reader finished, Mike was barely able to get up from his chair. But he did. Very haltingly, with the aid of an arm and his cane, he managed to navigate the crowd and safely descend the 20 steps to the ground floor, knowing that each step brought him closer to his goal, our vehicle, which would return him to the safety of home and his bed. His medication was wearing off and within minutes he would have serious difficulty walking.

As he contemplated the pouring rain outside the building, another 12 steps to the street, and the location of our car a block away he said, 'We've got to hurry... before I... I can't...

I couldn't understand him. I asked, 'Say it again?'

'Hurry, before I...'

'Ahh,' I said, 'Before you turn into a pumpkin?'

And he laughed, 'Yes that's it. Exactly.' No, I thought, it's the coach that turns into a pumpkin not Cinderella herself. I had a vision of Mike turning into a pumpkin as his meds wore off, literally losing his legs.

'Then,' he said, 'you'll have to roll me across the street.'

The following Wednesday, one day before Valentine's at 7:30 a.m., I carried my tea into the den and was greeted by a huge bouquet of red and white alstromeria. Mike was still sleeping but on the table beside the flowers was an envelope with my name on it. I opened the envelope and read the valentine:

'Will you be my Valentine and accompany me to dinner tonight at The Oyster Bar? I have a reservation for 6 p.m. so we can enjoy the evening, before I turn into a pumpkin.'

He must have set this stage in the middle of the night, because he can't sleep. He must have thought today was Valentine's Day. And so it will be.

The beauty of this story is that in spite of progressing Parkinson's, in spite of increasing forgetfulness, we shared a joke and it was clear to me that we are still a team. Hang on to humor; capitalize on it for as long as possible.

These exercises emphasize choices for the care receiver. The caregiver can provide as many choices as the individual seems to be capable of handling. In cases where the frail elder is not willing or able to make choices, obviously, another approach must be taken. We recommend the *harm criterion* for determining an elder's ability for such matters as driving and money management. If the loved one's behavior leads to harmful outcomes, the caregiver may have to change her thinking once again. Consider our fictional characters, Walter and Mae.

Walter, who suffered from Alzheimer's, liked to help. He took pride in his contribution in the kitchen and his wife, Mae, wanted to allow him as much latitude as possible. Mae noticed that Walter especially enjoyed and was comforted by the feeling of warm soapy water as he washed a few select pots and pans after dinner. Then Mae swooped in to load the dishwasher, add the detergent, close the door and start the wash cycle. Because the water calmed Walter, Mae was reluctant to curtail his dishwashing endeavors.

Increasingly, though, Walter played on the job, splashing bubbles in the air, blowing them into the windows, pouring soapy water back and forth from small pans to larger pans, then reversing the order with more and more water missing his target pan.

For quite a while, Mae seamlessly, wordlessly rescued Walter's efforts with deft mopping skills and piles of bath towels. But soon, Mae realized the water on the kitchen floor was rising to dangerous and damaging levels. Pretty soon, she imagined that to save Walter's dignity, they would have to wear wet suits and rubber waders to finish the dishes.

Gradually the water seeped through, separating the joints of the wood floor, eventually dribbling down into the basement, through the sheetrock near an electrical ceiling outlet. Ooops! Now, what to do?

Mae could not imagine Walter not playing in the water after dinner, as that routine was one he expected and enjoyed. It was a dependable, peaceful time in the evening when she could relax knowing he was content before the nightly task of getting him ready for bed. Mae also realized that the important elements for Walter were the warmth of the water, the enjoyment of the bubbles and accomplishing something useful. She had to retool her gracious intentions, swiftly, firmly but with sincere respect.

> *'Oh, Walter you do so well washing things. After dinner, would you consider helping me wash out the muddy socks in the laundry tub? That would be such a big help to me.'*

Using this shift of duties, Walter is asked to *consider* the option, although Mae must insist on the water activity being relocated to a deeper tub, on a tiled, impervious floor. The word "consider" takes away any threat to Walter's remaining autonomy and incorporates all the pleasant features of his former contribution. At the same time, Mae is exercising her retooling muscle and gaining confidence in her creative ability to shift her former caretaking routine to something safer and more manageable.

Rule of thumb: Be ready to allow for your own mistakes and be kind to yourself when you need to reassess a situation that resulted in negative outcomes.

A number of caregivers in this study made such shifts in the process of their care work. Instead of imposing rules, they allowed their sick elder to act with self-determination. Rather than "caregiver knows best," they practiced compassion to understand the feelings of the other. And, in place of complaining about their situation, they learned to conduct themselves as they would choose the other to treat them, were their roles reversed. Finally, they came to recognize the significance of their own contribution, and accepted caregiving as a spiritual, life-sustaining practice. To facilitate this shift, we now turn to the third approach to raising the happiness quotient: the practice of *mindfulness*. This offers an innovative set of teachings for improving mind power and emotional balance. The mindfulness approach will be explored in greater detail in Chapter 12. For now, let's consider some practical steps.

Checklist for Caregivers

Below is a check list of recommendations for allowing your loved one the optimum independence within the limits of his or her capacity. This requires three shifts in our thinking:

1. A shift from the sense that caregiving entails mainly isolated duties and responsibilities to adopting the care receiver's perspective about the amount and kind of help. This allows for the emergence of the loved one's capabilities and opportunities within his or her level of ability.

2. A shift from a single-minded focus on the care receiver's needs and requirements, toward juggling the multiple demands of a caregiver's life; and

3. A shift from **doing** good works to **being** a fully realized person, who acknowledges her own inner light and inner truths.

With practice, these essential shifts enhance the relationship between caregiver and care receiver. To allow your loved one optimum independence, you might consider the following:

- Respect the autonomy of the care receiver. Avoid invasive or exploitative tactics that impose the will of the caregiver, physician or other intervention specialist on the ill person. The elder needs support to maintain self-ownership and self-determination. The caregiver is in the best position to run interference for her vulnerable loved one, especially when dealing with medical or institutional personnel.

- Try to develop habits of sensitivity, moral discernment and response. The ethic of care entails not only recognizing the others' rights to non-interference, but also requires us to actively promote the welfare of the dependent, vulnerable elder. In many instances, his or her condition may *not* include the capacity for decision-making and moral judgments. Sensitivity and moral discernment, in turn, clarify the practice of caring as one in which *emotional connection*, not grim duty, is the grounding for sacrifice.

- Learn to recognize that it is not only *what* we do that plays a significant role for enhancing autonomy. It's also *how* we do what we do that makes a moral difference in giving care. Expressing the right emotions at the right time and the right place involves a keen self-awareness. Remember, we communicate by gesture, tone of voice, listening, demeanor and facial expressions.

- Focus your attention on *healing*, rather than *curing*; on patient integrity, not on forcing the care receiver to endure the latest surgical procedure or drug; on *comfort care*, not *heroic measures*.

- Remain ever-mindful of our attitudes and emotions, and how these are communicated to our loved one. This is, perhaps, the most difficult aspect of all for overwrought caregivers. By overriding our own negative emotions through empathy and compassion for ourselves, we can enter into the often subtle and hidden emotions of the person we are caring for. By tuning into our own indignation, grief, joy, anguish, fear, humiliation, hope and despair, we can become attuned to the feelings of our loved one.

- Cultivate an active concern for the good of others and develop an openness of heart. This approach allows a sympathetic and engaged mind for attending to the ways others experience their situations. Caring is not a medical procedure, but an extension of our capacity for love, forgiveness and generosity.

The goal for caregivers is to truly empathize with their sick elder. Approaching a seriously ill, usually vulnerable, even cantankerous, and sometimes dying loved one from the care receiver's perspective profoundly shifts the energy from self-absorption to loving concern for the other. With our hearts open, we may hand over the responsibility to our loved one that we once believed we alone could carry. This enables caregivers at all stages of the illness process to work on behalf of her loved one, but not attempt to *be* that dependent or dying person.

Caregiving as Priceless Opportunity

Finally, the awakened heart transforms the nature of caregiving from *duty* to *opportunity* as we now serve from our place of strength, abundance and wholeness. What, precisely, are the opportunities that await the elder caregiver? In addition to transforming the nature of caregiving, other benefits are in store for those willing to serve with open and awakened hearts.

First, caregiving offers an opportunity for reinvigorating the family and continuing the circle of life. This provides a unique chance to rebuild family relationships and heal old wounds. When family members come together in a crisis, bonds can be restored, or built among families with varying degrees of family dynamics—from well-integrated to troubled to even those with shattered relationships. As we develop our much-needed family support, we lighten our own load, and create connections among family members. Ideally, such support networks should be firmly in place at early stages of family building, perhaps in early childhood, as parents and family allies strengthen connections with grandparents and other elders. Generational conflicts, a product of modernization, can be eradicated when both younger and older generations recognize that their own extended family is but a microcosm of the larger human family.

The second opportunity for caregivers entails strengthening individual and family bonds with the community. When we reach out into the community for support, we forge common values and enduring friendships. As people come to recognize the inevitability of their own aging and vulnerability to decline, individuals and organizations are more likely to be persuaded to aid and nurture the sick and dying.

A third possibility for caregivers who form solid connections in the community involves widening their own horizons and becoming beacons of hope for others. Emboldened by the caregiver's strength that transcends the difficulties and hardships of giving care, the caregiver becomes a force for personal and social regeneration.

Fourth, values of caregiving, including empathy, sacrifice, and compassion, become a way of life for individuals, families and community groups. As we extend our goodwill from caring for a family member to all of our friends, neighbors, associates and human contacts, we certainly demonstrate the power to make the world a better place.

Finally, a commitment to service, whether at home, in the community or in the world allows one to "give back" to persons and society for the gifts we have received over the years. Caregiving is service that feeds the soul and liberates the mind. Let us remember this as we move into this newly formed caregiving model. The next chapter shows us how.

Chapter 12

The Ingenious Caregiver

There are only two ways to live your life. One is as though nothing is a miracle. The other is as though everything is a miracle.

~Albert Einstein

We cannot all do great things, but we can do small things with great love.

~Mother Teresa

Qualities of an Ingenious Caregiver

In the last chapter, we discussed the necessity to drastically change the nature of caregiving—away from burden and toward opportunity. This chapter considers a program, a "how to do it" course of action, for what I call *being* the *ingenious caregiver*. This agenda offers a new, even miraculous way of being in the caregiver role. First, let's define this newly remodeled person. This caregiver has moved from operating out of the burden of care mentality into the caring focus, drawing on wisdom of the heart to allow for the *ingenious caregiver* to emerge. The qualities of an ingenious caregiver involve a person who is both inventive and resourceful. She knows how to make things work, and she deals successfully with externally imposed problems. She also has a measure of cleverness to smooth conflict and ease tension, as well as a heart of generosity and love to overcome the daily grind and larger adversities she must face.

Once she moves beyond the caregiving burden with its dis-ease and suffering, the ingenious caregiver is now free to devise a new self; a self that moves freely from taking care of others to include taking care of self. Newly energized, she is open to developing positive care strategies, such as seeking help outside the family, putting aside time for herself and recognizing that her well-being is the essential element that permits caring for another in the first place. She fully appreciates that her energy is finite. She agrees with the admonition that "you can't give away what you haven't got," and understands that "you have to fill up your own cup first before you can share with others."

Because she knows she's in this caregiving relationship for the long run, she will need to modify her expectations. She will start with creating another checklist titled: "How Am I Doing?" On this checklist she will have two columns. The left hand column contains tasks and commitments for the loved one she is caring for; the right hand column contains the features of self-care that invigorate, renew and revitalize her. These include periods of "time outs," which may entail a few moments or hours or even entire weeks, if this can be arranged.

Since she has learned to turn over more responsibility to the care receiver, she can revel in the satisfaction of his greater independence and her own greater freedom. She may choose to advocate for her loved one, especially when in institutional care, but she also recognizes that much of the suffering her loved one has been enduring is an integral part of her loved one's journey. It is *not* a totally shared journey, because she understands that each of us has a distinct journey that is unique to that person. She can appreciate stepping back and being the witness, as well as the participant in the life of her loved one.

As compassionate observer, she can maintain her composure and clarify her comfort zone. She holds fast to spiritual practices that have served her throughout her life, or seeks new ones to meet her current challenges. And finally, she has a set of guidelines she can turn to throughout the day to raise her level of awareness for the caregiving task she has lovingly assumed. These guidelines, which help us to deeply tune into our body, mind and emotions, I call The Eight Strategies for Joyful Living.[1]

The Eight Strategies for Joyful Living

The *Eight Strategies* can be used by ingenious caregivers to both acquire and maintain powerful mental training toward achieving contentment—regardless of how dire her caregiving situation may be—as well as to adopt new habits and skills for self-renewal. At its most fundamental level, the *Strategies* is a program aimed to *overcome* suffering and to live in harmony with self, others and nature. We propose simple, sometimes humorous, exercises to help caregivers grasp each of the Strategies toward promoting problem-solving.

Strategy One: Clear Understanding. This guideline focuses on achieving clarity in all matters: recognizing and overcoming our negative habits, our childlike clingings and cravings, and especially our fears and expectations. Once we understand the temporary nature of all life and our own place in the cycle of life—both our own and others—we can more willingly accept old age, sickness and death. And, when we allow the reality to register that everything changes—our loved one, ourselves, our daily routines—we understand the futility of fixed outcomes. Being mentally clear, we confront the certainty that *nothing* is certain. No matter how well we plan the future, life rarely turns out as we anticipated.

The following exercise reinforces the nature of change that underlies our everyday caregiver reality, and shows how a caregiver can turn each negative event or exchange into a positive outcome. We call this the *Fortunately/Unfortunately* game.[2] Although the scenarios are fictional, the exercises point the way to practical, everyday solutions for caregivers' most frequent challenges.

Laura's 83-year-old mother, Kay, has Alzheimer's disease and is beginning to forget recent occurrences, such as who came to her birthday dinner party last night. Laura is becoming impatient with her mother's changing condition. The morning after the dinner party, Laura wanted to visit with her mother about some of the amusing things that happened, but Kay could not remember who came to the party. Fortunately, Laura kept the guest list. Unfortunately, two of the guests had insulted her mother during dinner. Fortunately, her mother did not remember the insults. Unfortunately, Kay requested that Laura, exhausted from the dinner party preparations of the evening before, prepare an old recipe of Kay's grandmother's for her dinner tonight.

Fortunately, Laura could report to her mother that the recipe was exactly what they had for dessert just the night before, and so she could make another one. Unfortunately, Kay had misplaced the recipe. Fortunately, Laura could use the Internet and, so found a similar recipe. Unfortunately, her mother did not like the new recipe, and refused to eat it. Fortunately, for her mother, the dessert was made with contaminated milk, and would have made her mother ill, if she had eaten it…

The outcome of this story? Everything is impermanent—no final fixes, change is our nature. So, let us look forward to change!

Strategy Two: Smart Thinking. Thinking can make us happy or miserable. To be a smart thinker as a caregiver, we need to cultivate three liberating thoughts:

1. Letting go of control over what happens to our loved one frees us from holding on to outmoded patterns and responses in our immediate relationship, as well as all of our other relationships;
2. Loving one person unconditionally is a gift that enables us to achieve a sense of interconnectedness with all persons we encounter, and thereby gives us energy from multiple sources; and
3. Cultivating compassion as a virtue leads to a spontaneous, wholesome melting of the heart at the suffering of others, coupled with a wish to alleviate their pain. At the same time, we recognize that while we can "suffer with," we are not that other person.

Specific ways to practice smart thinking include: project a friendly and loving manner to all persons, and develop compassion for yourself, your parents, your children, your partner and your care receiver. Compassion helps you relax and softens your heart, and is especially recommended for persons who act out in angry ways. As a caregiver, even if you do not *feel* particularly positive, loving or compassionate, *act as though you do*, and the result will be the same. You will have created an environment of comfort and ease that will enhance the well-being of your loved one and yourself.

"*The Opposite*" involves an exercise in which a negative thought or feeling can be reversed. Good comes out of bad. Our hypothetical caregiver, Susan, complains that her husband can no longer drive, and this requires her to take additional time to shop, drive him to the doctor's office, get a haircut, pick up the cleaning, and all the other everyday duties. She says: "I hate taking additional time out. I'm already too busy." How can Susan realize the benefits of her disrupted life?

Susan can shift her attitude, and think:

> How wonderful that I can get out of the house. Now, I have this opportunity to meet new people, relax in the barber shop while he gets his haircut and learn my way around the hardware store. I am much more confident. I work efficiently with the time I have at home, instead of dragging tasks out.

Susan can also take deep breaths, stop the old tapes and continue to find the plus side of changing events. She can also remember to use reversals whenever possible and focus on the truism that "every cloud has a silver lining."

Strategy Three: Reflective Speech. At the outset, this step requires that we abstain from all malicious and harmful speech, including lying, cruel words, harsh language and idle talk. A test of skillful speech is that you stop and ask yourself before you speak: "Is it true? Is it kind? Is it beneficial? Does it harm anyone? Is this the right time to say something?" To practice this skill conscientiously requires that we avoid mean-spirited conversations that contribute to making another person feel diminished. For caregivers, the skillful speech rule can be applied in every relationship: loved ones, friends, neighbors, medical staff and institutional caregivers, among others.

A quick rule of thumb for Strategy Three is: Never say anything you will regret later. One simple exercise to monitor "reflective speech" involves taking three to five deep breaths, breathing in through the nose and out through the mouth, ever so gently. During this time, we gather our effective vocabulary to speak our truth.

An additional component of skillful speech includes the *tone* with which we communicate. The words we use may convey only 25 percent of what we mean. Voice tone and body language convey the other 75 percent. Paying attention to the way others respond to us is often our first clue that what we are saying is being clouded by our body language. Caregivers can check for the following communication signals:

Are your arms crossed over your chest? You may appear guarded.

Is your body turned away when you speak? You may seem disinterested.

Is the other person backing away? You may be perceived as too aggressive.

When we become self-aware of language, gesture, tone and other communication signals, we can correct impressions that do not match the message we want to communicate. As caregivers, when we are consistent with our words and our body language, our loved one and families will be more at ease with us.

Strategy Four: Doing the Right Action. This strategy has two provisions. The first part involves *avoidance* of negative actions. For caregivers, these actions can run the gamut from ignoring our loved one to acting out our resentment and anger against him. Taking the right action entails not only following the Ten Commandments from the Old Testament or a similar set of principles, but also avoiding treating ourselves in injurious ways. Doing the right thing for each occasion is also related to cultivating a generous spirit toward others— not merely our loved one, but all those who care for him. Right action produces positive outcomes. Disjointed, mean or thoughtless action leads to negative results. For example, when caregivers attempt to reduce stress by misusing alcohol or legal drugs, or complain about the family members who fail to show up for help, they compound, not relieve, their burdensome feelings.

The second provision brings *intention* into all actions of our body, speech and mind; *intention* becomes the basis for all of our choices. Since every intentional action impacts us so strongly, good *intention* contributes to a relaxed physical state and peaceful mind. We are thus able to enhance our joy and increase our capacity for concentration or *focused attention*. In turn, focused attention enables us to overcome negative thoughts that lead to negative actions.

Our fictional caregiver, Caroline, has systematically avoided visiting her invalid elderly aunt who lives four blocks away, because she and the house smell bad. Caroline intends to be compassionate with Auntie Ruth, and so she searches for a solution to overcome her anticipated negative actions. Cleaning out a drawer, she finds a packet of lavender, and tucks it in her vest pocket. Now, she can visit freely and lovingly by taking regular whiffs of this calming herb.

Strategy Five: Right Livelihood. How we earn our living should not interfere with our spiritual development or relationships. Always ask: Does this job cause harm to others or to myself? Does the job make it difficult for me to feel balanced? Does the job cause physical or emotional anguish, or interfere with my caregiving commitments? Here's an illustrative scenario.

Alice confronts a dilemma many caregivers experience. Her demanding job drains her energy for looking after her dying mother on weekends, when the agency help is not available. Yet, she thoroughly enjoys her work, and feels reluctant to leave it. How does Alice shift this problem, using clear understanding and sound action? She spoke to her boss, who fortunately had a similar dilemma with her chronically-ill husband, and so was open to helping to solve Alice's problem. Together, they came up with a unique schedule that pleased them both. Alice now works alternate weeks with varying hours for each week, allowing her time to recoup, as well as balance the workload.

For women without flexible bosses, other situations may work: Find more help from family and friends, cut back hours and adjust the family budget, and or as last resort, quit the job, and find another, more flexible, one. During my caregiving tenure, I chose to continue work because college teaching offered great time flexibility, and the work itself re-energized me for the caregiving. Anne, my research assistant, has chosen a different path. She and Mike are deeply engaged in organizational work as Parkinson's disease advocates. Mike creates the yellow bird sculptures, while Anne markets the birds as fundraising incentives for foundations seeking to improve quality of life for those afflicted with the disease. Together, they have regenerated their energies and their marriage.

Strategy Six: Inspired Effort. Outmoded habits, restlessness, worry, self-centeredness, ignorance, ill will toward others, laziness and the "monkey mind" (or undisciplined mind) are, as we all know, wasted efforts, and are among the common mental hindrances that prevent a sense of balance and peacefulness. Inspired effort involves four essential steps:

1. Preventing negative states of mind;

2. Overcoming negative states of mind;
3. Cultivating positive states of mind; and
4. Maintaining positive states of mind.

How can we achieve this? We can begin by recognizing that we are working to deal with our own past conditioning. Hence, the intentional effort to change is paramount. Whereas thoughts come and go, the idea is to *choose* which thoughts we allow to proliferate. Always aim for substituting positive ideas over negative ones. This gives us a sense of mastery over ourselves.

We can develop insight by examining specifically problematic thoughts. Observe the rising, peaking and falling away of mental states, feelings and bodily sensations. When our conditioned responses continue to rear up, we can try several remedies. Ignore it. Divert the mind to something else. Replace the unproductive or negative idea with its opposite. Recognize that everything is in flux, including the annoying thinking. Finally, when all else fails, we have the advice of the Buddhist monk, Gunaratana, who says, "With clenched teeth, pressing the tongue against the upper palate, apply all your energy to overcome it."

We can also acknowledge that inspired effort is a self-taught skill that all of us can achieve. Recognize that this skill involves wisdom, patience and persistence. The most powerful aspect is to know that the more we deliberately bring up enjoyable states of mind, the more delighted with life we become, and the better we are at overcoming negativity and cultivating a positive perspective. Gunaratana says: "Every day, every moment, we can cultivate unbounded loving-friendliness, sympathetic joy, deep compassion and profound equanimity."[3]

As caregivers, we can focus our intention to develop the art of substituting our negative, old, grade B, 16-millimeter videotapes into positive, vivid, grade A, digital DVDs. We can make the effort to let the negative shrink and the positive blossom, and the work belongs to our own individual, creative minds. The following exercise shows you how one might go about doing this.

Janine, whose husband had been diagnosed with Alzheimer's disease four years ago, had just returned from the Alzheimer's caregivers' support group meeting. As usual, the news was all bad. After two years of attendance, Janine had decided not to return to the group, even though she knew how important it was for her to interact with other people.

After Janine read an article about exciting advances in the treatment and care of Alzheimer's patients, she decided to "rewrite her story" by imagining the possibilities for personal change. She also visualized the hope that she could bring to the support group. She vowed to pay close attention to the words and actions of the people around her, and let each positive encounter grow into a larger circle of friends. Janine returned to her support group and began enthusiastically sharing her new knowledge, basking in the glowing atmosphere of hope and joy she was bringing to the group.

Strategy Seven: Enlightened Mindfulness. Illuminating our lives on a daily basis can be achieved by *meditative practice.* Before we discuss specifics of meditation, let's first pursue what mindfulness is all about.

Mindfulness is a strategy for changing your life, because it raises your level of inner awareness. What we have learned about mindfulness is that if we confront our own suffering, including letting go of our erroneous or limited belief systems, as well as our idealized agendas and obsolete expectations, we have an amazing opportunity for joy. Once we let go of these limitations, we have emptied ourselves of illusions, and can more readily embrace the here and now. Bruce Lipton reminds us that our old belief system is often in control. But using the tools of consciousness and intention, we may gain the power to change how we think, how we respond and how we care.[4]

Once reserved for the province of Buddhist monks, mindfulness has now entered the mainstream as a means to master and restore ourselves. In spiritual circles, mindfulness is a path to inner awakening, and facilitates a shift to a higher level of ethics and compassion. Ram Dass points out that we can be of most service to others when we face our own doubts, needs and resistances. As these obstructions lessen a hold on us, our generosity will flow more spontaneously and effortlessly.[5]

The seeds for the current popularity of the practice were largely planted by the book *The Miracle of Mindfulness.* Its author, Thich Nhat Hanh, is a Vietnamese Buddhist monk, once nominated for a Nobel Peace

Prize by Martin Luther King, Jr.[6] Decades of research have shown that mindfulness decreases stress and reduces the symptoms of depression, anxiety and hostility. Mindfulness has been promoted as providing optimal conditions for learning, and developing such skills as:

- Heightened attention and concentration;
- Emotional and cognitive awareness and understanding;
- Bodily awareness and coordination;
- Interpersonal awareness, social responsibility and empathy;
- Deep relaxation and stress reduction;
- Improved ability to regulate physical and emotional pain; and
- Greater sense of the "big picture."[7]

In the medical community, mindfulness is seen as a path to physical health, as well as a supplement to traditional medicine. The Center for Mindfulness at the University of Massachusetts Medical School uses many techniques to teach this practice. One exercise involves taking 20 minutes to eat two raisins. Participants notice how the raisins look and smell. They feel the texture. And, finally, they taste and chew them. The Center's director, Saki Santorelli, emphasizes: "People who come to our clinic don't care about Buddhism or any '-ism.' They're suffering and want relief. Mindfulness helps them tap inner resources."[8]

At its most basic level, mindfulness involves an awareness of our internal environment of thoughts, bodily sensations and feelings as vibrating energy. Energy, by its nature, is in a constant state of motion, which changes from instant to instant. Thoughts are "things," which seek to manifest in material form. When we are in a state of mindfulness, we become the witness—the compassionate, non-judgmental observer— who lives in the moment. As a compassionate witness, we have no past and no future—in other words, no expectations. There is only **now**. We begin with a new slate each moment. Thus, once we are aware of our thoughts, attitudes, feelings and actions, we can change them.

For caregivers, this translates into a script *free* of regrets and resentments. Forget about what your loved one "used to do" or "used to be"—brilliant professor, recognized authority in medicine, beautiful or talented woman, leading-edge artist. Now, we contend with a new "character," our care receiver, who is hardly a paragon of virtue in his or her forgetfulness. Get to know that new person without judging or lamenting this changeling. We get entirely too caught up with what we have lost, rather than what we have gained. Our loved one may be far more gentle and loving than during his or her pre-illness state. Or, if the change is for the worse—physical and mental deterioration—then, it may be a matter of adjusting our mind and spirit to absorb the immediate reality of new needs and different modes of care. By attending to the immediate symptoms and behavior, we can make more informed decisions about care.

Strategy Eight: Mastering Concentration. To be truly free of cravings, resentments, illusions and other negative mental images, *skillful concentration* is the last essential step on the path to happiness. Skillful concentration involves having a single-minded focus to free us from the distractions and annoying thoughts that clog our consciousness.

Here's one visualization to help you acquire the peacefulness you seek. View the concentrated mind as a laser beam burning a very hard, resistant substance. Keep the laser on that spot until you feel it giving way. What is burned out is mental debris—distractions, attachments, unwholesome thoughts, negative emotions, suffering, self-centeredness, anger and resentment. Only when the debris has been burned out can joy, happiness and equanimity flow through our being.

Caregivers may take careful note of this Strategy, because freedom from distractions, attachments, worries and negative emotions can genuinely open the heart to compassion. Giving becomes a natural extension of the transformed self. Indeed, the cumulative effect of all the Strategies promises to be the end of suffering, and ultimately, the highest degree of peace and happiness.

Application of the Strategies for Caregiving

Rather than focusing on visible sources of discomfort, and our inevitable shortcomings—that ever-growing list of undone tasks, hemmed-in space, lack of time, work overloads, sleep shortages, and lack of appreciation—recognize that our *reaction* to the caregiving situation is the key. Reactions are merely unconscious responses to frustration and dis-ease. In reacting to situations, we become unconscious, not only to the needs of our loved one, but also to our own needs. But once we work the series of strategies toward mindfulness, we can become conscious of when we have shifted into "automatic pilot," and can gently bring ourselves into awakened consciousness.

Meditation for Caregivers

A crucial approach for bringing a burdened caregiver into awareness is meditation. Meditation sustains mindfulness by promoting a moment-to-moment awareness of our life without judgment. What are the prerequisites to this enlightened state of awareness? Quieting the mind is the foundation of mindfulness. When our minds are quiet, they are more receptive to absorbing new information and learning. The two key elements to quieting the mind are soft-belly breathing and focused listening. Allow yourself to simply sit and breathe deeply in a conscious way.

Meditation experts advise us to "follow the breath." Soft-belly breathing offers a deeply relaxed breathing pattern. First take a slow, deep breath through your nose and softly let the air out through the mouth. Air is emitted slowly, as though you want to cause a candle flame to flicker, but not go out. Make sure that you are breathing diaphragmatically by paying attention to the rise and fall of the belly. Continue soft-belly breathing until you have entered a deeper state of peacefulness.

Then, try doing a body scan, "listening" to the body as your attention moves from head to toes, front to back. You are now a witness to your body, rather than identifying with the body. Where is your body holding the tension? If you're feeling pain or discomfort, what part of the body has the sensation? Mentally concentrate on that part of the body that hurts. Do not judge the sensation or try to make it anything different from what it is. Extend loving, compassionate concern to the part of you that feels damaged or deficient. You can also use a repeated phrase, chanting, or even concentrate on a meaningful image or phrase to initiate or sustain the meditative state.

Instead of the caregiver feeling oppressed, she now becomes the observer, the compassionate witness, watching the caregiver being oppressed. This is a qualitative leap; a shift from you being the *doer* to you being the *watcher*. It is really nothing more than stepping out of yourself on a moment-by-moment basis, and accepting this moment just as it is right now. You are making an informed choice to be in charge of yourself. It takes little time to achieve this inner state of balance, and when done once or twice daily, the practice becomes easier.

Christian Contemplation

Some ingenious caregivers may find solace in Christian contemplation, instead of meditation as I have described it here. Christianity offers an extensive history of ritual and contemplative prayer toward cultivating a relationship with Christ, thus enhancing spirituality and peacefulness. These rituals include Scripture reading and reflection, charismatic worship—which emphasizes ecstatic religious experience and gifts of healing—and most recently, the method of Centering Prayer.

Developed by Father Thomas Keating, centering prayer, a type of contemplative practice, is the opening of mind and heart, thoughts, words and emotions—our whole being—to a greater awareness of the God within. This awareness is cultivated through repetition of a sacred word that allows for a "resting in God." Father Keating explains how this meditation practice works: "Sitting comfortably and with eyes closed, settle briefly and silently introduce the sacred word [God, Jesus, Peace or other] as a symbol of your consent to God's presence and action within."[9] During this prayer, Keating emphasizes, "We avoid analyzing our experience, harboring expectations or aiming at some specific goal, such as 'achieving a spiritual experience...' or other pre-determined outcomes."[10]

Prayer

Prayer may be one of the most underrated remedies of all. What does prayer do? The act or state of praying is a form of meditation focused on communion with a trusted and powerful creator, deity or spirit. Prayer has the power to lift our own spirits, to view our potential from a different perspective, to request intercessions and express gratitude for wisdom granted.

When we pray, we experience some level of relief—we know that we have asked for help and guidance with the expectation that we will do what we are able to change our own destiny. It is a universally accepted belief that prayer results in self-improvement, if accompanied by positive intention, active participation and hard work from the person praying. Under those circumstances, prayer is power, prayer is action, prayer works. Matthew Fox says that prayer connects us to a life of love, justice and joy.

> *The understanding of prayer as a radical response to life suggests... that a new commandment has been given to us: thou shalt love your life with all your strength and energy, growing daily in appreciation of the joys of life; and you shall allow and aid where possible your neighbor to love his and do the same, using common norms of justice to determine life's priorities.*[11]

Moreover, Fox says prayer involves living in abundance, respecting life's mysteries in an active, not passive manner, and letting the Spirit move through us. "In short, love life [as a mystic and prophet]—and do whatever you want."[12]

The *Daily Word*, a prayer guide for everyday use, offers an insightful message for the ingenious caregiver. It admonishes all of us to accept the good in our lives:

> *Nourished with divine wisdom, I anticipate and welcome good in my life.*
>
> *I care about my dear ones and give my time and energy in support of them. I honor and appreciate them, their present abilities...*
>
> *I care about myself also. To renew my own reservoir of physical, emotional and spiritual strength, I take time alone with God. I acknowledge that I need to honor myself with rest, patience and understanding.*
>
> *Releasing all thoughts and feelings of anxiety, I welcome good in my life.*
>
> *Choosing to be with people who are supportive and compassionate, I place myself in situations where I feel positive, nurtured and uplifted. I am doing the best I can in my moments of thought, decision or activity. Physical, mental and spiritual blessings are mine.*
>
> *I honor the friend and partner that I am. God is good. All is well.*[13]

Whatever meditation or prayer approach we choose, the mental and emotional effects can be rewarding. When we are relaxed, attentive and receptive, everyday scenarios that once could have plunged us into anxiety or depression are quickly resolved. We can far more readily alter our thinking, feeling and acting. At some point, all caregivers confront the reality of not receiving the gratitude we think we are due for all our efforts. At that point, we can step back and say in the third person: "Mary is upset about the lack of appreciation." But, remember, this has nothing to do with Mary or her diligence in the job of caregiving. Her reaction is not only a false perception, but also springs from a trigger response to a set of outmoded expectations. "John always used to compliment me when I served him his dinner. Now, he can't even speak." This does not mean that Mary's dinner is flawed; but rather, the care receiver lacks the capacity for the habitual response.

The Epilogue that follows offers additional relaxation suggestions for caregivers, including an Alphabet of Spiritual Affirmations and a Caregiver's Special Prayer. Daily affirmations and prayer may smooth the way to more compassionate and loving caregiving.

We extend a heartfelt recommendation: Let us banish martyrdom and grief. Take advantage of the great lesson of love and live in the moment. Love now. Never miss an opportunity to embrace each moment with our loved one. We will never regret the good that we have said and done, but only what was left unspoken and unfinished.

The Alphabet of Spiritual Affirmations for Caregivers

We all need some shorthand way to communicate to ourselves how we can overcome our own limitations as caregivers. Alphabet-generated affirmations offer a simple way to shift our energy from negative to positive. They can be memorized, typed up on small cards for easy access, or simply tacked on a desk or bathroom mirror for quick reference. You can also try creating some of your own affirmations that ring true for your life. The idea for this spiritual practice was created by Frederic and Mary Ann Brussat, "The Alphabet of Spiritual Practices." *Spirituality and Health*, December 2006. We claim the affirmations as our own.

A **Acceptance** of life, just as it is right now, contributes to peace and wholeness.

   Awareness of emotions allows feelings to cycle—rise, diminish, disappear—without excessive thinking about or attaching to them.

   Attention to thoughts, emotions and actions allows us to change those negative influences that undermine our lives.

   Affinity effect implies that my close attachment and deep love for my sick or dying loved one is sufficient to cause illness even without the caregiver burden.

   Attachment to outcomes is the great fabricator of illusion, say the wise.

B **Breath**, our greatest essential for life, is a function of energy, and should be cultivated as the basis for relaxation and well-being.

   Buoyancy means we can be cheerful and resilient in every situation.

C **Consciousness** of mind, emotions and body is the caregiver's creed.

Celebrate every opportunity that comes our way.

Compassion for self and others keeps the heart open.

Concentration facilitates a caregiver's single-minded purpose of giving loving care.

Change is a natural process. Embrace it as we go with the flow of life.

D **Dreaming** releases our spirit for creativity and our body for renewal.

E **Enlightenment** is possible through following Strategies for Joyful Living. These strategies for caregivers provide a gentle eight-step program for overcoming suffering.

Education for caregivers involves learning not only new facts and details about disease and the limits of medicine, but also new ways of being in the world.

F **Forgive** yourself your limitations in order to vanquish shame and self-denigration as a caregiver.

G **Generosity**, as selflessness, is opposed to greed and craving, and is the highest virtue.

Golden Rule stipulates that we do not speak or act in ways to our disabled elders that we would not want them to speak or act to us, if our positions were reversed.

Grieving is a natural response to loss and pain associated with caring for a disabled or dying loved one.

H **Happiness** can be moral, emotional and judgmental. Caregivers strive for moral happiness by making sound choices, emotional happiness by practicing mindfulness, and judgmental happiness through problem solving.

Honor the divine within ourselves and our disabled loved one.

Healing restores us to wholeness and frees us from grief and troubles.

Harmony means we are acting in accord with our highest moral decision to give selflessly and to love deeply.

I **Interdependence** between the caregiver and other family members allows everyone to have a stake in the well-being of the disabled elder.

Intimacy, even when lost between partners, becomes tangible in the caring and understanding acts that reassure family members that a safe and loving place exists for them.

J   **Journaling** allows for the expression of our deepest feelings, and a safe place to record the passing days of our life.

Joy is contagious, and spreads easily from one person to another.

K   **Knowing** our own strengths and weaknesses enables us to accurately perceive the strengths and weaknesses of our frail elderly loved one.

Knowledge of the medical and emotional needs of our love one comprises successful caregiving.

L   **Listening** reaps the benefits of understanding and empathy, by empowering our loved one to "speak out."

Love is the reason for caregivers' selfless giving.

Learning positive caregiving strategies require an open mind and heart.

Laughter lightens our burdens, wipes away our fears and delights our souls.

M   **Mystery** enfolds our relationship with our disabled or dying loved one.

Miracles just happen when we allow them, and are a product of grace.

N   **Normal** is the appropriate and desired goal for the caregiver.

O   **Outreach** into friendship and community groups strengthens our capacity to care for our loved one.

Overcoming our own fears of being "less than," means we can conquer anything that comes our way as caregivers.

P   **Perfect** happens when both body and mind are at peace. At such times, we are lacking nothing.

Prayer life for caregivers puts us in touch with a higher source of power that serves to balance our lives.

Presence is what we bring to those we care for, a healing tonic of love.

Q   **Quieting** oneself in meditation helps usher in a spirit of peacefulness and joy.

R   **Ritual** shared with loved ones recreates balance in our lives.

Responsibility entails making a moral choice to provide elder care;

it does not require that we take on every duty and activity associated with this care.

S **Silence** gives us essential space to acknowledge ourselves and our loved one.

Self-care or **self-help** enables us to care for others with renewed energy and love, because we have honored our own interests and needs.

Synchronicity reveals the interwoven patterns of our relationships and choices.

Spaciousness, a sense of unlimited possibilities, occurs with expanded consciousness.

T **Teamwork** among supportive family members and friends lightens the load of caregiving.

Trust that the process of giving and receiving enhances both caregiver and care receiver to achieve their highest and best good.

Training ourselves in the discipline of mindfulness keeps us emotionally intact.

Tenderness to oneself and our elderly loved one lightens the caregiver's burden.

U **Undoing** the past is not possible; unconditionally accepting the here and now puts us in a state of contentment.

Unity of purpose and intention allows us to focus on our loved one's needs.

V **Venerable** are the elders in our life, worthy of respect and honor.

Vent your feelings in a safe place without causing harm to ourselves, our frail elder or other family members.

W **Witness** without judgment the "movie" of your own life to achieve peace and happiness.

X X represents the symbol for a person or thing unknown, as when we first initiated our caregiving activities.

Y **Youthfulness** is a state of mind, and not merely a set of physical traits. If we cherish the youth in us, we energize our care efforts.

Z **Zealousness** in our fervent intention to serve and give attention to our loved one, are practices that glorify both our lives.

The Caregiver's Invocation

Help me recognize this time in my life as an opportunity

To look into the face of suffering

To listen to the voice of pain

To comfort the isolated and the afflicted

And to grow in patience and a new understanding of my own
potential for spirituality.

Help me recognize the divine light of guidance and my innate
ability to heed the messages.

Help me let my compassion grow and spread in an ever-widening
circle of influence.

May I be happy. May I be peaceful.

May I be confident and positive in my efforts and
accomplishments.

Amen.

Endnotes

Introduction

1. Beth Witrogen McLeod, *Caregiving: The Spiritual Journey of Love, Loss and Renewal* (New York: John Wiley & Sons, 1999).
2. *Altruism* has often been linked with extraordinary acts of heroism and taking ultimate risks. See, for example, Samuel P. Oliner and Pearl M. Oliner, *The Altruistic Personality: What Led Ordinary Men and Women to Risk Their Lives on Behalf of Others?* (New York: The Free Press, 1988); and Jennifer Lois, *Heroic Efforts: The Emotional Culture of Search and Rescue Volunteers* (New York: New York University Press, 2003).
3. See Sara Lawrence-Lightfoot, *Respect* (Cambridge: Perseus Books, 2000).
4. Emile Durkheim, *Selected Writings* (New York: Giddens Publishing, 1972).
5. Sara Lawrence-Lightfoot, *Respect*.
6. Oliner and Oliner, *The Altruistic Personality*.
7. Kristen Renwick Monroe, *The Heart of Altruism: Perceptions of a Common Humanity* (Princeton: Princeton University Press, 1996).
8. Family Caregiver Alliance, "Fact Sheet: Women and Caregiving: Facts and Figures." Online at http://www.caregiver.org/jsp/print_friendly.jsp?nodeid=892.
9. I discuss the retirement consequences of women's non-continuous participation in the workforce because of caregiving responsibilities for children and elderly relatives, as well as substandard wages received throughout their working years. Nanette J. Davis, "Cycles of Discrimination: Older Women, Cumulative Disadvantages and Retirement Consequences," *Journal of Education Finance* 31, No. 1 (Summer 2005), 65–81.
10. M. Navale-Waliser, *et al.*, "When the Caregiver Needs Care: The Plight of Vulnerable Caregivers," *American Journal of Public Health* 92, No. 3 (2002), 409–413.
11. K. M. Langa, *et al.*, "National Estimates of the Quantity and Cost of Informal Caregiving for the Elderly with Dementia," *Journal of General Internal Medicine* 16, No. 11 (2001), 770–778.
12. The Commonwealth Fund, "Informal Caregiving Fact Sheet" (1999).

Chapter 1

1. Toni M. Calasanti and Kathleen F. Slevin, *Gender, Social Inequalities and Aging* (Walnut Creek: AltaMira Press, 2001).

2. Fact sheets and statistics abound in this burgeoning demographic and health field. Some recommended sources for statistical overviews include the Metropolitan Life Insurance Company's study, "The Metlife Juggling Act Study: Balancing Caregiving with Work and the Costs Involved" (1999); AARP, "Beyond 50: A Report to the Nation on Economic Security," *Executive Summary* (Washington, D.C.: AARP Fulfillment, 2003); Administration on Aging, "A Profile of Older Americans: 2007." See also B. Coleman, "Helping the Helpers: State-Supported Services for Family Caregivers" (AARP Public Policy Institute, Washington, D.C. (#2000-07).

3. Reported in Stephen Howie, "Taking Time and Giving Care," *The Bellingham Herald*, February 11, 2007, 3.

4. The literature strongly supports the fact of women's overwhelming contribution to elder care, compared with men's participation. Elizabeth A. Watson and Jane Mears, *Women, Work and Care of the Elderly* (Aldershot, England: Ashgate Publishing, 1999); Francesca M. Cancian and Stacey J. Oliker, *Caring and Gender* (Thousand Oaks: Pine Forge Press, 2000); Elizabeth W. Markson, *Social Gerontology Today* (Los Angeles: Roxbury Publishing Company, 2003).

5. Reported in Michael Vitez, "U.S. Conference: Society Unprepared for Aging," *The Bellingham Herald*, March 15, 2007, A7.

6. *Ibid.*

7. Demographic change is discussed in Nancy R. Hooyman and H. Asuman Kiyak, *Social Gerontology: A Multidisciplinary Perspective*, Seventh Edition (Boston: Allyn and Bacon, 2005).

8. Lynn Brenner, "Do You Need Insurance for Long-Term Care?" *Parade*, February 17, 2008, 10.

9. B. Farber, "Microinterventions: Assistive Devices, Telematics and Person-Environment Interactions," chapter in K. W. Schaie, H. W. Wahl, H. Mollenkopf and F. Oswald, eds., *Aging Independently: Living Arrangements and Mobility* (New York: Springer, 2003), 248–262.

10. David E. Biegel and Richard Schultz, "Caregiving and Caregiver Interventions in Aging and Mental Illness," *Family Relations*, No. 48 (1999), 345–354.

11. AARP, "Beyond 50: A Report to the Nation on Economic Security,"

Executive Summary (Washington, D.C.: AARP Fulfillment, 2003).

12. Calasanti and Slevin (2001).

13. J. Dianne Garner and Susan O. Mercer, eds., *Women as They Age,*
    Second Edition (New York: Haworth Press, 2001).

14. Administration on Aging, "A Profile of Older Americans: 2007."

15. U.S. Bureau of the Census, *Statistical Abstract of the United States*
    (Washington, D.C.: U.S. Government Printing Office, 2000).

16. Administration on Aging, "America's Families Care: A Report on the
    Needs of America's Caregivers" (Washington, D.C., 2003).

17. *Ibid.*

18. *Ibid.*

19. *Ibid.*

20. Hearing Before the Special Committee on Aging, United States Senate
    (2003). In 1969, Robert Butler coined the term *ageism* to describe nega-
    tive attitudes toward the aging process, and aged persons in particular.
    He defined ageism as "a process of systematic stereotyping and discrim-
    ination against people because they are old, just as racism and sexism
    accomplish this with skin color." He said that ageism reflects a "deep
    seated uneasiness on the part of the young and middle aged—a personal
    revulsion to and distaste for growing old, disease, disability; and fear of
    powerlessness, 'uselessness' and death." In Robert Butler, "Ageism:
    Another Form of Bigotry," *The Gerontologist* 9, No. 3 (1969), 243–246.

21. Palmore reports in 2001 that in a sample of older Americans, 77 percent
    said they had experienced more than one incident of ageism. E.B.
    Palmore, "Ageism Survey: First Findings," *The Gerontologist* 41, No. 5
    (2001), 572–575.

22. Administration on Aging, "A Profile of Older Americans: 2007."

23. Center on an Aging Society, Georgetown University, "How Do Family
    Caregivers Fare? A Closer Look at Their Experiences," No. 3 (June
    2005). Online at http://www.aging-society.org.

24. The National Family Caregivers Alliance (NFCA) has led the way in
    developing statistical findings of caregivers on a state and federal level.
    "Executive Summary: Survey of Fifteen States' Caregiver Support
    Programs" (available from National Family Caregiver Alliance, 180
    Montgomery Street, Suite 1100, San Francisco, CA 94104). Other
    scholarly contributors include: S. R. Gregory and S. M. Pandya,
    "Women and Long-Term Care—Fact Sheet" (Washington D.C.: AARP
    Public Policy Institute, 2002); and Older Women's League, "Women

and Long-Term Care." Online at http://www.owl-national.org.

25. Andrew Weil, "Caring for the Caregiver," *Self-Healing* (August 2003), 4–5.
26. Administration on Aging, "A Profile of Older Americans: 2007."
27. The National Family Caregivers Alliance (2001).
28. *Ibid.*
29. *Ibid.*
30. Weil (2003).
31. Susan L. Hughes, *et al.*, "Relationship Between Caregiver Burden and Health-Related Quality of Life," *The Gerontologist* 39, No. 5 (1999), 534–545.
32. B. J. Kramer and J. D. Lambert, "Caregiving as a Life Course Transition Among Older Husbands: A Prospective Study," *The Gerontologist* 39, No. 6 (1999), 658–667.
33. Hughes, *et al.* (1999).
34. The National Family Caregivers Alliance (NFCA), "Clearinghouse Statistics" (2001).
35. Long-term care has been extensively discussed in Nancy R. Hooyman and H. Asuman Kiyak, *Social Gerontology*, Seventh Edition. This text discusses such aspects as institutional placements, community care options, expenditures, role of Medicaid, treatment of the "oldest old" and Japan's national policy, in which the overwhelming percent of elder care occurs at home, just as it does in the United States.
36. NFCA, "Clearinghouse Statistics" (2001).
37. Richard W. Johnson and Joshua M. Wiener, "A Profile of Frail Older Americans and Their Caregivers." *The Retirement Project,* Occasional Paper, No. 8 (Urban Institute, February 2006).
38. *Ibid.*
39. NFCA, "Public Policy Issues" (2001).
40. Editorial, "Doctor Shortage Hovering Along the Horizon," *Los Angeles Times,* June 3, 2006, C10; and S. Levine, "The Hidden Health Care System," *Medical Care* 21 (2002), 378.

Chapter 2

1. bell hooks, *remembered rapture: the writer at work* (New York: Owl Books, 1999).
2. This chapter relies heavily on statistical assistance from my very competent colleague, Lucky Tedrow, Department of Sociology, Western Washington University, Bellingham, Washington.

3. These questions have been addressed in a paper, "Families in Crisis: A
    Case Study of Elder Caregivers" by Nanette J. Davis and Anne C.
    Mikkelsen. We presented the paper to the Third International
    Conference on New Directions in the Humanities, University of
    Cambridge, England, August 2005. A revised version has been pub-
    lished (same title) in *International Journal of the Humanities* 3, No. 9
    (Summer 2007).

Chapter 3

1. Nancy L. Mace and Peter V. Rabins, *The 36-Hour Day*, Third Edition
    (Baltimore: The Johns Hopkins University Press, 1999), 322.
2. Toni M. Calasanti and Kathleen F. Slevin, *Gender, Social Inequalities and
    Aging* (Walnut Creek: AltaMira Press, 2001), 144.
3. Robin West, "The Right to Care," chapter in *The Subject of Care:
    Feminist Perspectives on Dependency*, Eva Feder Kittay and Ellen K.
    Feder, eds. (Lanham: Rowman & Littlefield Publishers, 2002), 88–114.
4. Mace and Rabins, *The 36-Hour Day* (1999).
5. See Eva Feder Kittay and Ellen K. Feder, eds., *The Subject of Care;* and
    David A. Karp, *The Burden of Sympathy* (Oxford: Oxford University
    Press, 2001).
6. A range of literature exists that depicts the various deleterious aspects
    of gendered caregiving ("women's work"). See, for example, Francesca
    M. Cancian and Stacey J. Oliker, *Caring and Gender* (Thousand Oaks:
    Pine Forge Press, 2000). See also Kittay and Feder, eds., *The Subject of
    Care.*
7. Arlie Russell Hochschild, *The Commercialization of Intimate Life*
    (Berkeley: University of California Press, 2003). Hochschild writes
    cogently about the commercial uses and misuses of human emotions,
    and emphasizes how heartfelt care, including love and devotion to
    family, has been displaced by "emotion management" in our troubled
    society. We have lost care rules, says Hochschild, and confront only
    ambivalence about "how" to feel in intimate situations.
8. *Ibid.*
9. Andrew Weil, "Caring for the Caregiver," *Self-Healing* (August 2003).

Chapter 4

1. Richard D. Ashmore and Lee Jussim, eds., *Self and Identity:
    Fundamental Issues* (New York: Oxford University Press, 1997).
2. *Ibid.*

3. Kurt Danziger, "The Historical Formation of Selves," chapter in Richard D. Ashmore and Lee Jussim, eds., *Self and Identity: Fundamental Issues* (New York: Oxford University Press, 1997), 137–159.

4. S. Stryker and R. T. Serpe, "Commitment, Identity Salience and Role Behavior: Theory and Research Example," chapter in W. Ickes and E. Knowles, eds., *Personality, Roles and Social Behavior* (New York: Springer-Verlag, 1982), 199–218.

5. Erik Erikson, *Childhood and Society* (New York: Norton, 1950).

6. Susan Harter, "The Personal Self in Social Context: Barriers to Authenticity," chapter in Richard D. Ashmore and Lee Jussim, eds., *Self and Identity: Fundamental Issues* (New York: Oxford University Press, 1997), 81–105.

7. Erving Goffman, *The Presentation of Self in Everyday Life* (Garden City: Doubleday, 1959).

8. Roy F. Baumeister, "The Self and Society: Change, Problems and Opportunities," chapter in Richard D. Ashmore and Lee Jussim, eds., *Self and Identity: Fundamental Issues* (New York: Oxford University Press, 1997), 191–217.

Chapter 5

1. National Mental Health Association (NMHA), "Co-Dependency" (Mental Health Resource Center, 2001 Beauregard Street, 12th Floor, Alexandria, VA 22311).

2. Melody Beattie, *Co-Dependent No More*, Second Edition (Minneapolis: Hazelden Foundation, 1992).

3. Depression is a common problem among partners in a co-dependent relationship. This is described by Elizabeth L. Jeglic, *et al.*, "A Caregiving Model of Coping with a Partner's Depression," *Family Relations* 54, No. 1 (January 2005), 37.

4. NMHA, "Co-Dependency."

Chapter 6

1. Chokyi Nyima Rinpoche and David R. Shlim, *Medicine and Compassion* (Boston: Wisdom Publications, 2004).

2. Nicholas D. Kristof, "Medicine's Sticker Shock," *The New York Times*, October 2, 2005.

3. *Ibid.*

4. See, for example, Liz Szabo, "Prices Soar for Cancer Drugs," *USA Today*, July 11, 2006, 14; and Liz Szabo, "Cost of Cancer Drugs Crushes All But Hope," *USA Today*, July 11, 2006, 15.

5. Hospice is a physical environment whereby a dying patient is allowed to die with dignity as defined by the patient and family. Hospice care focuses on comfort, rather than cure, and on patients—not doctors—controlling the end-of-life process. See Duane A. Matcha, *The Sociology of Aging* (Boston: Allyn & Bacon, 1997).

6. Nanette J. Davis and Clarice Stasz, *Social Control of Deviance* (New York: McGraw-Hill, 1990).

7. Research on the impact of medical control is provided by Peter Conrad and Rochelle Kern, eds., *The Sociology of Health and Illness: Critical Perspectives* (New York: St. Martin's Press, 1990).

8. The most articulate discussion of how old age, especially among women, marginalizes the elderly is offered by Toni M. Calasanti and Kathleen F. Slevin, *Gender, Social Inequalities and Aging* (Walnut Creek: AltaMira Press, 2001).

9. Deepak Chopra and David Simon, *Grow Younger, Live Longer: Ten Steps to Reverse Aging* (New York: Harmony Books, 2001).

10. Andrew Weil, *Healthy Aging* (New York: Anchor Books, 2006).

11. *Ibid.*

12. Nancy R. Hooyman and H. Asuman Kiyak, *Social Gerontology* (Boston: Pearson, 2005).

13. Critical analyses of the state of dis-ease under medical control is offered by Peter Conrad and Rochelle Kern, eds., *The Sociology of Health and Illness: Critical Perspectives* (Hampshire, England: Palgrave Macmillan, 1990).

14. S. Katz and B. Marshall, "New Sex for Old: Lifestyle Consumerism and the Ethics of Aging Well," *Journal of Aging Studies* 17, No. 1 (2003), 3–16.

15. *Ibid.*

16. Feminists emphasize the inherent inequality of female caregivers confronting institutional representatives because of power differences. See C. Brown, *Women, Feminism and Aging* (New York: Springer Publishing, 1998); and J.D. Garner, "Feminism and Feminist Gerontology," *Fundamentals of Feminist Gerontology* (New York: Routledge, 1999), 3–13.

17. Davis and Stasz (1990) among others, discuss the far-ranging effects of deviant labeling.

18. American Medical Student Association, "The Senior Boom is Coming: Are Primary Care Physicians Ready?" May 24, 2005. Online at http://

www.amsa.org/programs/gpit/seniors.cfm. Gregory James, American College of Osteopathic Family Physicians, "Addressing Barriers to Health Care for Our Elderly," May 15, 2005. Online at http://www.acofp.org. American College of Emergency Physicians, "Elderly Lack Medication Knowledge," May 14, 2005. Online at http://www.acep.org. American Academy of Medical Colleges, "Statement on Patients in Peril: Critical Shortages in Geriatric Care," paper submitted to the Special Committee on Aging (AAMC), May 12, 2002.
19. American Academy of Medical Colleges.
20. *Ibid.*
21. Rinpoche and Shlim, *Medicine and Compassion.*
22. Pauline W. Chen, *Final Exam: A Surgeon's Reflections on Mortality* (New York: Knopf, 2006).

Interlude 2
1. "Begin the Adventure of a Lifetime: The Second Half of Life." An Interview with Angeles Arrien, *Sounds True Catalog,* Summer 1998, 35.

Chapter 7
1. Marilyn Gardner, "Caregiving May Mean Overcoming Frayed Ties," *Christian Science Monitor,* July 11, 2004.
2. Karen Hansen writes in *Not So Nuclear Families* that networks of care vary enormously by social class, values, solidarity and "feeling rules." Whereas her focus is child care, the concept of care network can also be applied to elder care analysis. Hansen's study offers an in-depth portrayal of how viable care networks operate to create and maintain family stability. Karen V. Hansen, *Not So Nuclear Families* (New Brunswick: Rutgers University Press, 2005).
3. Anne Roschelle asserts that social policy presupposes the availability of kinship networks for sustaining young, old and disabled members, but this is not necessarily the case. Minority families, although highly family oriented, are often prevented participation in extended kin groups. She argues that among poor African-American, Hispanic and Non-Hispanic whites, economic disenfranchisement has contributed to fragmented families. Thus, minority family life is no longer characterized by extensive non-kin and kin networks that in the past have been so essential to their survival. Anne R. Roschelle, *No More Kin: Exploring Race, Class and Gender in Family Networks* (Thousand Oaks: Sage Publications, 1997).

4. Marilyn Gardner, *Christian Science Monitor.*
5. Karen V. Hansen, *Not So Nuclear Families.*
6. *Ibid.*

Chapter 8

1. Nicholas Christakis, *Death Foretold: Prophecy and Prognosis in Medical Care* (Chicago: University of Chicago Press, 1999).
2. Daniel Goleman, *Social Intelligence: The New Science of Human Relationships* (New York: Bantam Dell, 2006), 58.
3. *Ibid.*
4. *Ibid.*
5. Sheldon Cohen, *et al., Measuring Stress: A Guide for Health and Social Scientists* (Oxford: Oxford University Press, 1995).
6. *Ibid.*
7. See the Association for Alzheimer's Society Website. Online at http://www.nlm.nih.gov/medlineplus/alzheimersdisease.html
8. Leonard Syme and Lisa F. Berkman, "Social Class, Susceptibility and Illness," chapter in *The Sociology of Health and Illness*, Peter Conrad and Rochelle Kerns, eds., Third Edition (New York: St. Martin's Press, 1990).
9. Reported in *USA Today*, February 16, 2006.
10. "Weaving the Tapestry of Life: Living with Loss/Healing with Hope" (St. Paul: Elder Service Providers 2003 Conference, March 8, 2003).
11. Goleman, *Social Intelligence.*
12. Toni M. Calasanti and Kathleen F. Slevin, *Gender, Social Inequalities and Aging* (Walnut Creek: Alta Press, 2001).
13. Nicholas Christakis, "Mortality After Hospitalization of a Spouse," *The New England Journal of Medicine* 254 (2006), 719–730.
14. Goleman, *Social Intelligence.*

Chapter 9

1. Robert Goodin and Diane Gibson, chapter in Eva Feder Kittay and Ellen K. Feder, eds., *The Subject of Care: Feminist Perspectives on Dependency* (New York: Rowan and Littlefield, 2002), 246–256.
2. Barry Corbet, "Nursing Home Undercover: Embedded," *AARP Magazine* (January/February, 2007).
3. Family caregivers emphasized their desire for an ongoing relationship with staff members and interpreted staff behaviors in terms of high quality care based on the social and emotional care given to their

resident, as much as on the technical tasks involved in caring for them. This issue is discussed in M.T. Duncan and D.L. Morgan, "Sharing the Caring: Family Caregivers' Views of Their Relationships with Nursing Home Staff," *The Gerontologist* 34, No. 2 (1994), 235–244.

4. National Citizens' Coalition for Nursing Home Reform, "Nursing Homes: Getting Good Care There." For example, this group sponsored a Residents' Rights Week, October 1–6, 2006. Online at http://www.nccnhr.org.

5. Penelope A. Hommel, "Enhancing Legal Services for Vulnerable Elders: The Challenge for Aging and Legal Services Advocates," Clearinghouse Review, *Journal of Poverty Law* 30, No. 6 (October 1996), 635–652. See also Administration on Aging, "Long-Term Care Ombudsman Program" (e-mail: aoainfo@aoa.gov).

6. Michael McCarthy, "Report Finds Abuse in U.S. Nursing Homes Goes Unreported and Unpunished," *The Lancet* 359 (March 9, 2002).

7. Athena McLean, *The Person in Dementia: A Study of Nursing Home Care in the U.S.* (Peterborough, Ontario: Broadview Press, 2007).

8. *Ibid.*

9. This situation may be changing. Geriatric training programs are now available for family care physicians, who seek to develop a specialization in elder medical care. The University of California at Los Angeles has emerged as a leader in education and training for geriatric medicine. Online at http://www.psychiatry.ucla.edu.

10. McLean, *The Person in Dementia.*

11. National Citizens' Coalition for Nursing Home Reforms, "Nursing Homes: Getting Good Care There." Online at http://www.nccnhr.org.

12. Alliance for Aging Research (2021 K Street NW, Suite 305, Washington, D.C., 20006 and Rand Corporation). Online at http://www.hsph.harvard.edu/pgda/resources.htm.

13. An overview of nursing home abuse and lack of regulation is covered in Kieran Walshe, "Regulating Nursing Homes: Are We Learning from Experience?" *Health Affairs* (Nov/Dec 2001).

14. The media has actively responded to the reported "epidemic" of abuse in nursing home care, as early as the 1990s, but apparently with little impact on changing the abuse patterns. See Mark Thompson, *Time*, "Shining a Light on Abuse," August 3, 1998; Mark Thompson, *Nation/Time* Special Investigation, "Fatal Neglect in Possibly Thousands of Cases: Nursing Home Residents are Dying from a Lack of Food and

Water and the Most Basic Level of Hygiene," October 27, 1997;
National Public Radio, Talk of the Nation, "Analysis: Ensuring Proper
Care for the Elderly," March 5, 2002; and *San Francisco Chronicle,*
"Nursing Homes Found Lacking," April 17, 2001.
AARP has likewise joined the voices in opposition to the lack of oversight in nursing homes. See Steve Bates, "Nursing Home Horrors: Study
Finds Repeat Offenses Common," *AARP Bulletin,* September 1, 1999.
The federal government's Administration on Aging has responded with
a National Ombudsman Reporting System, with provisions for a long-
term care ombudsman program, while Medicare, a component of the
federal government's Department of Health and Human Services, has
the responsibility of monitoring and enforcing minimum requirements
for nursing homes that wish to provide services under Medicare and
Medicaid.

15. The single best source of nursing home abuse is found in the National
Center on Elder Abuse (1201 15th Street, N.W., Suite 350, Washington,
D.C. 20005; e-mail: ncea@nasua.org).

16. See the Internet advertisement by Schmidt and Clark regarding legal
services for nursing home abuse and neglect. The firm advises readers to
"Submit Your Case." Online at http://www.schmidtandclark.com/
Nursing-Home-Abuse/?OVRAW=Nursing%20Home%

17. Cox News Service, "Report: Nursing Home Abuse Jumps," *The
Bellingham Herald,* July 31, 2001, A7.

18. Martha Holstein and Phyllis Mitzen, "Care of Elders in the
Community: Moral Lives, Moral Quandaries," *Generations: Ethics and
Aging* 22, No. 3 (1998).

19. Liz Taylor, "A Small Hospital's Big Progress in Eldercare," *Seattle Times,*
November 6, 2006; and "Culture Change is on the Horizon for Long-
Term Health Care," *Seattle Times,* November 13, 2006.

20. Lyngblomsten Care Center, St. Paul, Minnesota, Synopsis of Program.
Online at http://www.culturechangenow.com/stories/lyngblomsten.
html

Chapter 10

1. Sharon Salzberg, *Faith: Trusting Your Own Deepest Experience* (New
York: Penguin Putnam, Inc., 2002).

2. Bruce Lipton, *The Biology of Belief* (Santa Rosa: Mountain of Love/Elite
Books, 2005).

3. Daniel Goleman, *Social Intelligence* (New York: Bantam Dell, 2006).
4. I have separated "religion" from "spirituality" to comply with caregivers' self-labeled designations. In this context, religion refers to a set of beliefs concerning the cause, nature and purpose of the universe, especially (1) involving a superhuman or supernatural agency; (2) devotional and ritual observance; (3) a moral code; and usually (4) an institutional affiliation. Spirituality may or may not involve any of the above, but at the core, spirituality entails a highly developed consciousness regarding the power of mind or soul, with or without a deity.
5. Salzberg, *Faith.*
6. Nanette J. Davis and Anne C. Mikkelsen, "Families in Crisis: A Case Study of Elder Caregivers." *International Journal of the Humanities* 1 (2006).
7. Michael E. McCullough and Jean-Philippe Laurenceau, "Religiousness and the Trajectory of Self-Rated Health Across Adulthood," *Personality and Social Psychology Bulletin* 31, No. 4 (April 2005), 560–573.
8. Paul Wink, Michele Dillon and Britta Larsen, "Religion as Moderator of the Depression-Health Connection," *Research on Aging* 27, No. 2 (March, 2005), 197–220.
9. Christopher G. Ellison and Linda George, "Religious Involvement, Social Ties and Social Support in a Southeastern Community," *Journal for the Study of Religion* 33 (1994), 46–61.
10. Ellen L. Idler, "The Many Causal Pathways Linking Religion to Health," *Public Policy and Aging Report* 12, No. 4 (1998), 7–12.
11. David James Duncan, *God Laughs and Plays* (Great Barrington: Triad Books, 2006).
12. *Ibid.,* 112.
13. Victor E. Frankel, *Man's Search for Meaning* (New York: Washington Square Press, 1993), 7–10.
14. Lipton, *The Biology of Belief.*
15. Goleman, *Social Intelligence.*
16. Socialization of youth is discussed in Nanette J. Davis, *Youth Crisis: Growing Up in the High Risk Society* (Westport: Praeger Publishers, 1999).
17. Goleman, *Social Intelligence.*
18. Kenneth R. Overberg, S.J., "The Mystery of Suffering," *Catholic Update* (Cincinnati: St. Anthony Messenger Press, July 2002).

19. I am deeply grateful for the seminar on suffering, led by Paul Fiorini, pastoral associate, Sacred Heart Catholic Church, Bellingham, Washington, February 2005.
20. *Ibid.* See also James Wintz, O.F.M., "Why Must I Suffer?" *Catholic Update* (Cincinnati: St. Anthony Messenger Press, 1987).
21. Matthew Fox, *Original Blessings: Primer in Creation Spirituality* (Los Angeles: J.P. Tarcher, 2000).
22. Stephen Batchelor, "The Four Noble Truths," *Religion & Ethics,* October 2, 2002. The full text (print and audio) is available online at http://bbc. co.uk/religion/religions/buddhism/beliefs/fournobletruths.shtml
23. *Ibid.*

Chapter 11

1. This chapter is co-authored with Anne C. Mikkelsen.
2. Matthew Fox, *Meditations with Meister Eckhart* (Santa Fe: Bear & Company, 1983).
3. Kent Nerburn, *Simple Truths: Clear and Gentle Guidance on the Big Issues of Life* (Novato: New World Library, 1996).
4. Matthew Fox, *Meditations with Meister Eckhart.*
5. From *Analects,* Book 2, Chapter 7, quoted in Nancy R. Hooyman and H. Asuman Kiyak, *Social Gerontology,* Seventh Edition (Boston: Pearson Education, Inc., 2005), 54.
6. *Ibid,* 58.
7. Carole Gilligan, *In a Different Voice: Psychological Theory and Women's Development* (Cambridge: Harvard University Press, 1977).
8. *Ibid.* See also Alise Carse, "Facing Up to Moral Perils: The Virtues of Care in Bioethics," chapter in Suzanne Gordon, Patricia Benner and Nel Noddings, eds., *Caregiving: Readings in Knowledge, Practice, Ethics, and Politics* (Philadelphia: University of Pennsylvania Press, 1996), 83–110.
9. Jack Jonathan and Sheelagh G. Manheim, *Find More Meaning in Your Life* (Kansas City: Stowers Innovations, Inc., 2005).
10. Daniel Gilbert discusses the three types of happiness in *Stumbling on Happiness* (New York: Alfred A. Knopf, 2006).
11. *Ibid.,* 37–38.
12. Ram Dass, *Still Here: Embracing Aging, Changing, and Dying* (New York: Riverhead Books, 2000).
13. *Ibid.,* 64.

Chapter 12

1. This way of being a caregiver was inspired by Bhante Henepola Gunaratana in his book, *Eight Mindful Steps to Happiness* (Boston: Wisdom Publications, 2001). I have also been inspired by my mentor and friend, Ron Wypkema, whose spiritual insights and practical suggestions animate this chapter.

2. John Kehoe and Nancy Fischer offer a number of "mind power" techniques for parents and teachers in *Mind Power for Children* (Vancouver, B.C., Canada: Zoetic, Inc., 2002). We have adopted a few of these generic techniques relevant for caregivers in this section.

3. Bhante Henepola Gunaratana, *Eight Mindful Steps to Happiness* (Boston: Wisdom Publications, 2001), 181.

4. Bruce Lipton, *The Biology of Belief* (Santa Rosa: Mountain of Love/Elite Books, 2005).

5. Ram Dass, *Still Here: Embracing Aging, Changing, and Dying* (New York: Riverhead Books, 2000).

6. Thich Nhat Hanh, *The Miracle of Mindfulness* (Boston: Beacon Press, 1999).

7. Association for Mindfulness in Education. Online at http://www.mindfuleducation.org.

8. "Mindfulness in the Mainstream." Online at http://www.beliefnet.com.

9. Thomas Keating, "The Method of Centering Prayer" (St. Benedict's Monastery, Snowmass, Colorado). Online at http://www.thecentering.org/centering_method.html.

10. *Ibid.*

11. Matthew Fox, *Prayer: A Radical Response to Life*, New Edition (New York: Jeremy P. Tarcher/Putman, 2001), 70.

12. *Ibid.*

13. Colleen Zuck, ed., *Daily Word: The Silent Unity Magazine* 145, No. 7 (July 2007), 23.

Index

ORDER FORM

House of Harmony Press
P.O. Box 29347 • Bellingham, WA 98228
www.houseofharmonypress.com
360.961.2561 (phone) • 360.715.1348 (fax)

SEND TO:

Name _____

Street Address_____

City/State/Zip _____

Phone _____ Country _____

E-Mail_____

PAYMENT:

Blessed Is She (ISBN 978-1-60145-466-9)   **$18.95 each**

Quantity: _____

Sub-total: $ _____

Sales Tax: $ _____
(8.4% for WA State Residents)

Shipping: $ _____
(Standard USPS Mail)

Total: $ _____

U.S. shipping is $5.00 for the first book; $1.50 for each additional copy. International shipping is $9.00 per copy for Canada/Mexico and $11.00 per copy for all other countries.

Please make check or money order in U.S. dollars payable to **House of Harmony Press.** Your contact information will not be sold to or shared with any third party.

Thank you for your order!

LaVergne, TN USA
21 September 2009

158559LV00008B/30/P